OFFICIAL (ISC)²® GUIDE TO THE
HCISPP℠ CBK®

Edited by
Steven Hernandez, HCISPP, CISSP, CAP, SSCP, CSSLP

CRC Press
Taylor & Francis Group
Boca Raton London New York

CRC Press is an imprint of the
Taylor & Francis Group, an **informa** business
AN AUERBACH BOOK

CRC Press
Taylor & Francis Group
6000 Broken Sound Parkway NW, Suite 300
Boca Raton, FL 33487-2742

© 2015 by Taylor & Francis Group, LLC
CRC Press is an imprint of Taylor & Francis Group, an Informa business

No claim to original U.S. Government works

Printed on acid-free paper
Version Date: 20140814

International Standard Book Number-13: 978-1-4822-6277-3 (Hardback)

Visit the Taylor & Francis Web site at
http://www.taylorandfrancis.com

and the CRC Press Web site at
http://www.crcpress.com

Contents

Foreword

Official (ISC)² Guide to the HCISPPSM CBK® Foreword

As the rapidly evolving healthcare industry faces challenges to keep personal health information protected – including growing volumes of electronic health records, new government regulations, and a complex IT security landscape – there is an increasing need to ensure knowledgeable security and privacy practitioners are in place to protect this sensitive information.

Over the next ten years, the global healthcare industry is forecasted to be among the fastest growing employers. At the same time, the risks and consequences of keeping protected health information secure are increasing. As a result, healthcare employers must find qualified personnel who can demonstrate the necessary competence to protect and secure this vital information.

Healthcare Information Security and Privacy Practitioners (HCISPPs) are at the forefront of protecting patient health information. These are the practitioners whose foundational knowledge and experience are instrumental to a variety of job functions:

- Compliance Officer
- Information Security Manager
- Privacy Officer
- Compliance Auditor
- Risk Analyst Medical Records Supervisor
- Information Technology Manager

- Privacy & Security Consultant
- Health Information Manager

This Official Guide to the Health Care Information Security and Privacy Practitioner (HCISPP) Common Body of Knowledge (CBK) textbook covers the diversity of the healthcare industry, the types of technologies and information flows that require various levels of protection, and the exchange of healthcare information within the industry, including relevant regulatory, compliance, and legal requirements. The six sections in the HCISPP CBK unite the best practices and techniques of healthcare information security and privacy under one body of knowledge and underscore the relationship between basic risk management methodologies and lifecycles:

- *Healthcare Industry* – Examines the diversity of the healthcare industry, types of technologies, flow of information, and levels of protection.
- *Regulatory Environment* – Addresses relevant legal and regulatory requirements to ensure policies and procedures are in compliance.
- *Privacy and Security in Healthcare* – Refers to security and privacy concepts and principles, including the types of information to protect.
- *Information Governance and Risk Management* – Addresses how organizations manage information risk through security and privacy governance and risk management lifecycles.
- *Information Risk Assessment* – Identifies risk assessment concepts, practices, and procedures.
- *Third-Party Risk Management* – Refers to the identification of third parties based on the use of information and the requirements for additional security and privacy assurances.

Countries around the world have attempted to improve the effectiveness of security and privacy controls through numerous laws, regulations, and best practice frameworks. The magnitude of risks borne by entities handling patient health information results in even more diligent and vigorous efforts to protect information.

The privacy and security of personal health information has become a globally recognized issue and priority. Government regulations and patient concerns have highlighted the potential ramifications of inadequate controls around patient health records. Combined with the growing volume of these records and the conversion to an electronic format, the need for proper security and privacy controls has never been greater.

— **W. Hord Tipton, Executive Director, (ISC)²**

Introduction

Health care delivery is changing lives. The quality, speed, accuracy, and efficiency of health care are increasingly being reviewed and studied as the global patient population grows and ages. Health care is greatly enhanced using information technology. When patient records are digitized, automated record operations become possible, records can be easily transmitted from one provider to another, and patients can receive a higher quality of care while lowering costs of administrating the records. While the positives of healthcare information technology are clearly worth investigating, they must be balanced with the risks of technology adoption.

Electronic Health Records (EHRs) and other healthcare information systems can also greatly increase the risk of operating a healthcare organization. Poorly configured information systems can lead to information breaches, system outages, and information corruption. The negative implications of poorly implemented and monitored healthcare information systems have caused several nations and economies to pass legislation and regulations affecting the use healthcare information technology. A few of these regulations and laws incentivize the adoption of health information technology, but the vast majority provides a framework by which organizations may be penalized if they breach protected health information. Healthcare information breaches have cost healthcare providers millions of dollars and in some cases have caused organizations to fail and close shop due to fines and lawsuits. The healthcare industry must evolve and must adopt technology while managing risk in a continuous fashion.

As the international healthcare market continues to evolve, the need for efficient and effective risk management will increase. Healthcare providers are expected to see increased demands to not only leverage effective information technology, but also to provide due diligence and due care in managing the risk accompanying their patients' records. The six domains of the HCISPP provide a foundation for healthcare practitioners' and their partners' risk management processes.

- *Domain 1* – **Healthcare Industry** covers the healthcare industry and the common terminology and entities participating in health centric marketplaces. Different forms of insurance, care delivery, information systems, reporting, and records management are covered. Domain one serves as an industry foundation for practitioners to ensure familiarity with the industry.

- *Domain 2* – **Regulatory Environment** covers perhaps the most visible aspect of the healthcare information technology risk environment - the regulatory environment. Internationally, healthcare practitioners do not only need to comply with healthcare specific laws and regulations such as HIPAA in the U.S., but also data privacy laws such as the United Kingdom's Data Protection Act, which covers all personal data to include healthcare data.

- *Domain 3* – **Privacy and Security in Healthcare** focuses on the critical aspects of securing and protecting the privacy of healthcare information. An overview of information security and privacy concepts is covered in addition to how the concepts of privacy and information security are related yet distinct. Domain 3 covers sensitive data handling and how healthcare organizations need to apply sound processes, technology, and trained individuals to ensure sensitive data is accurate and safely stored.

- *Domain 4* – **Information Governance and Risk Management** introduces information governance and risk management. Internationally, numerous frameworks exist for managing risk and establishing information governance. Domain 4 covers several different approaches for managing risk and provides a risk management approach for assessing risk and understanding risk treatment options. Threats, vulnerabilities, impacts, and risk are covered in terms of their relationship to each other and the healthcare environment.

- *Domain 5* – **Information Risk Assessment** covers information risk assessment. Risk assessment is the critical activity that provides insight into the risk an organization is accepting at a given moment. The HCISPP plays a critical and active part in the risk assessment process by either leading the risk assessment or participating as a subject matter expert for the organization. Different risk assessment frameworks are explored in Domain 5 as well as specific information related to technical, operational, and managerial controls over time.

- *Domain 6 – Third-Party Risk Management* analyzes the relationship of third parties to the healthcare organization. In a growing market of international outsourcing and cloud computing, healthcare organizations must be aware of their responsibilities when using third parties. Domain 6 covers knowledge and skills in the areas of third-party assessment, connectivity, and reporting. Further third-party risk is explored and how communication and written agreements are critical for both the primary organization and its third-party partners.

The (ISC)[2] HealthCare Information Security and Privacy Practitioner or HCISPP credential is designed to ensure healthcare practitioners have the knowledge, skills, and abilities to protect healthcare information in digital or hardcopy form. The credential is appropriate for any member of a healthcare organization who may process, store, transmit, or disseminate protected health information. The credential is designed to ensure the practitioner has a strong mix of risk management, information security, regulatory knowledge, and operational security to protect health information. The credential is extensible for organizations of all sizes. Whether an organization has thousands of information technologists supporting it, or a rural clinic has a single nurse practitioner responsible for patient information, the HCISPP credential provides validation of the critical skills and knowledge necessary to understand the regulatory environment, implement appropriate information security controls, and leverage risk management. The credential is also excellent for information assurance, information security, cyber security, and risk management professionals who may be seeking to expand their area of practice to include healthcare. For those with a background in information security, the credential will further validate the application of information security principles to the international regulatory and operational environments of healthcare organizations.

Authors

Steven Hernandez – *Author and Lead Editor*

Steven Hernandez MBA, HCISPP, CISSP, CSSLP, SSCP, CAP, CISA, is a Chief Information Security Officer practicing in the U.S. Federal Government in Washington DC. Hernandez has over seventeen years of information assurance experience in a variety of fields including international healthcare, international heavy manufacturing, large finance organizations, educational institutions, and government agencies. Steven is an Honorary Professor at California State University San Bernardino and affiliate faculty at the National Information Assurance Training and Education Center located at Idaho State University. Through his academic outreach, he has lectured over the past decade on numerous information assurance topics including risk management, information security investment, and the implications of privacy decisions to graduate and postgraduate audiences. In addition to his credentials from (ISC)^2, Hernandez also holds six U.S. Committee for National Security Systems certifications ranging from systems security to organizational risk management. Steven also volunteers service to (ISC)^2's Government Advisory Board and Executive Writers Bureau. Steven enjoys relaxing and traveling with his wife, whose patience and support have been indispensable in his numerous information assurance pursuits.

Jennifer Inserro – *Contributing Author*

Jennifer Inserro, CISSP, CISA, has more than 15 years of experience in Information Technology, the majority of it in information security, as well as a stint in privacy. Currently, she is the Director of Information Security

Compliance for a major health insurance payer. Some of her areas of expertise include third-party vendor management, policy development, and role-based access control management. Her passion is helping the business understand information security and privacy risks at a level that allows them to make informed decisions. Ms. Inserro, who is also an editorial content reviewer for the ISACA Journal, has a master's degree in Public Service Management from DePaul University in Chicago. She lives in the Chicago area with her husband, son, and daughter.

Patrick Kelly – *Contributing Author*

Patrick J. Kelly, CISSP, is a Lecturer in the Department of Computer Science and Senior Research Associate in the Cyber Security Policy and Research Institute at George Washington University. Additionally, he serves as a Critical Infrastructure Policy Analyst at the Office of the Comptroller of the Currency (OCC).

Prior to joining the OCC, Mr. Kelly served as an operations and payment systems analyst at the Board of Governors of the Federal Reserve System as well as the Senior Official for Privacy and Information Security Branch Chief at the Office of Inspector General for the Department of Health and Human Services.

Mr. Kelly volunteers with the Public Service Speakers Bureau through the Partnership for Public Service where he promotes cybersecurity careers in the federal government. He is a member of the (ISC)² U.S. Government Advisory Board for Cyber Security and Executive Writers Bureau.

Mr. Kelly attended Florida State University where he received a Bachelor's of Science in Political Science and George Washington University where he was a recipient of the CyberCorps: Scholarship for Service through the National Science Foundation and earned a Masters of Public Policy. Mr. Kelly lives in Arlington, Virginia with his family who all know not to click on suspicious links or give anyone their social security number. Ever.

Michelle Monsees – *Contributing Author*

Michelle Monsees is an information assurance professional working in the Washington DC area. She holds a Master's of Computer Science with an emphasis in Information Assurance from George Washington University and a Bachelor's of Computer Science from the University of Hawaii. Prior to moving to DC, Ms. Monsees worked in the financial sector performing systems integration and systems development work with several large financial firms. In DC, she held information assurance and risk management positions with the U.S. Department of Justice and the U.S. Federal Reserve Board of Governors. Her work and experience in the information assurance is focused heavily on systems assessment, mobile device assurance, cryptography, and risk management. Ms. Monsees is an active member of the United States' Scholarship for Service Cyber Corps. She also guest lectures on a variety of cyber security and federal information security laws to students at the University of Washington, George Washington University, and the University of Hawaii.

Jack Orlove – *Contributing Author*

Jack Orlove is currently a Director of Information Security at MAXIMUS Inc. and also the Vice President of Cyber Communication Inc., a small security consultancy in Sacramento, California. He is responsible for managing the risk, controls, privacy, and security for not just MAXIMUS' information assets, but he has also consulted on major initiatives for the State of California including the HIPAA Security Implementation Project Manager for the state for two years, Lead HIPAA Security Auditor for multiple state agencies, a healthcare Expert Witness for the state and Disaster Recovery Expert and Datacenter Architect for many major initiatives. Prior to Cyber Communication, Jack held roles in application development, networking architecture, and data center design. He has worked with the U.S. State Department in Africa and the Middle East, the Department of Defense in Europe and Latin America, and supported General Schwarzkopf in Operation Desert Storm.

Jack is currently an Adjunct Professor at the University of San Francisco teaching Information Security at the master's degree level, and he also teaches Disaster Recovery for DRI International. Jack received his bachelor's degree from San Jose State University and graduated as the MBA Valedictorian from Nova Southeastern University in 1993. Jack was an officer in the Sacramento Chapter of the Information System Security Association for seven years and currently holds certifications from (ISC)^2, ISACA, DRII, and SANS. He also serves as a ski patroller for the National Ski Patrol in Tahoe, is a member of the Community Emergency Response Team for Sacramento, California, is a presenter for (ISC)^2's Safe and Secure Online program to help children ages 7-14 learn how to protect themselves online, and is currently piloting a similar program for senior citizens. Jack shares his life with two exceptional children and would never have gotten this project done without the help of his lifelong partner, Ingela.

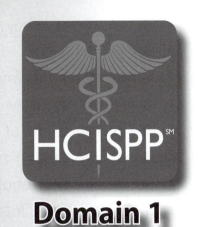

Domain 1

Healthcare Industry

THE HEALTHCARE INDUSTRY is exceedingly diverse, consisting of various organizations such as small physician practices and large health systems, laboratories, pharmaceuticals, biomedical companies, private and public payers, regulators and public health organizations, all of which rely on the efficient and effective exchange of patient-related information. Throughout the world, healthcare organizations are striving to use technology to help improve patient care while increasing efficiencies and reducing errors. Electronic health records and associated technologies are being adopted internationally at an astonishing rate as some countries require their usev and others provide substantial financial incentives to adopt them. The market, economic, patient satisfaction, and cost drivers are all moving healthcare towards a digital future.

The Healthcare Environment domain of the HealthCare Information Security and Privacy Practitioner (HCISPP) covers an international view of healthcare models, insurance models, and payment approaches. Numerous markets and industries such as business associates, pharma, insurance, nursing, assisted care,

1

laboratory testing, and more make up the healthcare environment. While each industry may vary from the other, they all have one common element of risk: the possibility of exposing confidential patient information to the public. Workflow management and an overview of the regulatory environment will be discussed to help further frame the international healthcare industry, while industry specific taxonomies and practices such as ICD-10 and Public Health Reporting will be covered. Understanding the healthcare environment is a critical necessity in ensuring the HCISPP can manage risk in and ultimately protect the business and operations of an organization.

TOPICS

- Understand the Healthcare Environment
  - Types of Organizations in the Healthcare Sector
  - Health Information Technology
  - Health Insurance
  - Coding
  - Billing, Payment, and Reimbursement
  - Workflow Management
  - Regulatory Environment
  - Patient Care and Safety
  - Clinical Research

- Understand External Third Party
  - Vendors
  - Business Partners
  - Data Sharing
  - Regulators

- Understand Foundational Health Data Management Processes
  - Information Flow and Life Cycle in the Healthcare Environments
  - Health Data Characterization
  - Data Interoperability and Exchange
  - Legal Medical Records

OBJECTIVES

According to the Candidate Information Bulletin (Exam Outline), the HCISPP candidate should be able to understand:

- The diversity of the healthcare industry,

- The types of technologies and flows of information that require various levels of protection, and

- How healthcare information is exchanged within the industry.

The Healthcare Industry

Today's doctor visit looks very different than it did several generations ago and even in the past few decades. Long gone are the house calls and long visits with the family doctor. Health care today is very specialized with highly technical procedures and tools that enable diagnosis that is more precise and treatment in a way that is more impersonal, yet it extends our lifespan. Because of this, patients' physical health and quality of life have been improved such that living an active life into their 70s and 80s is not uncommon. Many of the changes are driven by government programs such as Medicare and the Affordable Health Care Act in the United States (U.S.). Employers and insurers are responding to the changes in regulations in order to make consumers more price-conscious of what they are spending on both health care and health insurance.

These trends towards consumer-driven health care are supported in large part by innovations in technology. Social media, mobile technology, data analytics, and cloud tools have changed how healthcare organizations interact with patients and with each other. This new technology has created a rising demand for a digital-savvy healthcare workforce that can leverage technology to engage with patients and respond to changing demands in a faster, cheaper, and more user-friendly manner. Healthcare companies will need to think more like startup companies as changes force experimentation into areas that they have not needed to go in the past, yet they will continue to see that the adoption of technology will drive a more efficient and a better patient experience.

Not only is the provider and industry going through rapid change, but also a growing world population of sick and aging people is increasing the demand as well as stress on the healthcare industry. Considerably faster growth of healthcare spending outside of the U.S. in countries such as China and Brazil is also an area where there is a substantial amount of change. As the population grows and expectations rise due to new treatment options that are available, this industry will continue to become more complex. These drivers have been building for years and help explain the rise of high-technology healthcare industry innovations.

The world of healthcare has become one of the fastest growing industries today and is full of opportunities and risks. As new business models for healthcare companies and consumers of health care continue to emerge on the market, companies will be forced to respond. This new face of medicine will emphasize specialty products and new information transparency, which is good, but it could also pose new risks as electronic medical records, data analytics, and informatics could expose healthcare to new threats. The HCISPPs will need to guide their organization through these situations and provide oversight to the multiple flows of data and multiple missions.

Understand the Healthcare Environment

The basic health care responsibilities today are not much different than they were in the past. It still involves the maintenance and restoration of health by the treatment and prevention of disease by trained and licensed professionals.[1] Healthcare professionals, as with any industry, are looking for ways to make their product faster, more economical, and provide a better result that meets their customers' needs. These goals are constrained by resource issues such as standardization, technology, and qualified staffing.

Healthcare providers are embracing companies with specialized services for better ways to provide health care to the public in a plentiful and high quality manner, but these efficiencies come with a price. Medical information must be standardized and communicated to many stakeholders; this communication must be very specific and detailed so that miscommunication is minimized and quality is maintained. Many industries self-regulate much of this complexity by developing standards and requirements, but as one can imagine, healthcare today is not just one industry but instead is comprised of many different trades. The complex and detailed information generated from the process must traverse so many industries, specialists, and intermediaries that regulatory bodies had to step in to provide standards and regulations.

The definition of the healthcare environment has been expanded by regulators to include the many specialized companies and support services that are involved in traditional healthcare organizations as well as companies that generate and handle the mass of information or data generated from the process. General industry consensus states that any organization that handles patient data protected by some regulation, statute, or standard should be considered as part of the healthcare environment. This definition makes it one of the most heavily regulated industries in the world. These regulations stem from efforts to ensure quality, affordability, portability, and security and dictate the government's oversight role responding to increased demand for their health care services.

---

1   http://www.merriam-webster.com/medical/health%20care

Types of Organizations in the Healthcare Sector

Several types of organizations exist in the healthcare sector. Some organizations, such as large general hospitals, provide a wide range of acute care and other services spanning many parts of the continuum of care. Other organizations, such as hospices, are specialized and only provide a narrow range of services in one part of the continuum. Hospitals may also be specialized, such as for only psychiatric or only rehabilitation services. Medical group practices and physician offices are another type of healthcare organization. These practices might provide many medical services, such as cardiology, pulmonology, and neurology, or instead focus on a single specialty. Many medical groups now offer diagnostic testing, on-site therapy services, outpatient surgery, and other care.

Ambulatory healthcare organizations provide health care services to people who come for care and do not stay overnight. One example is an outpatient diagnostic center, which performs lab tests, medical imaging tests, and other services to help diagnose health problems. Other ambulatory options include ambulatory surgery centers, urgent-care facilities for minor problems, mental health clinics, and primary care clinics. Home care organizations provide an array of nursing and therapy services in people's homes. Some organizations, such as nursing homes, provide services for people (not all of whom are elderly) needing care for an extended period.

In addition to healthcare organizations that provide hands-on health care services to patients and directly affect health, other types of essential healthcare organizations indirectly affect people's health. Organizations such as the American Cancer Society and American Lung Association affect people's health by funding research, developing educational programs, and assisting people who need treatment. Medical supply firms and pharmaceutical companies produce and distribute the thousands of supplies, drugs, and equipment that other healthcare organizations use to provide health care. Many companies make high-tech equipment such as magnetic resonance image (MRI) scanners and robot surgical systems. Other companies make less sophisticated devices, catheters, intravenous solutions, wheelchairs, antibiotics, bandages, and many other items.[2]

Health insurance companies are another type of healthcare organization. These businesses assist in the financing and payment for health care services and include health maintenance organizations (HMOs), preferred provider organizations (PPOs), and point of service (POS) plans. An HMO is a type of health organization that includes several hospitals, insurance plans, and physicians. A PPO consists of a network of physicians and hospitals. A POS plan is a combination of both HMO and PPO.

---

2   http://www.ache.org/

Trade organizations, such as the American Hospital Association, and professional associations are other types of healthcare organizations. Colleges and universities prepare people to work in hundreds of distinct healthcare jobs, while other organizations accredit, license, and regulate healthcare organizations.

Another industry has emerged in the last 20 years that supports traditional health care and has had staggering growth. This industry consists of specialized activities in support of the healthcare providers and includes providing services such as billing, insurance processing, storage, and imaging and several others.

Health Information Technology

Today medical "data," or the information contained in an electronic format, is controlled by the Health Insurance Portability and Accountability Act (HIPAA) Security Rule in the United States (U.S.), as well as many other regulations worldwide. The ones and zeros in a health record are combined to tell everything about a patient's medical history, including what the patient may say to the doctor in the privacy of an exam room or issues that the patient would never want to be exposed to a perspective employer. Today there is great value in that information, and many people are willing to pay top dollar to obtain it. Not only is there sensitive personal information, but also included in that healthcare data is everything that a credit card fraud criminal would want to commit identity fraud, including social security number, date of birth, and address.

The data used in a healthcare environment is pervasive and is handled by many entities through many channels; all require security and protection in its many forms. Although there are prescribed best practices in a variety of industries, the healthcare security practitioner focuses much of his or her attention on the electronic versions of this data, but keep in mind that the definition of "electronic" is getting more and more complex. For example, take the simple fax that is transmitted from one entity to another as part of the health care process. This fax goes from a paper format to an electronic format, traverses the phone line, and then pops out in the other office as a piece of paper. At what point in the process did the paper form become electronic data, how was it transferred (or in HIPAA terminology, placed in transit) and upon receipt, when did the format change again into paper? This may appear to be a simple question with an obvious answer, but if the fax was sent over the phone line as a dual-tone multi-frequency (DTMF)[3] signal, it was always considered as a paper transmission and falls under the HIPAA Privacy Rule. On the other hand, if the transport was in a Voice over Internet Protocol transmission (VoIP) or was converted into data and

---

3   DTMF is used for telecommunication signaling over analog telephone lines in the voice-frequency band.

sent over a carrier's data circuit, as is done in almost 100% of cases in the U.S., then the transmission falls under the HIPAA Security Rule with many different requirements for access and control. The simple question becomes one with many possible and sometimes complicated answers.

The Healthcare Information Security and Privacy Practitioner (HCISPP) will focus on the unauthorized release of data as the most severe threat, utilizing a risk-based approach to determine threats, but the technology of healthcare is changing so quickly that the threats will emerge from a variety of places not previously considered. Today, doctors have the capability to implant devices inside bodies that are Internet protocol (IP) addressable and wireless. Imagine the benefit of a device implanted in a patient's body that delivers insulin based on his or her individual needs to keep blood sugar under control. Now imagine the device being manipulated by a hacker so that all the insulin contained in the device is delivered in one injection. This possibility, which could kill an individual, poses a technological threat that far exceeds the typical confidentiality, integrity, and availability (CIA) triad that is so familiar to information security professionals. The CIA triad is a mainstay of the information security industry and stipulates that information must be kept confidential from exposure to individuals who do not need to have access to it, must maintain its integrity and not be changed unless authorized, and ensure that the information is available when necessary. Finally, imagine the financial ramifications to a hospital or organization if this threat is extended to other IP addressable implants and medical devices. It would not take long for the organization to be buried in a legal quagmire and go out of business.

Many people use the terms electronic health record (EHR), electronic medical record (EMR), and personal health record (PHR) interchangeably; however, they are very different items. The EMR is an electronic record of an episode of medical care that occurs in the particular office, clinic, or hospital and is mostly used for diagnosis and treatment. The EHR contains information from all the clinicians involved in a patient's care and can be accessed by all the authorized clinicians. The EHR is also appropriately shared with insurance companies, government agencies, laboratories, specialists, patients, and employers and follows the patient as the patient moves to different facilities or locations. The PHR contains the same types of information as the EHR, but it is designed to be set up, accessed, and managed by the patient in a private, secure, and confidential environment.[4]

---

4   http://www.healthit.gov/providers-professionals/faqs/what-are-differences-between-electronic-medical-records-electronic

Electronic Health Records and Health Information Exchange

The difference in the healthcare technology between yesterday and today is vast and requires many different technologies and interoperable standards to control the entire CIA security triad. Formatting the data and how the data is handled is a major concern as legacy systems try to communicate with newer state-of-the-art technology. The interoperability of systems that are manufactured by a variety of vendors, all connecting to form a complex health care delivery system, is only becoming infinitely more complex. These disparate systems interoperating with each other are a major concern today and a major focus of the conversations and the announcements at the 2013 annual conference of the Health Information Management and Systems Society (HIMSS).[5] Some organizations are turning to large software providers, such as Epic,[6] in order to solve these problems, but a variety of system manufacturers have started creating an open standard to solve the issue. A consortium of manufacturers has developed an open standard for interoperability using the EHR format. These vendors are opening up their systems for improving the functionality of their systems working with other manufacturers' systems.

Similar to the standards for data formatting described above between system manufacturers, the Health Information Exchange (HIE) is a self-regulating standard for the interconnection of electronic data transmission between government and private organizations. The HIE is a confederation of stakeholders including federal agencies; state, regional, and local integrated-delivery networks for health information organizations; and private organizations. Through the HIE mechanism, stakeholders are coming together to develop and implement standards, services, and policies that foster secure and interoperable health information exchange over the Internet.[7] HIE includes the following generic benefits:

- Providing a vehicle for improving quality and safety of patient care;
- Providing a basic level of interoperability among electronic health records (EHRs) maintained by individual physicians and organizations;
- Stimulating consumer education and patients' involvement in their own health care;
- Helping public health officials meet their commitment to the community;

---

5   http://www.himssconference.org/

6   Epic is a privately held healthcare software company founded in 1979 and offers an integrated suite of healthcare software centered on a legacy database.

7   http://www.healthit.gov/providers-professionals/health-information-exchange

- Creating a potential loop for feedback between health-related research and actual practice;
- Facilitating efficient deployment of emerging technology and healthcare services; and
- Providing the backbone of technical infrastructure for leveraging by national and state-level initiatives.

Another popular method developed to maintain and control healthcare data is done by the patients themselves in a personal health record (PHR). As personal devices that monitor such metrics as caloric intake, sleep cycles, blood sugar, and fitness level continue to become more popular, they provide a rich data store for preventative health control. The health data embedded in the information is stored electronically in order to achieve a variety of goals such as:

- Correlating various different pieces of information into one central location;
- Allowing various electronic monitoring devices to report to a data repository;
- Providing the patient with a convenient place on the Internet that allows connectivity from almost anywhere in the world; and
- Eliminating paper records.

Health Insurance

Until recently, the most important of all U.S. access-enhancing healthcare policies came in the mid-1960s. In 1965, Congress passed Title XVIII of the Social Security Act, better known as Medicare. Medicare provided for the reimbursement of medical care costs to persons 65 years of age or older and to those disabled persons deemed eligible by the Social Security Administration. In 1965, Congress also passed Title XIX of the Social Security Act, creating Medicaid. The goal of this amendment was to provide access to needed medical care for the indigent (families with dependent children and the aged), the blind, and the disabled. During the next decade, healthcare policy shifted toward cost effectiveness. The 1970s saw cost-containment policies focused on utilization review, rate control, and capital-expenditure control.

The 1980s and into the 1990s saw fostered growth in competitive medical plans and health maintenance organizations (HMOs) with the aim of bringing market forces to bare in the pursuit of cost-containment objectives. The U.S. federal government began to recognize the limited ability of regulations in achieving cost controls and, more importantly, in limiting its own healthcare expenditures. The passage of the Social Security Act of 1983 established a system of prospective payment based on diagnosis-related groups (DRGs) for care provided to Medicare recipients. The original objective of DRGs was to develop a classification system that identified the "products" that the patient received.[8] Intended as a tool for measuring the efficient use of hospital resources, DRG research was supported by the U.S. federal government, which shifted its focus to the prices that the government paid for Medicare services. This action was clearly aimed at reducing federal support for Medicare and at controlling healthcare costs at the federal level. Hospitals were forced to leave the "nearly risk-free world of cost reimbursement"[9] and learn to live in a world where health care was provisioned and cost was managed.

Healthcare Models

Many of the tools used to manage healthcare costs in the past exist today in modern models, where codes are used to identify treatments and standards are used to regulate the provisioning of health care. The variety of methods allowing for the delivery of health care has included socialized medicine, community medicine, pay-for-service, and both private and public health plans. All of these models have strengths and weaknesses in terms of quality and cost. Many Scandinavian and European nations use a national healthcare model where the state controls the delivery of various services. This model can promote better preventative health care and limit the cost, but scarce or specialized services can be delayed. Other systems, such as the system used in the U.S., has provided immediate service and quality but at a high cost. This commentary is not meant to be a political one, but it is meant to demonstrate some of the strengths and weaknesses in various models. In the U.S., there are millions of Americans without any insurance or the ability to pay for services, either by choice or by economic status. When these Americans become ill or injured and eventually seek treatment, many times their only option is to go to the local emergency room. Because emergency centers are required to provide basic care, they provide the necessary services, but the costs are passed on, not to the consumer who received the services but to the other consumers serviced by the hospital and to society's taxpayers as a whole.

As costs continue to rise in the delivery of health care, new models will continue to be created and used with varying levels of success. The HCISPP will need to understand these models, their strengths and weaknesses, and how both privacy and security must be implemented.

---

8   http://en.wikipedia.org/wiki/Diagnosis-related_group

9   Department of Health Policy and Management, School of Public Health and Health Services, George Washington University, Washington, DC, USA. Journal of healthcare finance 02/1999; 25(3):10-6.

Traditional Group Healthcare Plans

Many industrial nations in the world provide some form of healthcare to their citizens, and most Americans obtain health insurance from their employers. Private insurance has been prohibitively expensive for many Americans. The World Health Organization (WHO) ranked U.S. healthcare 37th in the world, and in a recent comprehensive, comparative study, the Commonwealth Fund ranked the U.S. healthcare system last based on 21 indicative factors.[10] Analyzing the countries that have surpassed the U.S. in these rankings highlights a puzzling reality - what places these other countries ahead of the U.S. is not just their universal healthcare systems but also their significantly lower healthcare costs. Various models have been in place for some time, but as healthcare becomes more expensive and prohibitive for U.S. employers, many Americans are looking to move to something provided from the new health insurance exchanges.

The Affordable Health Care for America Act

American models for health insurance have changed dramatically since enrollment in private health plans were made available for sale on new insurance exchanges. The Obama Administration introduced the Affordable Health Care for America Act, generally referred to as "Obamacare," in October 2009, and projections expect that the federal and state run exchanges will enroll many Americans into healthcare insurance plans for the first time ever. These exchanges allow private insurance companies to compete for individuals in an organized marketplace and allow a person to join a group plan instead of purchasing an individual plan, which tends to be cost prohibitive. Group plans have been in existence for years under employer or trade association groups and, as a rule, are able to maintain lower costs by pooling together groups of older and younger, as well as healthier and chronically ill patients, thereby allowing a sharing of resources and theoretically standardizing the cost structure of such plans.

Payment Models

America's healthcare system is high cost and high volume, but statistically it is not high value. In 2012, the U.S. spent more than $8,000 per person on health care, which is more than twice the average of $3,400 per person in other developed nations. However, spending more on health care has not made most individuals healthier. Even within the U.S., different areas of the country spend very different amounts on health care, again with no correlation to better outcomes. One of the key reasons for the high level of healthcare spending and its rate of growth is the predominance of the fee-for-service payment

---

10   http://www.businessinsider.com/best-healthcare-systems-in-the-world-2012-6?op=1

system, which rewards quantity over quality, especially for high-cost, high-margin services. Under this system, healthcare insurers, including Medicare and Medicaid, pay doctors, hospitals, and other healthcare providers separately for different items and services provided to a patient. As of 2008, 78 percent of employer-sponsored health insurance was fee-for-service.[11]

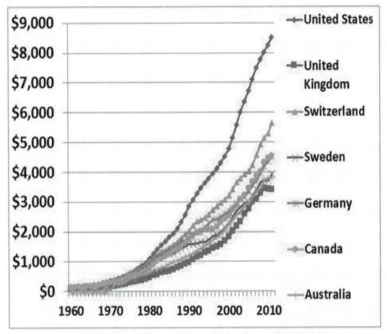

Source: OECD Health Data 2012 in U.S. Dollar purchasing power parity

Figure 1.1 – **1960 to 2012 Healthcare Spending Per Capita (US$)**

Three payment models exist in the U.S. for paying medical practitioners: fee-for-service, capitation, and salary. The fee-for-service is based on paying for the service that is received when it is received, hence the name. This system is used quite often to supplement the second method, capitation.

The capitation method pays each provider in the "network," or who is a provider in the associated plan, a flat fee, sometimes based on an adjustment for factors such as gender and age of the patient. The capitation system allows healthcare plans to control the overall level of primary health expenditures and the allocation of funding among doctors, based on patient registrations. However, under this approach, many specialists are oversubscribed, and patients are unable to have immediate access to their services. This approach is very cost effective as long as specialty services and the under-subscription of

---

11   http://www.americanprogress.org/issues/healthcare/report/2012/09/18/38320/alternatives-to-fee-for-service-payments-in-health-care/

general practitioners are controlled. If this system stays in balance, both doctor and patient can benefit; but if the system is not controlled, imbalances occur and health care becomes scarce. This is one of the reasons that fee-for-service is sometimes mixed with the capitation system in many countries.

The third form of payment model is a salary arrangement, which is the method of choice in many developing countries. In a salary arrangement, the provider is paid a fixed weekly or monthly amount, regardless of the number of patients that are seen or the services provided. However, this payment model has many shortcomings as salaried physicians have no financial incentive to improve their treatment methods or see more patients. Additionally, providers that receive a very good reputation for their service quickly become oversubscribed, while doctors with a bad reputation quickly become undersubscribed and quality control becomes an issue.[12]

Coding

Medical Coding

Medical coding, also called medical classification, is the process of transforming descriptions of medical diagnoses and procedures that are taken from the patient's health care record into universally accepted, industry-standard medical code numbers. The codes are primarily used to submit health care claims to third-party payers, but they are also used to gather statistical information, such as the tracking of specific diseases and therapeutic actions, the surveillance of epidemic or pandemic outbreaks, and discerning developing trends in treatment protocols. These codes are used by government health programs, private health insurance companies, workers' compensation carriers, and others.

Medical codes are utilized in every aspect of healthcare; every disease, every condition and procedure is assigned a specific numeric code. These codes are used by medical professionals worldwide to communicate with each other and with insurance providers. When it comes to patient care, coding determines which health care services are reimbursed and how much is paid. If an error is made in the coding diagnosis or treatment, patients could be incorrectly treated, payment could be denied, or too much could end up being paid for services. The HCISPP should understand how medical codes have unified the practice of healthcare internationally and established a standard for billing and payment from private and government programs.

---

12 http://www.geom.uiuc.edu/usenate/payreport/how.html

The History of Coding

In 1893, the International Statistical Institute approved a standardized system for classifying deaths. The list was called the Bertillon Classification, as it was prepared by Jacque Bertillon, a Paris statistician. By 1900, 26 countries had implemented the Bertillon Classification. In 1928, a study sponsored by the Health Organization of the League of Nations discussed how the Bertillon Classification could be expanded to include the tracking of diseases as well as deaths.[13]

In 1949, The World Health Organization (WHO) established the Manual of the International Classification of Diseases, Injuries, and Causes of Death (ICD).[14] The ICD became the universally accepted method of distinguishing all manners of injuries and diseases.

The Need for a U.S. National Standard

Prior to HIPAA, most payers of U.S. healthcare claims had developed their own standards for claims and other healthcare transactions, which created a great deal of confusion as every insurer had unique requirements for the processing of claims. The result was a mix of terms or "taxonomy" that added complexity and cost to providers. Thousands of different claim forms and procedure codes were in use that complicated medical care and frustrated everyone involved - patients, insurers, employers, and providers.[15]

Prior to HIPAA, there were over 400 different ways to submit a claim in the U.S., but with the advent of HIPAA's Administrative Simplification provision, there became only one way to conduct electronic claims. Everyone covered by HIPAA was required to follow the standard formats for processing claims and payments, as well as for the maintenance and transmission of electronic healthcare information and data. Under HIPAA, if a covered entity or their business associate conducts one of the adopted transactions electronically, they must use the adopted standard. These transactions include:

- Claims and encounter information;
- Payment and remittance advice;
- Claims status;
- Eligibility;
- Enrollment and disenrollment;

---

13   http://www.cdc.gov/nchs/data/misc/classification_diseases2011.pdf

14   http://www.who.int/classifications/icd/en/HistoryOfICD.pdf

15   http://www.cms.gov/Regulations-and-Guidance/HIPAA-Administrative-Simplification/ EducationMaterials/downloads/HIPAA101-1.pdf

- Referrals and authorizations;
- Coordination of benefits; and
- Premium payment.

Medicare now requires all bills to be sent electronically, and in return, they electronically transmit payments to providers. Most insurance companies also require electronic billing.

Different Types of Code Sets

HIPAA's Administrative Simplification provision also included Electronic Transactions and Code Sets requirements that simplified the medical coding process as local codes were replaced by standard U.S. national codes.

A code set is any set of codes used to identify specific diagnosis and clinical procedures on claims and encounter forms. Different code sets for procedures, diagnoses, and drugs were adopted under the Administrative Simplification requirement to include:

- *International Classification of Diseases (ICD)* – Created by the World Health Organization (WHO) and updated every 10 years, the ICD-9 is used in the U.S. for coding diagnostic and hospital inpatient procedures but is primarily utilized for billing purposes.
- *Current Procedural Terminology (CPT)* – Created by the American Medical Association (AMA), the CPT is updated every year and describes medical services and procedures. It is used by doctors and other healthcare practitioners to describe, and bill for, medical procedures. The latest version is the CPT-4.[16]
- *Healthcare Common Procedure Coding System (HCPCS)* – Produced by the Centers for Medicare and Medicaid Services (CMS), HCPCS codifies ancillary services and procedures. HCPCS are Medicare codes that are utilized by doctors and other healthcare providers and are divided into two levels: Level I and Level II. Level I is comprised of Current Procedural Terminology codes (HCPT) and is based on the CPT; these codes are used for doctors' services and outpatient procedures and are used in hospitals and the diagnostic process. Level II codes are used primarily by medical vendors and suppliers, and they identify products, supplies, and services not included in CPT.[17]

---

16 http://www.ama-assn.org/ama/pub/physician-resources/solutions-managing-your-practice/coding-billing-insurance/cpt.page

17 http://www.cms.gov/Medicare/Coding/MedHCPCSGenInfo/index.html?redirect=/MedHCPCSGeninfo/

- *Current Dental Terminology (CDT)* – Developed by the American Dental Association (ADA), the CTD is updated every year. CDT codifies dental procedures and services.[18]
- *Diagnostic and Statistical Manual of Mental Disorders (DSM-IV-TR)* – The DSM-IV-TR is used by mental healthcare professionals.[19]
- *The International Classification of Functioning, Disability, and Health (ICF)* – The ICF relates to disabilities.[20]
- *National Drug Code (NDC)* – The NDC is administered by the U.S. Food and Drug Administration and identifies drug products.[21]
- *Systematized Nomenclature of Medicine* – Clinical Terms (SNOMED CT) - SNOMED CT is a comprehensive, multilingual clinical healthcare terminology that provides the core general terminology for the EHR and formal logic-based definitions organized into hierarchies.[22]

A Transition for the U.S. in 2014

In 2013, most providers in the U.S. used ICD-9 for coding patient problems, and all providers used ICD-9 for billing. In 2014, a transition is occurring as the Center for Medicare & Medicaid Services (CMS) has set a target date of October 1, 2014 for full execution of ICD-10-PCS, which is replacing ICD-9 for billing. ICD-10-PCS is the American version of the new coding and is expanded and has had fundamental changes to the structure and concepts.[23]

Additionally, in 2014 the U.S. is adopting the use of SNOMED CT for coding patient problems. The SNOMED-CT coding system is a comprehensive vocabulary used to express clinical and medical terms. It contains over 300,000 codes, terms, synonyms, and definitions covering diseases, findings, procedures, microorganisms, and substances in order to provide for consistent information interchange and an interoperable electronic health record.[24]

---

18 http://www.ada.org/glossaryforprofessionals.aspx

19 http://www.psych.org/practice/dsm

20 http://www.cdc.gov/nchs/icd/icf.htm

21 http://www.fda.gov/drugs/informationondrugs/ucm142438.htm

22 http://www.nlm.nih.gov/research/umls/Snomed/snomed_main.html

23 http://www.ama-assn.org/ama1/pub/upload/mm/399/icd10-icd9-differences-fact-sheet.pdf

24 http://www.healthfusion.com

Codes Utilized in Other Countries

Codes for billing, diagnostics, and procedures are also used in other countries. Examples of some of the coding systems utilized in other countries include:

- *ICD-10* – The latest version of the ICD, ICD-10, is used worldwide except in the U.S., which will fully adopt it in 2014. Some countries, including Australia and Canada, have developed their own adaptations of ICD, which contains more procedure codes for classification of operative or diagnostic procedures.[25]

- *Systematized Nomenclature of Medicine (SNOMED)* - Several countries throughout the world have been using SNOMED for several years. Licenses to utilize SNOMED are issued by the International Health Terminology Standards Development Organization (IHTSDO).[26]

- *Anatomical Therapeutic Chemical Classification System (AT, or ATC/DDD)* –Administered by the WHO, the ATC/DDD classifies therapeutic drugs. The purpose of the ATC/DDD system is to serve as a tool for drug utilization research in order to improve the quality of drug use.[27]

- *Drug Identification Number (DIN)* – Administered by the Health Canada under the Food and Drugs Act, the DIN uniquely identifies the following product characteristics: manufacturer, product name, active ingredient(s), strength(s) of active ingredient(s), pharmaceutical form, and route of administration.[28]

Billing, Payment, and Reimbursement

Medical Billing

Healthcare providers contract with insurance companies to provide health care services, and they in turn receive reimbursement from the insurance company for the services performed. Medical billing is the process of the healthcare provider submitting a claim to the insurance company in order to receive payment for those services. The medical billing process is usually the same whether the insurance company is a private company or a government-sponsored program.

The medical billing process starts after a patient visits a healthcare provider. Medical codes are assigned to the patient's medical record based upon the diagnosis of the patient and the procedures performed. A claim is then sent via

---

25 http://www.ama-assn.org/ama1/pub/upload/mm/399/icd10-icd9-differences-fact-sheet.pdf

26 http://www.ihtsdo.org/

27 http://www.who.int/classifications/atcddd/en/

28 http://www.hc-sc.gc.ca/dhp-mps/prodpharma/activit/fs-fi/dinfs_fd-eng.php

electronic transmission from the healthcare provider to the patient's insurance company or to a healthcare clearinghouse for processing prior to submission to the patient's insurance company. A healthcare clearinghouse is a contracted vendor who reformats the meaning of the claims data into the specified HIPAA transaction format and forwards it electronically to the third-party payer. Once the data is submitted to the patient's insurance company, the insurance company reviews and processes the claims, and the medical codes assist the insurance company in determining the patient's insurance coverage as well as the medical necessity of the service. Approved claims are reimbursed for a certain percentage of the billed services while failed or denied claims result in a notice being sent to the provider, who then makes any required corrections and resubmits the claim.

Payment and Reimbursement

Rates for reimbursement to a healthcare provider for services rendered are pre-negotiated between the healthcare provider and the insurance company. When the allowed payment is made by the insurance company, the healthcare provider also receives an Explanation of Benefits (EOB) or Electronic Remittance Advice (ERA) that outlines the transaction made.

If the patient has a co pay, deductible, or a coinsurance, the insurance payment is reduced and the healthcare provider is responsible for collecting the out-of-pocket expense from the patient. If the patient has a deductible, it is his or her responsibility to pay for any charges until the deductible is met, and the insurance company would issue payment for future charges. A coinsurance is a percentage of the allowed amount that the patient must pay.

Workflow Management

The typical office handles tens of thousands, or even hundreds of thousands, of documents and images each year, including patient charts and information forms, treatment authorization forms, insurance claim forms, and explanation of benefits, just to name a few. In the past, the majority of this information passed from one office or organization to another through cumbersome and manual processes. HIPAA's Administrative Simplification provision addresses the security and privacy of health data that includes knowing how, when, where, and to whom the data is moving in order to improve the efficiency and effectiveness of the nation's healthcare system. Effective workflow management practices enable healthcare providers to store, access, manage, and share critical documents across a broad range of functions, departments, and locations.

What is Workflow Management?

Workflow management is the process of managing healthcare data as it moves from one process or entity to another. It includes the management of information as well as knowledge as it is communicated with the provider, payer, clearinghouse, and other entities that require access to the data. Patients are also included in the healthcare workflow because they have rights of access, amendment, and account under the HIPAA Privacy Rule. Workflow management includes the ability to efficiently manage the input and output of data and provides the ability to effectively manage items such as:

- Physician orders, referrals, and x-ray and lab results;
- Image-based workflow systems that transfer traditional media such as health insurance claims to digital 'images' and then routes them based on text-fields associated with the images;
- Medical records and internal communications specific to individual patients;
- Discharge processes; and
- Notice of Privacy practices that are sent out to patients.

Security, Privacy, and Workflow Management

Workflow management is part of the CIA triad, and it improves clinical decision-making by ensuring that the data is available to authorized users when it is required. It also decreases clinical and administrative errors by ensuring the integrity of the data and that information is changed only in a specified and authorized manner, and it guarantees the confidentiality of the patient's data by controlling who has access to the information.

"Minimum necessary use" is the heart of privacy and is essentially a workflow matter because the best way to achieve security is to have appropriate workflow management. Minimum necessary use, also called "least privileged access," requires covered entities to evaluate their practices and enhance safeguards as needed in order to limit unnecessary or inappropriate access to, and disclosure of, protected health information. Essentially, minimum necessary use maintains security so only those that require the information have access to the information that they require in order to do their job, while at the same time it restricts access to information that they do not require.

"Separation of duties" is another information security practice that should be included in proper workflow management. Separation of duties has the potential to restrict fraud and conflicts of interest, especially in regards to the cash handling process. Adequate separation of duties could require that one staff member accept payments from clients while another staff member reconciles the bank deposits to the computer-generated daily receipts journal and makes the bank deposit.

Workflow Management and a Common Language

HIPAA's Administrative Simplification provision included an Electronic Transactions and Code Sets requirement that simplified the medical coding process. Workflow management works in conjunction with transactions and code sets in order to aid in coordination and communication efforts by providing a common language. This common language includes sending code sets and transaction envelopes via electronic data interchange (EDI), which defines the different types of transactions that are covered under HIPAA and stipulates the exact format for each transaction record.

A medical transaction may change in the format and meaning (or taxonomy) many times as a patient's treatment moves from the provider side to the billing side of an encounter. Verification of eligibility and insurance must take place when a patient is scheduled for an appointment. After verification, the patient's care is provided and an appropriate disposition or medical description is rendered for that encounter. The healthcare provider documents the care provided, and the information in turn is coded into a standards based encounter data (in the U.S., this would be a HIPAA compliant code set such as the ICD-10). As shown in *Figure 1.2*, when the coding process is completed, the facility sends the data to complete the billing process. For facilities using electronic billing, the information is sent via electronic HIPAA 837 (an EDI healthcare claim transaction) compliant transmission to a clearinghouse, potentially changing the codes and words describing the patient encounter. The clearinghouse forwards it electronically to the third-party payer, and the third-party payer then prepares the Explanation of Benefit (EOB) statement for the patient and may provide a paper remittance advice and payment back to the facility.

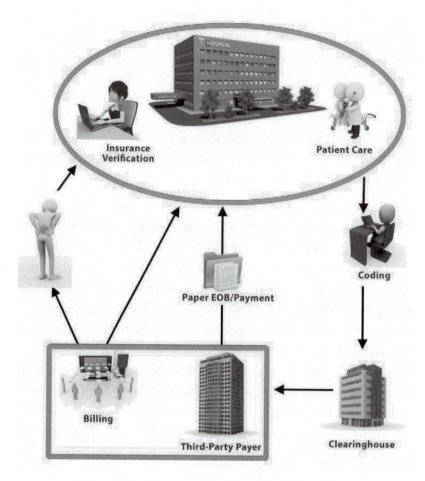

Figure 1.2 – **An example of medical data flow**

Regulatory Environment

Privacy and Security in a Regulated World

Throughout the world, society is becoming more and more aware of the sensitive nature of our healthcare data. Canada has the Personal Information Protection and Electronic Documents Act (PIPEDA),[29] the U.S. has the HIPAA Privacy and Security Rules, and the European Union (EU) has the Directive on Data Privacy[30] as well as the Charter of Fundamental Rights of the European Union.[31] For example, everyone in the EU has the right of access to the data, which has been collected concerning him or her, and the right to have it rectified. These rights may include the ability of a person to request the removal from any record in an organization's database if some proposed

---

29 http://www.priv.gc.ca/leg_c/leg_c_p_e.asp

30 http://ec.europa.eu/justice/data-protection/

31 http://ec.europa.eu/justice/fundamental-rights/charter/

legislation, currently being considered, passes into law. Everyone has the right for respect of his or her private information regarding his or her family life, home, and communications.[32] The goals of these articles are to establish a framework that supports the protection of confidentiality of patient information use and disclosure in the EU, similar to HIPAA in the U.S.

Health Insurance Portability and Accountability Act

The Health Insurance Portability and Accountability Act (HIPAA) was passed by the U.S. Congress in 1996. This law, more than any other, has reshaped the requirements for privacy and security in the U.S. healthcare industry in order to protect health-related data. Prior to HIPAA, various states in the U.S. had laws to protect that state's citizen information, but until the federal government established HIPAA, such laws were applied across the U.S. inconsistently. It established a federal floor of safeguards to protect the confidentiality of medical information. HIPAA also amended the Employee Retirement Income Security Act (ERISA) in order to provide new rights and protections for participants and beneficiaries participating in health plans. Two of the major elements of HIPAA are the Privacy Rule and the Security Rule that require that healthcare providers and organizations ensure the CIA of their healthcare information.

Prior to the adoption of HIPAA, personal health information could be distributed, without either notice or authorization, for reasons that had nothing to do with a patient's medical treatment or health care reimbursement. For example, unless otherwise forbidden by state or local law, patient information held by a health plan could, without the patient's permission, be passed on to a lender, who could then deny the patient's application for a home mortgage or a credit card, or to an employer who could use it in personnel decisions. Without HIPAA, typical medical situations could escalate into gross breaches of privacy and possibly cause undue embarrassment to the patient. With that in mind, HIPAA has the following goals:

- Providing portability or the ability to transfer and continue health insurance coverage for millions of American workers and their families when they change or lose their jobs;
- Reducing healthcare fraud and abuse;
- Mandating industry-wide standards for healthcare information on electronic billing and other processes; and
- Requiring the protection and confidential handling of protected health information.

---

32 EU Article 8 Protection of Personal Data

Covered Entities

Not all organizations in the U.S. are bound by the regulations stipulated in HIPAA. The U.S. Department of Health and Human Services (HHS) determined that only certain organizations deal with healthcare data and defined those organizations as "covered entities." HHS divided these covered entities into three groups:

Direct Covered Entities		
1. Health Plans Includes an individual or group plan who provides and pays for health care (Medicare and the components of government agencies)	2. Providers of Services Radiologists, Physicians, Laboratories, etc.	3. Health Information Clearinghouses Organizations that can be used to translate either to or from the standard format
Business Associates		
Companies that work on behalf of or subcontract with a covered entity		

Table 1.1 – **Covered entities as determined by the Department of Health and Human Services (HHS)**

1. ***Health Plans*** – Any individual or group plan that provides or pays the cost of health care (e.g., a health insurance issuer and the Medicare and Medicaid programs), which includes:
    - Health insurance companies
    - Health maintenance organizations (HMOs)
    - Company health plans
    - Government programs that pay for health care, such as Medicare, Medicaid, and the military and veterans' healthcare programs

2. ***Providers of Services*** – any provider of medical or other health care services or supplies who transmits any health information in electronic form in connection with a health care transaction such as:
    - Doctors
    - Clinics
    - Psychologists
    - Dentists
    - Chiropractors
    - Nursing Homes
    - Pharmacies

3. ***Healthcare Information Clearinghouses*** – Entities that process nonstandard health information they receive from another entity into a standard (i.e., standard electronic format or data content), or vice versa.

Health Insurance Portability

Portability refers to the portion of HIPAA that addresses the ability of a person to retain health coverage and provides rights and protections for participants and beneficiaries in group health plans. HIPAA also includes protections for coverage under group health plans that limits exclusions for preexisting conditions, prohibits discrimination against employees and dependents based on their health status, and allows a special opportunity for individuals in certain circumstances to enroll in a new plan. HIPAA may also give individuals the right to purchase individual coverage if they have no group health plan coverage available and have exhausted other continuation coverage possibilities.[33]

Healthcare Fraud and Abuse

HIPAA established a comprehensive program to combat fraud committed against all health plans, both public and private. The legislation required the establishment of a national Healthcare Fraud and Abuse Control Program (HCFAC), under the joint direction of the Attorney General and the Secretary of the Department of Health and Human Services (HHS) acting through the Department's Inspector General (HHS/OIG). The HCFAC program is designed to coordinate federal, state, and local law enforcement activities with respect to healthcare fraud and abuse.[34]

The Office of the Inspector General (OIG) has the authority to exclude individuals and entities who have been convicted of healthcare fraud from participation in all U.S. federal healthcare programs. Such healthcare fraud includes criminal offenses such as Medicare or Medicaid fraud, patient abuse or neglect, and felony convictions relating to unlawful manufacture, distribution, prescription, or dispensing of controlled substances. The OIG maintains a list of excluded individuals and entities called the List of Excluded Individuals and Entities (LEIE). Healthcare companies routinely check the LEIE to ensure that new hires and current employees are not on the excluded list, as any company who hires such individuals may be subject to civil monetary penalties.[35]

---

33   http://www.dol.gov/dol/topic/health-plans/portability.htm

34   http://oig.hhs.gov/reports-and-publications/hcfac/index.asp

35   http://oig.hhs.gov/exclusions/background.asp

Protection and Confidential Handling of Health Information

The HIPAA Security and Privacy Rules require that healthcare providers and organizations, as well as their business associates, develop and follow procedures that ensure the confidentiality and security of protected health information (PHI) when it is transferred, received, handled, or shared. This applies to all forms of PHI, including paper, oral, and electronic. Furthermore, only the minimum health information necessary to conduct business is to be used or shared. HIPAA confidentiality and privacy is covered by the following rules:

- The Privacy Rule;
- The Security Rule;
- The Omnibus Final Rule, which includes the Enforcement Rule and the Breach Notification Rule; and
- The HITECH Act.

HIPAA Privacy Rule

HHS issued the Privacy Rule in December 2000 to carry out HIPAA's mandate that HHS establish minimum national standards for protecting the privacy of individually identifiable health information with the goal of:

- Giving patients more control over their health information;
- Setting boundaries on the use and release of health records;
- Establishing appropriate safeguards that healthcare providers and others must achieve to protect the privacy of health information;
- Holding violators accountable, with civil and criminal penalties that can be imposed if they violate patients' privacy rights;
- Striking a balance when public responsibility supports disclosure of some forms of data (for example, to protect public health);
- Helping patients make informed choices when seeking care and reimbursement for care based on how personal health information may be used;
- Enabling patients to find out how their information may be used and about certain disclosures of their information that have been made;
- Limiting release of information to the minimum reasonably needed for the purpose of the disclosure;
- Giving patients the right to examine and obtain a copy of their own health records and request corrections; and
- Empowering individuals to control certain uses and disclosures of their health information.

The HIPAA Privacy Rule created national standards to protect individuals' medical records and other protected health information (PHI). Under the Privacy Rule, the primary concern is with written information and verbal information addressing patient data, such as:

- Information that identifies or can be used to identify an individual; and
- Information that relates to that individual's
  - Past, present, or future physical or mental condition;
  - Health care that he or she received; and
  - Payment for health care.

All patient data collected and maintained for the operation of a covered entity or business associate is protected from unauthorized disclosure, but HHS makes specific reference to 18 identifiers that constitute PHI. These identifiers are:

- Name;
- Address, which includes street address, city, county, zip code (more than 3 digits) or other geographic codes;
- Dates directly related to patient (except year), including date of birth, admission or discharge date;
- Telephone and facsimile numbers;
- Driver's license number;
- Email addresses;
- Social security number;
- Medical record number or client identification number;
- Health plan beneficiary number;
- Account number;
- Certificate or license number;
- Any vehicle or device serial number, including license plates;
- Web addresses;
- Internet protocol (IP) address;
- Finger or voice prints;
- Photographic images;
- Any other unique identifying number, characteristic, or code; and
- Age greater than 89 (as the 90-year-old and over population is relatively small).

The 18 identifiers mentioned above, whether individually or in combination, constitute PHI, but this data can be de-identified for research purposes or to release it to non-covered entities. The HHS's Office of Civil Rights (OCR) provides guidance and explains and answers questions regarding two methods that can be used to satisfy the Privacy Rule's de-identification standard: Expert Determination done by statistical analysis and Safe Harbor where any reference to the 18 identifiers is removed. The two methods to achieve de-identification in accordance with the HIPAA Privacy Rule are depicted in the figure below.[36]

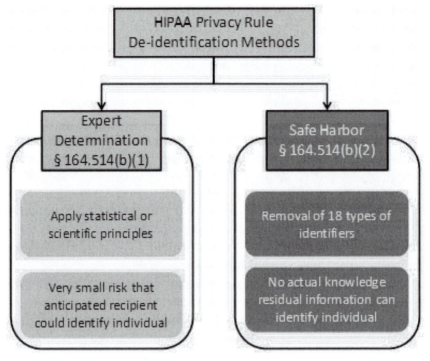

Figure 1.3 – **The process of de-identification**

The process of de-identification has its own challenges, and a very real threat of re-identification exists if not done properly. Re-identification of anonymized data may expose companies to increased liability, as the information may no longer be treated as anonymous. In addition, companies may violate their own privacy policies by releasing anonymous information to third parties that can be easily re-identified with individual users. The potential for third parties to re-identify anonymous information with its individual source indicates the need for both increased privacy protection of anonymized information and increased security for databases containing anonymized information.[37]

Directing the emphasis on the security of PHI, a covered entity's staff must be clear on when PHI can and cannot be disclosed, when it can be released, and to whom information can be released. The basic premise behind when to release PHI is based on a need-to-know basis and the minimum amount needed to conduct operations. Below are samples of information that under certain circumstances require special precautions:

36   http://www.hhs.gov/ocr/privacy/hipaa/understanding/coveredentities/De-identification/guidance.html

37   http://digital.law.washington.edu/dspace-law/bitstream/handle/1773.1/417/vol5_no1_art3.pdf

When PHI CAN Be Disclosed	When PHI CANNOT Be Disclosed
■ To conduct work as outlined in the contract between a covered entity and its business associate. ■ To the individual that the information is about (after the verification process has been satisfied). ■ With a third person, provided that permission has been received from the individual that the information is about.	■ The selling of information for any reason. ■ If used for any work not related to normal business operations or in violation of HIPAA. ■ For discussion with anyone beyond those with the right or need to know.

Table 1.2 – **When PHI can and cannot be disclosed**

HIPAA Security Rule

HHS issued the Security Rule in February 2003 in order to establish national standards to protect individuals' electronic personal health information that is created, received, used, or maintained by a covered entity. The Security Rule requires appropriate administrative, physical, and technical safeguards to ensure the confidentiality, integrity, and security of electronic protected health information.[38] The format of the PHI is where the Security Rule and the Privacy Rule differ in context. While the Privacy Rule focuses on the printed and verbal nature of the information, the Security Rule focuses on the electronic data or the electronic protected health information (e-PHI). The HIPAA Security Rule (and its definitions) tends to be more "conforming and procedural" than the HIPAA Privacy Rule or the Breach Notification Rule (see below). Because this rule focuses on the procedures of securing data, more than 50% of the rule focuses on policies and procedures and applies to all HIPAA covered entities.

Help from the National Institute of Standards and Technology

The National Institute of Standards and Technology (NIST) has published Special Publication (SP 800-66) that summarizes the HIPAA security standards and explains some of the structure and organization of the Security Rule. The publication not only helps to educate federal, state, and local government readers about the HIPAA Security Rule, but it can also improve understanding the meaning of the security standards set out in the Security Rule.[39] This publication is intended as an aid to understanding security concepts discussed in the HIPAA Security Rule and does not

---

38 The Security Rule is located at 45 CFR Part 160 and Subparts A and C of Part 164.

39 http://www.hhs.gov/ocr/privacy/hipaa/administrative/securityrule/nist80066.pdf

31

supplement, replace, or supersede the HIPAA Security Rule itself. While the Centers for Medicare and Medicaid Services (CMS) mentioned several NIST publications in the preamble to the HIPAA Security Rule, CMS does not require their use in complying with the Security Rule.[40]

HIPAA Enforcement Rule

On February 16, 2006, HHS issued the "Final Rule" regarding HIPAA enforcement. It became effective on March 16, 2006, and this Enforcement Rule sets civil monetary penalties for violating HIPAA rules and establishes procedures for investigating HIPAA violations.

Since HIPAA's Privacy Rule compliance date in April 2003, HHS has received over 87,597 HIPAA complaints,[41] and they have resolved 94 percent of those complaints. From the compliance date to the present, the compliance issues investigated most are:

1. Impermissible uses and disclosures of protected health information

2. Lack of safeguards of protected health information

3. Lack of patient access to their protected health information

4. Uses or disclosures of more than the minimum necessary protected health information

5. Lack of administrative safeguards of electronic protected health information

The most common types of covered entities that have been required to take corrective action to achieve voluntary compliance are, in order of frequency:

1. Private Practices

2. General Hospitals

3. Outpatient Facilities

4. Health Plans (group health plans and health insurance issuers)

5. Pharmacies

---

40 The HIPAA Security Rule mentions NIST documents as potentially helpful guidance but not mandatory for compliance, at 68 Federal Register pages 8346, 8350, 8352, and 8355 (February 20, 2003).

41 http://www.hhs.gov/ocr/privacy/hipaa/enforcement/highlights/, as of October 31, 2013

Healthcare Industry

There are other provisions of HIPAA, for example when stronger state laws such as California's Civil Code 1798 (requiring certain breach notifications), and those covering genetic information continue to apply and in some cases are stronger than (or preempt) HIPAA.

The healthcare industry has many other laws that cover the privacy of medical conditions and the data that describes the patient's condition. Many countries have requirements when dealing with specific illnesses or conditions such as:

- HIV/AIDS
- Sexually transmitted diseases (STDs)
- Alcohol or drug addiction
- Mental illness
- Genetics

The Health Information Technology for Economic and Clinical Health Act (HITECH Act)

The Health Information Technology for Economic and Clinical Health Act (HITECH Act) was enacted under Title XIII of the American Recovery and Reinvestment Act (ARRA) of 2009. The HITECH Act has expanded the responsibilities described in Title II's Administrative Simplification provision and added business associates to the list of those who are directly culpable for compliance to HIPAA.

Prior to the HITECH Act, HIPAA was often cited as ineffectual because enforcement capabilities were very limited. Covered entities and business associates had requirements that went into effect under HHS' regulatory arm, but there were very few enforcement actions taken. However, when the Office of Civil Rights (OCR) took control of the enforcement arm of HIPAA via the HITECH Act, enforcements started with dramatic effect. This shift in enforcement has business associates and covered entities playing catch-up to the requirements.

The HITECH Act requires business associates to implement each of the three information safeguards (the CIA triad) under the HIPAA Security Rule that already applied to covered entities. Now business associates are required to undertake a detailed analysis of the standards and implementation specifications listed in HIPAA and implement those safeguards as appropriate for their organizations, including written policies and procedures that document their compliance with the information safeguards. This change in the law is sweeping and dramatically changes the landscape of HIPAA when considering all of the healthcare organizations and the business associates that support those organizations.

The HITECH Act also imposes new requirements for covered entities to limit disclosures of PHI "to the extent practicable" to a limited data set or, if needed by the covered entity, to the minimum necessary to accomplish the intended purpose.

The HITECH Act has other sweeping changes to HIPAA's Title II rules such as providing individuals with the right to obtain their PHI in electronic format, enhancing fines and penalties for breaches, and dramatically changing the definition of a "breach," which is now broadly defined as an acquisition, access, use, or disclosure of unsecured PHI that is not otherwise permitted under HIPAA that compromises the security or privacy of the PHI.

HIPAA Breach Notification Rule

The HIPAA Breach Notification Rule did not exist prior to the HITECH Act and requires a covered entity to provide notification to affected individuals and to the Secretary of HHS following a discovery of a breach of unsecured PHI. In some cases, covered entities are also required to provide notification of a breach to the media.

In the case of a breach of unsecured PHI by a business associate of a covered entity, the business associate is required to notify the covered entity. The HITECH Act also states that a breach is "discovered" as of the first day that the breach is known or should have been known based on the exercise of reasonable diligence. Additionally, the "risk of harm" to the patient or beneficiary is taken into account and in essence has changed the accepted definition of a breach. Breaches are now presumed reportable unless, after completing a risk analysis by applying four factors, it is determined that there is a low probability of PHI compromise. The four factors are:

1. The nature and extent of the PHI involved, including the sensitivity of the information from a financial or clinical perspective and the likelihood the information can be re-identified;

2. The person who obtained the unauthorized access and whether that person has an independent obligation to protect the confidentiality of the information, such as another provider or insurance provider;

3. Whether the PHI was actually acquired or accessed; and

4. The extent to which the risk has been mitigated, such as by obtaining a signed confidentiality agreement from the recipient.

One example of a breach involves Sutter Health in the Sacramento, California area in October 2011. Sutter Health had encrypted its laptops and Blackberry devices and was in the process of encrypting its desktop computers when a desktop computer that was not yet encrypted was stolen from an administrative office at a Sutter Health facility. The stolen computer contained a database with information for 4.2 million patients, including names, addresses, dates of birth, etc. Sutter Health was required to notify 943,000 patients by mail.[42] Sutter Health may need to pay approximately $1,000 for each compromised record in a lawsuit.

The cost of healthcare breaches can be significant. For a recent breach of 1.5 million medical records, a U.S. health insurance firm incurred the following fines and penalties due to the loss of an unencrypted portable drive:

- Lawsuits: $250,000
- Letters to affected clients: $319,000
- Identity theft monitoring for affected clients: $1 million[43]

HIPAA Omnibus Rule

Early in 2013, HHS issued its "Final Rule" to modify HIPAA. This Omnibus Rule implements a number of provisions of the HITECH Act and is a wake-up call to any covered entities who handle protected healthcare information and their business associates. It makes the interim changes introduced by the HITECH Act permanent to the HIPAA Privacy, Security, and Breach Notification Rules. The sweeping changes that were proposed in the interim HITECH Act had a compliance date of October 2013 (unless the agreement between a covered entity and its business associate was signed after January 2013, in which case the compliance date is October 2014). After this date, business associates are susceptible to the same financial penalties associated with the rule violations that applied to covered entities. The OCR can now audit a business associate, just as they could a covered entity, and can investigate and penalize business associates directly. Increasing penalties for noncompliance is based on the level of negligence with a maximum penalty of $1.5 million U.S. per violation.

The area that concerns the HCISPP regarding information security and privacy regulatory requirements is specifically addressed in HIPAA's Title II under the Administrative Simplification provision as well as in the final HITECH and Omnibus Rules.

---

42 http://www.healthcareinfosecurity.com/computer-theft-affects-42-million-a-4250?webSyncID=38269b6b-8d5d-4ebd-9118-85db68bd56a4&sessionGUID=2661747d-1d9e-e423-749c-377c0e18a15b

43 http://www.secureworks.com/assets/pdf-store/other/infographic.healthcare.pdf

Patient Care and Safety

The Hippocratic Oath is an oath historically taken by healthcare professionals swearing to practice medicine honestly. Of historic and traditional value, the oath is considered a rite of passage for practitioners of medicine in many countries; although these days, the modernized version of the text varies among them.[44] Part of the oath refers to the healthcare professionals' obligation to benefit the sick and keep them from harm. This is the foundation for why many countries will not withhold basic health care and why patients must be treated in U.S. emergency rooms.

Patient care and safety is the primary goal and objective of the Hippocratic Oath, but unfortunately, harm to patients can be an unwelcomed byproduct of health care as a business. While there is a general acceptance of the need to improve our ability to deliver care in a safer, cost effective manner, a major barrier to progress in safety has been the ability to effectively measure harm.[45] This has resulted in a shift from initiatives focused exclusively on analysis of errors to those targeting events linked to harm. There is a growing recognition of a distinction between errors and adverse events as they often represent unique concepts fostering different strategies for improvement of safety.

Conventional approaches to identifying and quantifying harm, such as individual chart audits, incident reports, or voluntary administrative reporting, have often been less successful in improving the detection of adverse events. As a result, a new method of measuring harm, called the trigger tool, has been developed.[46] In this system, specific events including the ordering of certain drugs or certain abnormal laboratory values, for example, can serve as triggers to initiate a more detailed chart audit. Each time a trigger event is found in a pharmacy or physician order sheet, it is counted and audited for errors. The trigger tool can be easily customized and taught, enabling consistent and accurate measurement of harm.

Clinical Research

Interruption of clinical research due to a technical issue or failure can be a catastrophic event for any medical firm. Complex administrative approval processes and the sheer volume of the data that must be protected can put smaller companies out of business. There is so much at stake; it is easy to see how the CIA triad discussed earlier becomes a critical concern for a research firm and the HCISPP professional.

Clinical research and the documented outcome data from one stage of the trial to the next stage can create new hurdles for the technical support team. Infrastructure, team members, locations, and participants can all change through the different stages of a typical research study to include:

- Pre-clinical testing;
- Investigational new drug application;
- Phase I (assess safety);
- Phase II (test for effectiveness);
- Phase III (large-scale testing);
- Licensing (approval to use);
- Approval (available for use); and
- Post-marketing studies (special studies and long-term effectiveness/use).

The pre-clinical and drug application stages could take between three to six years; clinical trials Phase I to Phase III could take six to seven years; the licensing and approval stages could take between half a year to two years; and the post-marketing studies are indefinite.[47] Extensive amounts of sensitive information from long-term studies that can last for decades must interoperate and be preserved accurately and confidentially in a secure manner. Stages can be postponed, moved to different locations, and the data can involve hundreds of locations at the same time. This complexity of environments coupled with the variety and sensitivity of the data can generate significant risk for the security professional.

Healthcare Records Management

Healthcare records management is the art and science of managing all information relating to the operation of a healthcare practice. This includes filing and storing patient charts, scanning medical records, ensuring adherence to regulations and retention schedules, and managing the destruction of medical records after their retention period. Healthcare records management also involves effective administration of a practice's non-clinical information, including accounting records, contracts, and other business-related documentation.

Everything about a patient is housed in his or her records. In the past, this was completed by hand, on paper, and kept in a physical file. While many healthcare organizations continue to operate this way, many others are upgrading to electronic data management systems in order to provide immediate access to the patient's records that is accessible to all healthcare providers.

---

47   http://www.phrma.org/innovation/clinical-trials

Electronic health records (EHR), electronic medical records (EMR), and personal health records (PHR) were described previously, as well as the requirement to maintain the security of these healthcare records. HIPAA requires that covered entities and their business associates must take security measures to protect healthcare records and other data, and encryption is probably the most common way to achieve this safeguard through technical means. Encryption is the process of converting plain text data into a form called a ciphertext that cannot be easily understood by unauthorized people.[48] Encryption is utilized on items such as servers, laptops, desktops, personal devices, backup media, and data in transit from one point to another.

One challenge for healthcare and other organizations has been the retention of healthcare records. HIPAA does not require that healthcare records are retained for a specific period; however, local laws often govern how long those records should be retained, and it varies between days to years, depending on the location. Maintaining this vast storehouse of records in a secure environment can be a costly and challenging endeavor for many organizations. Healthcare organizations need to utilize administrative, physical, and technical safeguards to keep their records secure. An administrative safeguard that an organization should use is a records retention policy that includes information such as how records will be securely retained and the duration of time that they will be retained.

Once records have been designated for destruction in a records retention policy, it is imperative that they are destroyed in a secure manner. Examples of proper disposal methods under HIPAA may include, but are not limited to:

- For PHI in paper records, shredding, burning, pulping, or pulverizing the records so that PHI is rendered essentially unreadable, indecipherable, and otherwise cannot be reconstructed.
- Maintaining labeled prescription bottles and other PHI in opaque bags in a secure area and using a disposal vendor as a business associate to pick up and shred or otherwise destroy the PHI.
- For PHI on electronic media, clearing (using software or hardware products to overwrite media with non-sensitive data), purging (degaussing or exposing the media to a strong magnetic field in order to disrupt the recorded magnetic domains), or destroying the media (disintegration, pulverization, melting, incinerating, or shredding) should be required.

---

48 http://searchsecurity.techtarget.com/definition/encryption

Understand External Third Parties

Healthcare is an inherently decentralized and porous system, and because there are so many parties that are involved, it is inherently insecure. Healthcare institutions, networks, exchanges, and portals all involve many players that are sharing data, entering new data, and connecting through multiple endpoints to access data. Because of the inherent risk with data that affects everyone in the healthcare industry, many nations have enacted laws to protect the privacy and the security of this information. Security and privacy requirements are becoming more serious with each new iteration of regulations around the world. Not only are regulations helping secure sensitive data, but also an expectation to identify and protect against reasonably anticipated threats to the security or integrity of e-PHI is expanding.

An even broader and more complex privacy and security concern involves the third parties who handle, store, transmit, or process e-PHI on the behalf of covered entities. For example, because data center service providers typically store and transmit e-PHI, they must comply with the Security Rule and Breach Notification portions of the HITECH Act, but if service providers of network services only provide transport of the data, they may not be culpable. These fine lines to the rule demonstrate why everyone in the healthcare industry or doing business with a covered entity should be aware of these new legal requirements. The impact of not paying attention to the HITECH Act includes fines and penalties administered by the OCR, scrutiny from a large group of regulators, and loss of confidence if the organization has a breach.

Third-Party Liability

Third-party culpability to legal requirements is not a new concept, and insurance companies have been insuring against third-party liability and loss for as long as there has been insurance. At the international level, confidentiality of information takes on a different and sometimes conflicting nature where international laws and the movements of data are very complicated. Multinational organizations should consult experts to understand their liability.

The consequences involving who is liable for what legal requirement, from where the negligent act originated, when in the regulatory timeline that the breach occurred, and the motivation of the breach have all dramatically changed since the implementation of the Omnibus Rule. For example, in the U.S. if a business associate of a covered entity were to experience a material data breach involving e-PHI in 2010, he or she would not be liable for the associated costs and penalties unless otherwise required to by his or her contract; the covered entity would. However, if that same breach happened after September 2013, the business associate would not be considered a third party anymore and as such, could be fined and penalized by HHS and other regulatory authorities under the laws of HIPAA. This would be true even if the business associate had never signed a business associate agreement or understood that they were culpable to HIPAA. Simply because they are performing the functions of a business associate of a covered entity, they can be held liable to the laws of HIPAA.

This broad interpretation, simply based on the work performed, requires that all organizations understand the value-add that they are performing for their customers, the data that they maintain on behalf of their customers, and the necessity to perform due diligence on their customer selection.

Vendors

The healthcare industry is one of the fastest growing industries in the world and offers many opportunities, but the requirements of HIPAA could be very daunting for the organization with limited resources. Vendors with business operations that include some form of exposure to healthcare information should identify their regulatory and compliance risks. For example, a review of the HITECH Act reveals approximately 1,350 occurrences of the term "business associate." Each reference emphasizes the obligation that vendors have to ensure compliance to these requirements, usually by assessing their situation in a comprehensive risk assessment. Vendors who do expose themselves to these compliance and conformance issues must incur the cost associated with mitigating their risks. HHS estimates that the total cost of compliance with the Omnibus Final Rule for covered entities and business associates could be between $114 and $225 million in the first year and approximately $14 million for each year going forward. That means the rule qualifies as an "economically significant" one under Executive Order 12866.[49] The reason for this new level of security is basic: healthcare security and privacy has experienced serious deficiencies through the years, and healthcare has become a prime target for theft.

Healthcare poses new risks and challenges worldwide with additional regulatory hurdles, and many vendors have taken advantage of this opportunity. Vendors have responded by providing everything from applications infrastructure and storage to complete solutions in the cloud. Services are available to provide expertise and assume risk from the various medical entities and their partners. Vendor specialization can be a very cost effective way for organizations to transfer the increased risk that they may not have the internal expertise or staffing to mitigate. Understanding the products and services that are available to respond to the growing threats to healthcare information falls under the responsibility of the HCISPP professional. Some of the secure services that have been created to assume these risks are:

---

49   http://www.forbes.com/sites/danmunro/2013/05/01/hipaa-support-widens-in-cloud-vendor-community/

- *Hosting Service Providers* – Hosting services are very popular for a variety of data stores and applications and are referred to as Software as a Service (SaaS). Today, covered entities without the necessary security and infrastructure expertise can host their sensitive databases with organizations that do have the necessary expertise as well as geographical diversification in order to provide secure application support and availability. If interested in this type of service, a healthcare organization should focus on hosting service providers that are fully auditable and provide service level agreements.

- *Encryption in Transit Solution Providers* – Strong encryption can reduce the chances of a data transmission being compromised and is a requirement of many regulations. National and international requirements allow the use of 128-bit encryption, but utilizing a minimum 256-bit premium service is recommended and, in the U.S., is Federal Information Processing Standard (FIPS) Publication 140-2 (FIPS 140-2) compliant.

- *Encryption at Rest Solution Providers* – The requirement that all data is encrypted in storage is mandatory in some countries and by security best practices. This data-at-rest encryption reduces the likelihood of e-PHI being accessed by unauthorized persons in the event of hacking or theft. Many vendors provide both hardware and software that enables all databases and file systems to be encrypted.

- *Audit Solution Providers* – After a breach has occurred, the ability to audit who did what and when they did it is required in the healthcare industry, and having the ability to proactively gather intelligence is imperative. Providers of these tools are able to assist in both the discovery and investigation of correlated events and to reduce the risk of data leaving the organization. Additionally, auditors with independence and industry expertise provide greater assurance to regulators of an organization's compliance to regulations.

- *Security Solutions* – Many tools are currently available to allow for immediate awareness of, and reaction to, security threats. Providers of both hardware and software are making great strides in providing significant amounts of data specific to events that can cause harm, but all this data can require significant resources to process and understand. Some vendors have heuristic tools that can analyze the typical behavior of the network and applications so if the behavior becomes abnormal, these tools can block activity and alert the information security or network team.

1

Healthcare Industry

- **Security Incident Response** – Once a breach has occurred on an organization's IT systems and data, whether by an outside assailant or a malicious insider, a computer security incident response service can provide structured guidance for mitigating the attack. These services can efficiently filter through the volumes of data and can respond quickly with strong solutions.

- **Secure Backup (and Off-Site Retention) of Sensitive Data** – Long-term secure retention of data for as long as 25 years may be required by privacy regulations. Encrypting data archives and ensuring that the solution meets sensitive data requirements is a service provided by a variety of solutions and vendors.

- **Restricting Access to Authorized Users/Unique User Identification** – Tools and services that restrict access to authorized users, dual-factor authentication, and tracking-use software are essential to providing a secure network. Additionally, having the ability to securely access information in a disaster or remotely is an essential part of the CIA triad.

- **Secure Email** – Applications that are built to send email securely or services that enable email communication to be encrypted and read by authorized staff have become the normal way to do business. Many email service providers are available to provide for such services.

Breaches of Healthcare Information by Vendors

Due to the rising expectations of patients and regulators, the unauthorized release or breach of sensitive data has become heavily regulated. The opportunity to misuse data in order to steal identity or commit medical practice fraud has reached the point where regulators were required to respond. In the U.S., the Secretary of HHS is required by the HITECH Act to post a list of breaches of unsecured protected health information affecting 500 or more individuals.[50] These breaches are now posted in a new, more accessible format that allows users to search and sort on the names of covered entities and their business associates who have reported breaches of unsecured protected health information to the Secretary.[51] Such breaches often result in the loss of patients and customers and can seriously damage an organization's brand name.

---

50 http://www.hhs.gov/ocr/privacy/hipaa/administrative/breachnotificationrule/breachtool.html

51 http://search.hhs.gov/

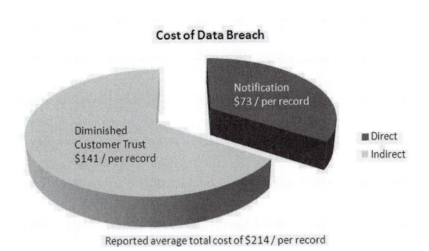

Figure 1.4 – **Cost of a Data Breach**
(Source: Ponemon Institute 2011 Cost of Data Breach Report)

Business Partners

As the network of the healthcare business becomes more complex and diverse, the advantage of sharing expertise and risk becomes an essential form of doing business. The ability to collaborate with another individual or group does just that, but the definition of partnership can become convoluted. A partnership typically has some degree of involvement with another entity's business dealings.

The term 'business partner' is frequently used for two businesses that cooperate, to any degree, and commit to the relationship, but it can refer to a legal structure for a business of two or more individuals, which is called a general partnership when used without a qualifier such as "limited" or "limited liability."[52] The main implication is that the relationship shares responsibilities and liabilities. Many legal requirements involving privacy and security grow from this relationship and require a clear assignment of responsibility for any issues that may arise.

In the U.S., the HHS felt that this relationship needed formalization despite any legal definition held between the partners. When both partners are providing the same health care service, the situation is resolved by providing the same covered entity requirements to both. However, in the situation where both partners are providing dissimilar health care services or supported health care in a close business relationship, HIPAA defines the role of the business associate. Using regulations, HHS gives clear direction that both now share accountability and responsibility for the privacy of the data in their charge. They also face similar fines in the event of a breach of their shared data.

---

52 Definition provided by Nolo's Plain-English Law Dictionary.

Contractually, this relationship can be very challenging as each entity desires to keep its processes proprietary, providing both a cost and efficiency advantage. This desire for control can lead to a potential for conflict as each entity may emphasize different operational goals. For example, one partner might focus on compliance and security of sensitive data assets, but the other partner might focus on cost savings, which is too often a divergent goal to security and privacy. The requirement for both partners to clearly identify their specific goals at the beginning of the relationship can mitigate much discord later on in the relationship. Trust must be a strong part of these relationships, and the verification through audit and transparency is the key to maintaining that trust. The old adage, "trust, but verify" is critical, and the ability to perform audits in order to verify compliance to the contract must be part of any long-term business partnership.

Business allies both bring a unique value to the partnership, and in the U.S., the business associate contract serves to clarify and limit that relationship between the parties. These partnership arrangements, due to the HIPAA Omnibus Rule and the Health Information Technology Economic and Clinical Health (HITECH) Act, have regulated activities or services that could fall under very restrictive requirements. If a breach of sensitive information is discovered, each responsible party is independently responsible and can be fined directly by the Office of Civil Rights (OCR), an office of HHS. This regulatory authority is new to many organizations, and the HCISPP should be able to understand the types of technologies and flows of information between both partners and be able to identify who has what responsibilities for security and privacy. Contractual language should always be in place to spell out all partners' responsibilities in order to protect the privacy and security of health information.

Data Sharing

Healthcare data sharing concerns surface in a variety of ways. The obvious concern is those business associates who require access to patient data from many different locations around the world. The ability of an organization to authorize, authenticate, and transfer data securely, timely, and in a useable format is a requirement for the application of quality health care. The use of data format and transfer protocols, such as Electronic Data Interchange (EDI), between partners to exchange data has made great strides in all but eliminating the need for paper flows and faxes.

In 1993, the Workgroup for Electronic Data Interchange (WEDI) made the first attempt to standardize electronic healthcare data exchange. HIPAA now requires the use of EDI for electronic transmission of patient care and insurance information.

The scientific community has a long history of sharing data with other agencies and research organizations, and they have guidance for methods sharing data. HHS and other U.S. federal agencies are collaborating with one another to develop an interoperable data infrastructure to support research and data sharing. Varieties of agencies and organizations have developed guidance on the sharing of this research data to include:

- The National Institute of Health (NIH) endorses the sharing of research data;
- The National Science Foundation now requires grant applications to include a data sharing and management plan;
- The Center for Disease Control (CDC) standards for how research is done in their counseling, testing, and referral (CTR) data protocol include data sharing policies;
- The Medical Research Council (MRC) is developing a more comprehensive set of guidelines to govern management and sharing of research data;
- The Economic and Social Research Council (ESRC) has revised its longstanding research data sharing policy and guidelines;
- The Engineering and Physical Sciences Research Council (EPSRC) in the United Kingdom (UK) is preparing a policy framework for management, sharing, and access to research data;
- The Commission Nationale de l'informatique et des libertes (CNIL), also known as the French Data Protection Authority, monitors the security of information systems by checking that all precautions are taken to prevent the data from being distorted or disclosed to unauthorized parties.[53]

Even with the standards defined from industry associations and self-regulating bodies, interoperability issues remain today. Unique proprietary standards and various levels of data maturity have continued to provide obstacles in the sharing of sensitive data between healthcare organizations. Providers and business partners in the healthcare industry still need guidance, and regulators will need to continue to provide more guidance.

Regulators

Owners of organizations, chief information officers (CIO), and IT professionals within the healthcare environment are tasked with achieving a balance between the demand for universal access to information and the need to ensure security and privacy. Added to this is the challenge of achieving compliance

---

53 http://www.cnil.fr/english/the-cnil/role-and-responsabilities/

with increasing regulatory requirements, such as HIPAA, the HITECH Act, and the Omnibus Act in the U.S., and the European Commission's Data Protection Directive as well as the European Commission's unveiled General Data Protection Regulation (GDPR) that will supersede it in 2016. A sampling of some of the regulators responsible for the healthcare industry is:

- **The Department of Health and Human Services (HHS)** is the U.S. government's principal agency for protecting the health of all Americans and providing essential human services;[54]
- **The Office of Civil Rights (OCR)** is the U.S. government's enforcement arm for the HIPAA Privacy and Security Rules. OCR helps to protect the privacy of health information held by health insurers and certain healthcare providers and insurers;[55]
- **The National Institute of Standards and Technology (NIST)** is a federal government standards organization that conducts world-class research, often in close collaboration with industry that advances the nation's technology infrastructure and helps U.S. companies continually improve products and services. The NIST Special Publications are mandated guidance to federal agencies and provide guidance to other state and local governmental agencies;[56]
- **The Federal Information Processing Standards (FIPS)** are publicly announced standardizations developed by NIST after approval by the Secretary of Commerce pursuant to Section 5131 of the Information Technology Reform Act of 1996;[57]
- **The Federal Trade Commission (FTC)** is the U.S.'s chief privacy policy and enforcement agency and author of the U.S./EU Safe Harbor Program;
- **The European Commission** established common EU rules to ensure that personal data enjoys a high standard of protection everywhere in the EU. Since 2009, new requirements have been introduced and are being implemented by the Commission under the EU Data Protection Regulation;[58]
- **The Commission Nationale de l'Informatique et des Libertes (CNIL)** supervises compliance with the law by inspecting IT systems and applications. The Commission also uses its inspection and investigation powers to investigate complaints.[59]

---

54 http://www.hhs.gov/about/

55 http://www.hhs.gov/ocr/office/index.html

56 http://www.nist.gov/

57 http://csrc.nist.gov/publications/PubsFIPS.html

58 http://ec.europa.eu/about/index_en.htm

59 http://www.cnil.fr/english/the-cnil/role-and-responsabilities/

- **The Information Commissioner's Office (ICO)** is the UK's independent authority set up to uphold information rights in the public interest.[60]

This sample is a representative set of the many regulators that an organization may need to deal with for privacy and security issues worldwide. There are other regulators depending on which country that an organization conducts business in. The challenge as a HCISPP is to secure access to data resources, to protect confidential patient information, and to ensure the systems are available to all who need it, and to conform and comply with sometimes-conflicting laws and regulations.

Foundational Health Data Management Processes

With an estimated 50 petabytes of data in the healthcare industry, data is growing exponentially and will continue to play a large role in transforming health care. Some of the causes of this data growth are a direct result of where it is used, stored, and generated and are influenced by:

- The surge mobile device adoption as well as the prevalence of internet access, which has created an anywhere-and-anytime expectation of data availability;
- Cloud applications, portable storage devices, and email communication that have sent our data to storage devices located in any office, state, or country with a variety of privacy requirements;
- The fact that our data is generated and stored directly in multiple smart devices with multi-vender interoperability challenges; and
- Medical data that can be generated directly in our bodies and communicated wirelessly from the biological environment to the business environment for uses that could not be conceived of only a few short years ago.

This growth in data and multiple uses of data that go far beyond the traditional doctor's office has caused regulatory and technical challenges that confront healthcare management today. Security and privacy of this "big data"[61] results in new safeguard requirements and standards from a regulatory environment that is in flux, and healthcare data flows today require the HCISSP to go beyond what was not even imagined yesterday.

---

60 http://www.ico.org.uk/

61 Big data is a term that has grown to describe the huge amounts of data being generated and the analytics and predictive statistical analysis that comes from the research and examination of that data generated.

So, where does this data originate from and how does it flow throughout the delivery of health care? Below is a sanitized and simplified diagram showing data flows in an actual insurance claims process. Data flows into the organization from partners or patients; the electronic 835 files on the left of the diagram are one example of this flow. The example 835 files are received, adjudicated, imaged, and can go through several different processes. The final output goes to the patient and various partners on the right of the diagram. Today, this process could involve many more steps, be transmitted to a vast array of partners and be stored in a variety of repositories. Each step in this process exposes the data to security and privacy risks that require safeguards to mitigate those risks.

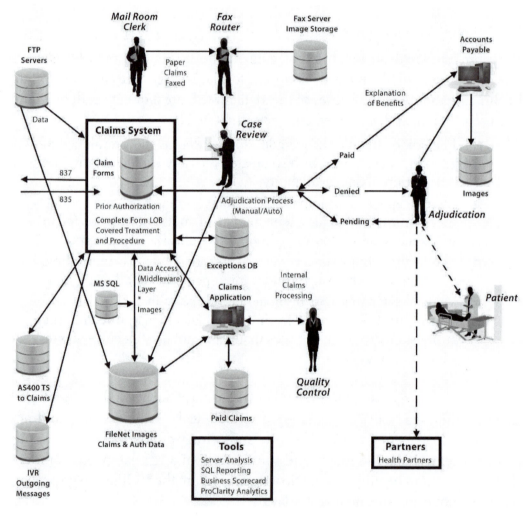

Figure 1.5 – **Healthcare Claims Business Process Flows**

Information Flow and Life Cycle

Controlling patient data and the different data flows that are necessary in the healthcare ecosystem is sophisticated and challenging. The key to this ecosystem is understanding the relationship between the patient, the provider, and the healthcare organization and how services are delivered, tracked, and paid for digitally. It is vital to effectively manage these data flows and enforce patient privacy preferences for their data exchange. As the world moves toward the broad adoption of various standards for this exchange of electronic data, the Centers for Medicare & Medicaid Services (CMS) in the U.S. has established an incentive program to help organizations adopt the Electronic Health Record (EHR) standard. EHRs are real-time, patient-centered records that make information available instantly, whenever and wherever it is needed.[62] The goals for the new EHRs are:

- Contain information about a patient's medical history, diagnoses, medications, immunization dates, allergies, radiology images, and lab and test results;
- Offer access to evidence-based tools that providers can use in making decisions about a patient's care;
- Automate and streamline providers' workflow;
- Increase organization and accuracy of patient information; and
- Support key market changes in payer requirements and consumer expectations.

Most U.S. health providers and hospitals will eventually standardize on the EHR standard as the U.S. government currently covers 46% of U.S. healthcare expenditures.

The U.S. government is also promoting the health information exchange (HIE) system through the American Recovery and Reinvestment Act (ARRA). HIE facilitates the movement of healthcare information electronically across organizations within a region, community, or hospital system. This exchange (not to be confused with a health insurance exchange) facilitates the flow of electronic healthcare information across many government and private organizations. This facilitation of data exchange is still finalizing, but many regional systems called regional health information organizations (RHIOs) are using it and it includes over 14,000 physicians.[63]

---

62 http://www.healthit.gov/providers-professionals/learn-ehr-basics

63 Trends in Health Information Exchanges; http://www.innovations.ahrq.gov/content.aspx?id=3944

Widespread adoption and "meaningful use"[64] of health information technology (HIT) makes it possible for healthcare providers to improve management of patient care through secure use and sharing of health information. HIT includes the use of EHRs instead of paper medical records to maintain people's health information. This secure electronic exchange of health information will improve healthcare coordination, clinical outcomes, and the patient experience.

Healthcare information has various regulated requirements for the retention of healthcare data, and various country requirements range from six years under HIPAA to forever under some EU articles. This requirement is one of the primary drivers for the growth of data and its storage requirements. The need to quickly recall data that may be years old and necessary for chronic diseases, imperative for a statistical understanding of trends, or required to aid in the ability to support medical services can be as critical as data just created. The lifecycle management of healthcare information involves long-term availability, security, and stewardship from the provider.

Today, with the desire for more availability and the need to drive down costs, many providers are turning to the various cloud providers. The cost savings promised by these providers are very tempting, but if the solution does not adequately protect the data, a breach can occur. HIPAA data breaches result in providers and health plans suffering significant fines, reduction of trust, and damage to their reputation.

Health Data Characterization

There is a variety of health data used internationally for numerous reasons. Classification of that data can be done according to any criteria. For example, data can be broken down by its physical characteristics, such as file type, operating platform, average file size, when it was created, when it was last accessed or used, which department last used it, etc. The National Center for Health Statistics (NCHS) serves as the WHO's center for the classification of data and health related activities, which in the U.S. uses the ICD codes to classify health data. Through their effective use, providers can make better decisions and provide a higher level of care by classifying different healthcare data types for different uses. Healthcare data's production, collection, storage, and use are necessary in fulfilling their mission in an efficient way. However, because healthcare data is some of the most valuable assets owned by the healthcare industry, laws, standards, and policies mandate privacy and protection as another method to classify health data. This is a more practical way for the HCISPP to classify data as it is based on risk management, legal discovery, and compliance issues.

---

64 Meaningful use is the set of standards defined by the Centers for Medicare & Medicaid Services (CMS) Incentive Programs that governs the use of electronic health records.

Classifying data based on its need for privacy is the first step in determining the data's need for protection. The healthcare data is classified based on the information contained in the data elements, such as:

- **Social Security Number Data** – the nine digit code unique to each American and used for social security benefits and other identification purposes;
- **Credit Card Transaction Data** – the information contained on the credit card and other transnational data used to document the payment of services;
- **Patient Health Data** – The data designated by HIPAA as the 18 identifiers and other sensitive data used for health care; and
- **Financial Data** – personal sensitive data used for payment and credit history.

Within the data Workflow Management in the U.S., HIPAA has a classification requirement for providers to use a special taxonomy code called the National Provider Identifier (NPI), which is part of HIPAA's Administrative Simplification provision. The Healthcare Provider Taxonomy code divides healthcare providers into hierarchical groupings by type, classification, and specialization, and assigns a classification code to each grouping. It is designed to uniquely identify a provider based on three distinct levels.

- **Level 1** is provider type
- **Level 2** is classification
- **Level 3** is the area of specialization

This use of a Healthcare Provider Taxonomy code is designed for use in an electronic environment, specifically within ASC X12N[65] healthcare transactions. This includes the transactions mandated under HIPAA.

With all of the health data being generated by patients, providers, health plans, and insurance organizations, another major use of healthcare data is to provide an understanding or predictor of future performance, done by reviewing past performance. This study of the data is called analytics and predictive modeling, and they are both experiencing major developments in the evolution of data management and information technology utilization. Huge data warehouses or data collection repositories of electronic medical records data are being analyzed and characterized by various analytical tools with hopes of using that data to predict care and behavior.

---

65   Accredited Standards Committee (ASC) X12 is a membership based not-for-profit organization chartered in 1979 by the American National Standards Institute (ANSI) to develop uniform data standards and specifications for cross-industry electronic exchange of business transactions. See http://www.x12.org/

Data Interoperability and Exchange

Interoperability describes the extent to which systems and devices can exchange data as well as interpret that shared information. Hospitals and other healthcare provider organizations typically have many different computer systems used for everything from billing records to patient tracking. All of these systems should communicate and interoperate with each other, but not all do. There are standards that enable the data exchange and interpretation of classification codes to be seamlessly used by disparate systems, many of which have been adopted by the vendor community, some by the international community and still others are only supported by individual jurisdictions. Three data interoperability methodologies are HL7, DICOM, and IHE.

HL7

Health Level 7 (HL7, named after the 7th application layer of the ISO IP Model) specifies a number of flexible standards, guidelines, and methodologies by which various healthcare systems can communicate with each other.[66] HL7 includes approximately 500 corporate members who represent more than 90% of the information systems vendors serving healthcare[67] and most equipment types support this standard of data control. Most HL7 standards are now considered as open standards and, since April 2013, are available for free from the HL7 website.[68]

The HL7 v3 confidentiality code vocabulary is a "structured code set" designed to restrict access to healthcare information. The confidentiality codes can be used to associate data elements to privilege and access permission rights with document, message, and record level metadata. The application of the codes enables organizations within a HIE to establish a uniform vocabulary that can restrict information access by context, role, rule, permission, purpose, information type, and patient type through structured directive rules at a granular level for various types of data elements.

HL7 messages utilize metadata in the transmission of documents as a way for a sender to inform a receiver of how to handle the data's access controls. In this way, the publisher of a document can indicate the sensitivity classification of the document. Confidentiality codes can be applied in various situations to protect information by:

- Restricting access based on the specific role of the requestor;
- Restricting access by the patient's consent directive; and
- Restricting access by the type of information (general access directives).

---

66 http://en.wikipedia.org/wiki/Health_Level_7

67 http://www.hl7.org/about/index.cfm?ref=nav

68 http://www.hl7.org/

The Common Terminology Services (CTS) Release 2 standard, also developed by HL7, provides a suite of standards for sharing data across different health IT systems and provides a way to federate the development of common international standards as well.[69]

DICOM

Digital Imaging and Communications in Medicine (DICOM) standards specify many different formats for image data. DICOM is the international standard for medical images and related information (ISO 12052) and provides document capture and enterprise content management solutions that were adopted by the National Electrical Manufacturers Association (NEMA) and the American College of Radiology for computerized axial tomography (CAT).

DICOM defines the data and quality formats for medical images exchanged for clinical use and utilizes metadata in the transmission of documents similar to HL7. It is implemented in radiology, cardiology imaging, and radiotherapy devices, and increasingly in devices in other areas of medicine such as ophthalmology and dentistry.[70] This protocol enables interoperability, which is important in reducing the cost and increasing efficiency of health care by sharing patient data and optimizing workflows. The DICOM standard is also utilized by cloud-based medical image exchange services, making it easy to access medical images, but it also creates more exposure to malicious exploits.

IHE

Another technical framework called Integrating the Healthcare Enterprise (IHE) defines a common information model and a common vocabulary for systems to use in communicating medical information. It was founded in 1997 by the Healthcare Information and Management Systems Society (HIMSS) and the Radiological Society of North America (RSNA) in order to enable the collaboration of healthcare providers and industry leaders to work together to improve the interoperability and exchange of health information. IHE specifies how DICOM and HL7 are to be used by information systems to complete a set of well-defined transactions that accomplish a particular task and documents how to use established clinical information workflows, standards, tools, and services for healthcare data interoperability.

---

69 http://www.hl7.org/implement/standards/product_brief.cfm?product_id=10

70 http://medical.nema.org/Dicom/about-DICOM.html

IHE utilizes a framework for standards-based interoperability of healthcare IT systems, which is being adopted and implemented worldwide.[71] Rather than create new standards, IHE drives the adoption of existing standards to address specific technical needs. It is multi-domain with integration profiles for radiology, cardiology, laboratory, and information technology infrastructure, which enable interoperability both within an organization and across multiple enterprises. Profiles also specify how standards are to be used to address clinical needs, reducing configuration and interfacing costs and ensuring a higher level of interoperability. The IHE technical framework is process oriented and defines a set of protocols that must interact with each other to successfully complete the process. The protocols interact by means of a well-defined set of transactions that are based on DICOM and HL7 messages.

Legal Medical Records

Today, fewer medical records are being stored in paper format and more are being stored in computer databases that allow for greater efficiencies in the processing of clinical and financial services. Electronic storage of medical records also has other unintended consequences that include the threat of patient privacy and the increased potential for misuse. Healthcare organizations that store and use medical records have had to establish security measures, prompted by an inconsistent patchwork of legal standards that vary from industry to industry, state to state, and country to country. There is widespread concern that the various legal entities that regulate the use of these legal medical records have unrealistic and sometimes conflicting requirements, even though HIPAA mandated that the administration develop regulations regarding the control of these medical records.

In the U.S., the legal medical record is a subset of the designated record set and is the set of records that would be released for legal proceedings or in response to a request for patient medical record release. The legal medical record may include records maintained in an electronic medical record system. An example would be an electronic system framework that integrates data from multiple sources, captures data at the point of care, and supports caregiver decision making.

The designated record set is a group of records that include PHI and that is maintained, collected, used, or disseminated by, or for, covered entities for each individual that receives care from them. The DRS includes:

---

71 http://www.iheusa.org/about.aspx

- The legal medical records and billing records about individuals maintained by or for a covered entity (including in a business associate's records);
- The enrollment, payment, claims adjudication, and case or medical management record systems maintained by or for a health plan; or
- The information used, in part or in whole, to make decisions about an individual's care.

Internationally, medical record privacy and security measures control and regulate the use and transfer of healthcare and personal data. In the EU, everyone has the right to the protection of his or her personal data. Under EU law, personal data can only be gathered legally under strict conditions and for a legitimate purpose. Additionally, persons or organizations that collect and manage personal information must protect it from misuse and must respect certain privacy rights. The EU's Data Protection Directive also regulates specific rules for the transfer of personal data outside of the EU in order to ensure the best possible protection of patient data when it is exported abroad.

On April 11, 2011, India adopted new privacy regulations, known as the Information Technology Rules (Reasonable Security Practices and Procedures and Sensitive Personal Data or Information). The Rules impose wide-ranging regulations on any corporation that "collects, receives, possesses, stores, deals or handles" personal information. These regulations require companies to provide privacy policies, restrict the processing of sensitive personal data, and restrict international data transfers. The rules introduce a HIPAA Omnibus style privacy law that is also similar in many respects to EU data protection laws, but it specifically targets India's numerous outsourcing vendors and their customers.[72]

Many other nation states are enacting or have enacted several privacy laws regarding the right to restrict the way data in a patient's medical record or history is used.

---

72 http://cis-india.org/internet-governance/blog/comments-on-the-it-reasonable-security-practices-and-procedures-and-sensitive-personal-data-or-information-rules-2011

Domain 1 – *Review Questions*

1. A Health Information Exchange (HIE) is an example of _____.

    A. Health Information Technology (HIT).
    B. Personal Health Record.
    C. An exclusion under HIPAA.
    D. An implantable medical device.

2. Information security and privacy **MOST** benefit the healthcare industry by _____.

    A. Increasing organizational information technology costs.
    B. Allowing the organization to meet legal mandatory requirements.
    C. Ensuring risk is identified and managed in an appropriate and timely manner.
    D. Transferring risk from the organization to another party.

3. Two of the **MOST** important features of an Health Information Exchange are

    A. Scalability and patient "ease of use."
    B. Scalability and security.
    C. Interoperability and security.
    D. Interoperability and patient "ease of use."

4. Which of the following **BEST** describes the general benefits of a Health Information Exchange?
   A. Providing a vehicle for improving quality and safety of patient care, providing a basic level of interoperability among electronic health records (EHRs) maintained by individual physicians and organizations, and reducing healthcare fraud and abuse.
   B. Providing a vehicle for improving quality and safety of patient care, reducing healthcare fraud and abuse, and providing the backbone of technical infrastructure for leveraging by national and state-level initiatives.
   C. Reducing healthcare fraud and abuse, providing a basic level of interoperability among electronic health records (EHRs) maintained by individual physicians and organizations, and providing the backbone of technical infrastructure for leveraging by national and state-level initiatives.
   D. Reducing healthcare fraud and abuse, providing a basic level of interoperability among electronic health records (EHRs) maintained by individual physicians and organizations, and providing the backbone of technical infrastructure for leveraging by national and state-level initiatives.

5. Select the **BEST** response from the following to complete the phrase: Medical coding _____.
   A. Is used as part of an organization's information security and privacy risk management process.
   B. Has unified the practice of healthcare internationally and established a standard for billing and payment from private and government programs.
   C. Provides an effective way to determine data classification
   D. Provides a standard to determine an information's confidentiality, integrity and availability impact.

6. When designing a workflow for sensitive patient information, which of the following is **MOST** important in terms of privacy?
   A. Data integrity checks and audit logs.
   B. "Minimum necessary use" and data integrity checks.
   C. Audit logs and availability tests.
   D. "Minimum necessary use" and audit logs.

7. In the United States under HIPAA, Doctors, clinics, pharmacies and psychologists are **BEST** defined as _____.
   A. Health information clearing houses.
   B. Providers of services.
   C. Healthcare Plans.
   D. Business Associates.

8. How does the U.S. HIPAA privacy and U.S. HIPAA security rule differ?
   A. No difference exist; they mandate the same requirements
   B. The privacy rule applies to electronic transmissions while the security rule applies to physical and verbal matters.
   C. The security rule applies to electronic transmissions while the privacy rule applies to physical and verbal matters.
   D. The privacy rule contradicts the security rule regarding electronic health records.

9. The U.S. HIPAA Privacy Rule de-identification requirement
   A. allows patient data to be used for research without consent if the data is from less than eighteen people.
   B. allows patient data to be used for research without consent if an expert determines the data has been de-identified or if eighteen specific identifiers are removed.
   C. allows research on data of individuals over the age of eighteen without their consent.
   D. allows the selling of fully identifiable patient data to non-covered entities.

10. Which of the following **BEST** explains the relationship between the U.S. HIPAA and U.S. HITECH laws?
    A. HIPAA enhances HITECH by specifying that the U.S. Food and Drug Administration must administer a PHI breach notification and enforcement program.
    B. HITECH nullifies HIPAA and acts as a holistic replacement designed with electronic health records in mind.
    C. HITECH enhances HIPAA by specifying the U.S. HHS Office of Civil Rights as the enforcer of HIPAA privacy and security rules.
    D. HIPAA nullifies HITECH and acts as a holistic replacement designed with electronic health records in mind.

Domain 2

Regulatory Environment

THE CURRENT CHAPTER covers the domain of healthcare information security, legal, regulations, standards, and compliance. The healthcare regulatory environment domain addresses general computer crime legislation and healthcare data handling and disclosure regulations; the focus is on concepts and internationally accepted methods, processes, and procedures. It is important to highlight the international focus of this chapter early to ensure the HCISPP has a general grasp on global requirements. This chapter will avoid in-depth discussions of country- or region-specific laws, legislation, and regulations. Although some regional examples are presented to clarify certain discussion points, these will be limited to the emphasis of principles common across most, if not all, jurisdictions.

The chapter has been logically broken down into broad categories, each with several subsections. The major sections set the stage for subsequent sections and deal with the major legal systems of the world. The intention is not to turn readers into international law experts but to introduce the context and backdrop for the remainder of the chapter. Under the major legal systems and healthcare regulatory environments, the reader will examine, at a high level, principles of common law; civil or code law; and customary, religious, and mixed legal systems. Similarities and differences between these systems that are important for information security professionals will be briefly introduced.

Later sections deal specifically with healthcare law and regulations as they relate to information systems. Patient treatment, payment, operations, and related healthcare functions, such as data analytics and research, often require the routine exchange of sensitive patient health information. As a result, the healthcare industry receives a significant amount of oversight in many countries around the globe, and there are numerous laws, regulations, and best practice frameworks that specifically address the privacy and security of patient health information impacting what, when, how, and with whom this information may be exchanged. HCISPP candidates should be able to identify and understand relevant legal and regulatory requirements related to health information, including requirements for trans-border data exchange, and help ensure their organization's policies and procedures are in compliance.

TOPICS

- Identify applicable regulations including those related to:
  - Legal issues that pertain to information security and privacy for healthcare organizations
  - Data breach regulations
  - Personally identifiable information
  - Information flow mapping
  - Jurisdiction implications
  - Data subjects
  - Data owners/controllers/custodians/processors
- Understand international regulations and controls including:
  - Treaties (e.g., Safe Harbor)
  - Regulations
  - Industry specific laws (mental health, substance abuse, pregnancy, HIV)
  - Legislative
    - EU Data Privacy Directive
    - HIPAA/HITECH
- Compare internal practices against new policies and procedures
  - Policies (information security and privacy)
  - Standards (information security and privacy)
  - Procedures (information security and privacy)
- Understand compliance frameworks including:
  - ISO
  - NIST
  - Common Criteria
  - IG Toolkit
  - Generally Accepted Privacy Principles (GAPP)
- Understand response for risk-based decisions
  - Compensating controls
  - Control variance documentation
  - Residual risk tolerance
- Understand and comply with codes of ethics/conducts in a health information environment
  - Organizational code of ethics
  - (ISC)² code of ethics

OBJECTIVES

According to the (ISC)[2] Candidate Information Bulletin, a HCISPP candidate is expected to identify and describe relevant legal and regulatory requirements regarding:

- Healthcare information
- How organizational policies and procedures are in compliance
- Frameworks that are used within the healthcare industry to ensure compliance

Identify Applicable Regulations

The healthcare industry is consistently changing, whether it is advances in technology for devices, electronic health records, or healthcare organization payment frameworks. All of these changes pose challenges for healthcare organizations and professionals to ensure they comply with changing regulatory requirements for not only the country they live in; depending on the organization's role, regulatory requirements of other international countries may need to be considered. In addition to the complications of the international regulatory environment, there are other requirements and standards for industry technology, information types, or codes of ethics that may need to be taken into account, as illustrated in *Figure 2.1*.

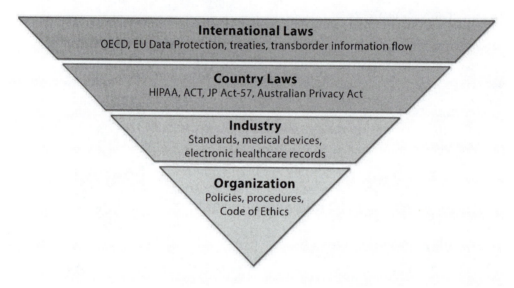

Figure 2.1 – **Healthcare Regulatory Model**

Legal Issues That Pertain to Information Security and Privacy for Healthcare Organizations

Navigating the regulatory environment is a complicated and convoluted process for most healthcare organizations that definitely requires the participation of all employees. The level of participation and tasks is dependent on the employee's job function. In any situation, it is necessary for the organizations to identify the applicable legal issues that pertain to information security and privacy for the organization and to create the framework for their policies and procedures that employees need to adhere to and ensure compliance. The involvement of legal expertise, whether outsourced or within the organization, is generally necessary to assist with the identification of information security and privacy issues associated with the information types the organization collects, stores, transmits, and deletes.

Healthcare organizations often have sensitive information about their patients relating to their health records that may be health, personal, or financial information. In any of these cases, that information is sensitive and protected by laws and regulations to protect an individual's information from malicious or accidental loss or theft. Part of information security is protecting the integrity of information and preventing data from being accidentally modified. Another part of information security is protecting the confidentiality of the information. For example, information containing a person's test results including his or her personal information is emailed to the wrong person. This is also an issue from a privacy point of view. Although it may have been an accident, it is still a legal issue with repercussions for individuals or organizations from a financial or credibility aspect. Malicious loss and theft of personal information is often for the purpose of identity theft, which may result in major financial impacts to individuals and organizations, depending on the amount of information lost or stolen. Identity theft may be a simple use of a credit card number, or it may be a complete use of a person's identity. In either case, it is a serious crime and easy to accomplish given today's interconnected world. The 2013 Identity Fraud Report, released annually by Javelin Research, reported more than 12 million identity fraud victims, resulting in $21 billion U.S. dollars in stolen money.[1] When information, personal, health, financial, or otherwise, is lost or stolen, the laws and regulations surrounding enforcement and protection vary significantly between countries and are even nonexistent in some.

Data Breach Regulations

Most countries that have laws concerning the accidental or malicious loss of personal information refer to the incident as a data breach. Data breaches may contain financial information, PHI, or personally identifiable information (PII), which is discussed further in the next section. A recent data breach occurred in December 2013 affecting the U.S. company Target. 40 million credit and debit card accounts were stolen, which has resulted in Target stock prices dropping and, at this time, an unknown financial impact to cover fraud protection, settlements, and other costs. The Ponemon Institute estimates the highest average cost of a single record for a data breach to be at $194 in the U.S., with Germany as a close second at $191 per record.[2] In addition, an organization may have impacts to its customer loyalty or credibility, resulting in loss of business. Many of the data protection laws have requirements for breach notification of individuals and law enforcement.[3]

---

1   https://www.javelinstrategy.com/brochure/276

2   http://www.symantec.com/content/en/us/about/media/pdfs/b-ponemon-2011-cost-of-data-breach-global.en-us.pdf

3   http://www.bakerlaw.com/files/Uploads/Documents/Data%20Breach%20documents/International-Compendium-of-Data-Privacy-Laws.pdf

Personally Identifiable Information

With the proliferation of technology and the increasing awareness that people's personally identifiable information (PII) is stored online or electronically in some way, shape, or form, there is growing pressure to protect personal information. Almost weekly, there are media reports worldwide of databases being compromised, files being lost, and attacks against businesses and systems that house personal, private information. This has spurred concerns over the proper collection, use, retention, and destruction of information of a personal or confidential nature including Protected Health Information (PHI). PHI not only includes an individual's medical records, but also his or her billing history and information. This public concern has prompted the creation of regulations intended to foster the responsible use and stewardship of personal information. In the context of this discussion, privacy is one of the primary areas in which business, in almost all industries, is forced to deal with regulations and regulatory compliance.

The actual enactment of regulations or, in some cases, laws dealing with privacy depends on the jurisdiction. Some countries have opted for a generic approach to privacy regulations—horizontal enactment (i.e., across all industries, including government), while others have decided to regulate by industry—vertical enactment (e.g., financial, health, publicly traded). Regardless of the approach, the overall objective is to protect a citizen's personal information while at the same time balancing the business, governmental, and academic or research need to collect and use this information appropriately. Unfortunately, there is no one international privacy law, resulting in a mosaic of legislation and regulations. Some countries have been progressive in dealing with privacy and personal information, while others have yet to act in this area. Given the fact that the Internet has created a global community, our information and business transactions and operations may cross several different borders and jurisdictions—each with their own sovereign concerns, societal standards, and laws. Therefore, it is prudent that we have a basic understanding of privacy principles and guidelines and keep up to date with the changing landscape of privacy regulations that may affect our business as well as our personal information.

Privacy can be defined as "the rights and obligations of individuals and organizations with respect to the collection, use, retention, and disclosure of personal information." Personal information is a rather generic concept and encompasses any information that is about or on an identifiable individual. Although international privacy laws are somewhat different in respect to their specific requirements, they all tend to be based on core principles or guidelines. The Organization for Economic Cooperation and Development (OECD) has broadly classified these principles into the collection limitation, data quality, purpose specification, use limitation, security safeguards, openness, individual participation, and accountability. The guidelines are as follows:

- There should be limits to the collection of personal data, and any such data should be obtained by lawful and fair means and, where appropriate, with the knowledge or consent of the data subject.
- Personal data should be relevant to the purposes for which they are to be used and, to the extent necessary for those purposes, should be accurate, complete, and kept up to date.
- The purposes for which personal data is collected should be specified not later than at the time of data collection, and the subsequent use limited to the fulfillment of those purposes or such others as are not incompatible with those purposes and as are specified on each occasion of change of purpose.
- Personal data should not be disclosed, made available, or otherwise used for purposes other than those specified above except:
  - With the consent of the data subject.
  - By the authority of law.
- Personal data should be protected by reasonable security safeguards against such risks as loss or unauthorized access, destruction, use, modification, or disclosure of data.

There should be a general policy of openness about developments, practices, and policies concerning personal data. Means should be readily available for establishing the existence and nature of personal data, and the main purposes of their use, as well as the identity and usual residence of the data controller.

- An individual should have the right:
  - To obtain from a data controller, or otherwise, confirmation of whether the data controller has data relating to him or her.

To be told of data relating to him or her:

- Within a reasonable time
- At a charge, if any, that is not excessive
- In a reasonable manner
- In a form that is readily intelligible to him or her
- To be given reasons if a request made is denied and to be able to challenge such denial
- To challenge data relating to him or her and, if the challenge is successful, to have the data erased, rectified, completed, or amended. A data controller should be accountable for complying with measures that give effect to the principles stated above.

2

Regulatory Environment

69

It should be noted that the OECD is very cautious about not creating barriers to the legitimate trans-border flow of personal information. The OECD also cautions members to be aware of, and sensitive to, regional or domestic differences and to safeguard personal information from countries that do not follow the OECD guidelines or an equivalent.

These principles should form the minimum set of requirements for the development of reasonable legislation, regulations, and policy, and nothing prevents organizations from adding additional principles. However, the actual application of these principles has proved more difficult and costly in almost all circumstances; there has been a vast underestimation of the impact of the various privacy laws and policies both domestically and with cross-border commerce. This is not an excuse to abandon, block, or fail to comply with applicable laws, regulations, or policies. However, the HCISPP needs to appreciate that business practices have changed due to the need to be in compliance (often with international regulations) and that budgets must be appropriately increased to meet the demand.

Information Flow Mapping

Understanding information flow is critical to ensure information stays within legal jurisdictions desired by an organization. In order to understand information flow mapping, it is necessary to understand general information security models and that their focus is on defining allowed interactions between subjects (active parties) and objects (passive parties) at a particular moment in time. Consider a simple example of a user trying to access a file on a computing system. As the active party, the user would be the subject while the file would be considered the object. The following types of security models approach the problem in slightly different ways.

- ■ ***State Machine Model:***[4] State describes a system at a point in time. A state machine model, then, describes the behavior of a system as it moves between one state and another, from one moment to another. Typically, it uses mathematics to describe system states and the transition functions that define allowed or unpermitted actions. When it is used in security modeling, the purpose is to define which actions will be permitted at any point in time to ensure that a secure state (a point in time when things are secure) is preserved. The role of time in a state machine model is very important. According to its rule set, which is determined by a security policy, a model system's secure state can only change at distinct points in time, such as when an event occurs or a clock triggers it. Thus, upon its initial start-

---

4   http://openlearn.open.ac.uk/mod/oucontent/view.php?id=397581&section=9.1

up, the system checks to determine if it is in a secure state. Once the system is determined to be in a secure state, the state machine model will ensure that every time the system is accessed, it will be accessed only in accordance with the security policy rules. This process will guarantee that the system will transition only from one secure state to another secure state.

- ■ ***Multilevel Lattice Models:***[5] Multilevel security models describe strict layers of subjects and objects and define clear rules that allow or disallow interactions between them based on the layers they are in. These are often described using lattices or discrete layers with minimal or no interfaces between them. Most lattice models define a hierarchical lattice with layers of lesser or greater privilege. Subjects are assigned security clearances that define what layer they are assigned to, and objects are classified into similar layers. Related security labels are attached to all subjects and objects. According to this type of model, the clearance of the subject is compared with the classification of the data to determine access. They will also look at what the subject is trying to do to determine whether access should be allowed.

- ■ ***Noninterference Model:*** Noninterference models[6] may be considered a type of multilevel model with a high degree of strictness, severely limiting any higher-classified information from being shared with lower-privileged subjects even when higher-privileged subjects are using the system at the same time. In other words, these models not only address obvious and intentional interactions between subjects and objects, but they also deal with the effects of covert channels that may leak information inappropriately. The goal of a noninterference model is to help ensure that high-level actions (inputs) do not determine what low-level users can see (outputs). Most of the security models presented are secured by permitting restricted flows between high- and low-level users. A noninterference model maintains activities at different security levels to separate these levels from each other. In this way, it minimizes leakages that may happen through covert channels because there is complete separation between security levels. Because a subject at a higher security level has no way to interfere with the activities at a lower level, the lower-level subject cannot get any information from the higher level.

---

5   http://dimacs.rutgers.edu/Workshops/Lattices/slides/meadows.pdf

6   http://www.cs.cornell.edu/andru/cs711/2003fa/reading/1990mclean-sp.pdf

■ **Matrix-Based Models:** While lattice-based models tend to treat similar subjects and objects with similar restrictions, matrix-based models focus on one-to-one relationships between subjects and objects. The best-known example is the organization of subjects and objects into an access control matrix. An access control matrix is a two-dimensional table that allows for individual subjects and objects to be related to each other. It lists the subjects (such as users or processes) down the left-hand side and all the resources and functions across the top in the table. A matrix is a concise way to represent the capabilities that subjects have when accessing particular objects. To make this easier, an individual subject may be put into groups or roles, and the matrix is built according to role or group membership. This provides ease of management and simplification.

Most matrix-based models provide more than simple binary rules (such as allow or deny). Sometimes it is beneficial to specify how the access will be performed or what capabilities the subject will require. Perhaps some subjects are allowed read only, while others can read and write.

The list of access methods will be what is appropriate to the organization. Typical access methods for content are read, write, edit, and delete. Recording this type of information requires extending the access control matrix to include the appropriate permissions in each cell. It is important to note that this model does not describe the relationship between subjects in the model, such as if one subject created another or gave another subject access rights.

■ **Information Flow Models:**[7] While most models are concerned with subjects-to-objects relationships, information flow models focus on how information is allowed or not allowed between individual objects. Information flow models are used to determine if information is being properly protected throughout a given process. They may be used to identify potential covert channels, unintended information flow between compartments in compartmented systems. For example, although compartment A has no authorized path to do so, it may send information to compartment B by changing a variable or condition that B can see. This usually involves cooperation between the owners of the compartments in a manner that is not intended or anticipated by the managers of the system. Alternatively, compartment B may simply gather intelligence about compartment A by observing some condition that is influenced by A's behavior.

---

7   http://users.cis.fiu.edu/~smithg/papers/sif06.pdf

Examples of Security Models

There are hundreds of security models. The following are a few examples that have had a major impact on the ways that security services have been developed over the years.

Bell–LaPadula Confidentiality Model[8]

Bell–LaPadula model is perhaps the most well-known and significant security model as well as being one of the oldest models used in the creation of modern secure computing systems. Like the Trusted Computer System Evaluation Criteria (or TCSEC), it was inspired by early U.S. Department of Defense security policies and the need to prove that confidentiality could be maintained. In other words, its primary goal is to prevent disclosure as the model system moves from one state (one point in time) to another.

It starts by describing four basic components in defining the main actors and how they are distinguished from each other. Subjects are the active parties, while objects are the passive parties. To help determine what subjects will be allowed to do, they are assigned clearances that outline what modes of access (read, write, or read/write) they will be allowed to use when they interact with objects assigned a classification level. The model system uses labels to keep track of clearances and classifications and implements a set of rules to limit interactions between different types of subjects and objects.

Using this set of basic components, Bell–LaPadula model explores the rules that would have to be in place if a subject is granted a certain level of clearance and a particular mode of access. They describe these as different properties, depending on whether the subject in question has the ability to read, write, or read/write objects in the model system. In the simple security property (*Figure 2.2*), Bell and LaPadula considered a subject with the ability to read information (but not write it).

8   http://www.acsac.org/2005/papers/Bell.pdf

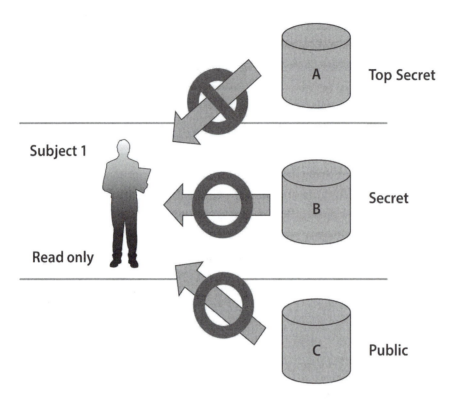

Figure 2.2 - **The simple security property according to Bell–LaPadula. Subject 1 has been assigned a clearance level of secret and the ability to read only from a set of objects. In order to prevent disclosure, the subject may read information from objects classified.**

To prevent disclosure, that subject would be able to read information from objects at a similar classification level or at lower levels but would be barred from reading any information from objects classified at a higher level of confidentiality. For example, if employees have a government security clearance of secret, they may be allowed to read secret and documents classified at lower levels. They would not be allowed to read top secret information as this would result in disclosure.

In the "*" property" (so named as the story goes because the authors never replaced the asterisk with another term in the manuscript before it was published,)[9] the same subject has the ability to write information, but not read it (*Figure 2.3*).

---

9   http://www.acsac.org/2005/papers/Bell.pdf - page 3

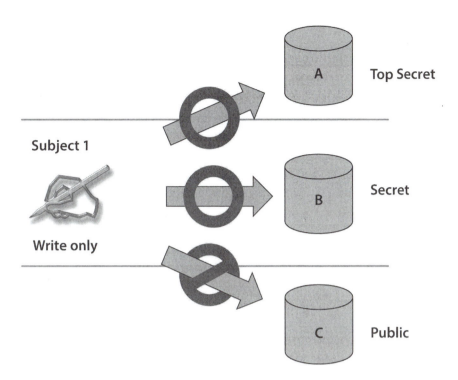

Figure 2.3 - **The * property according to Bell–LaPadula.**
Subject 1 has been assigned a clearance level of secret and the ability to write only to a set of objects. In order to prevent disclosure, the subject may write information to objects classified as secret or top secret, but is prevented from writing information classified as public.

To prevent disclosure, the subject would be able to write information to objects at a similar classification level or higher levels but would be barred from writing any information to objects classified at a lower level of confidentiality. This can seem very odd at first glance, but remember that the goal is to prevent disclosure. Writing something at a higher level will not result in disclosure, even if it makes it impossible for the original subject to read it. It also has some practical value in some cases. For example, an organization's president may wish for a set of subordinate officers to make reports to their superiors in such a way that they cannot read each other's reports while still allowing their superiors to read and collate information across reports from their subordinates.

In the strong * property (*Figure 2.4*), they consider the same subject with the ability to read or write to objects in the model system. To be mathematically certain that the subjects could never disclose information, they must be restricted to objects at a similar classification level and not be allowed to interact with any other objects in the model system.

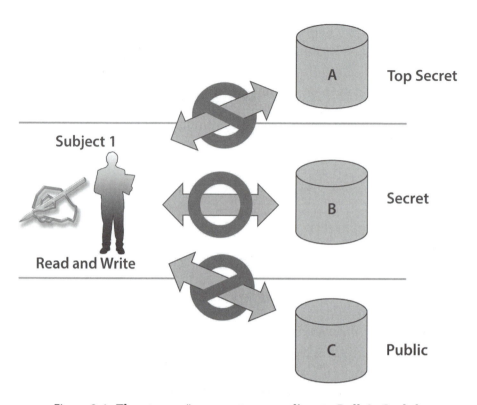

Figure 2.4 - **The strong * property according to Bell–LaPadula. Subject 1 has been assigned a clearance level of secret and the ability to read or write to a set of objects. In order to prevent disclosure, the subjects may only access information classified at their own level, in this case objects classified as secret.**

Bell–LaPadula is not without its limitations. It only concerns confidentiality and makes no mention of other properties (such as integrity and availability) or more sophisticated modes of access. These have to be addressed by other models. More importantly, it does not address important confidentiality goals such as need-to-know, the ability to restrict access to individual objects based on a subject's need to access them. Because Bell–LaPadula does not provide a mechanism for a one-to-one mapping of individual subjects and objects, this will also need to be addressed by other models.

Biba Integrity Model[10]

Biba's model is just enough like Bell–LaPadula to possibly confuse the two. Like Bell–LaPadula, Biba is also a lattice-based model with multiple levels. It uses the same modes of access (read, write, and read/write) and also describes

---

10 Read more about the Biba Integrity Model here: http://www.dtic.mil/cgi-bin/ GetTRDoc?AD=ADA166920 - page 27

interactions between subjects and objects. Where Biba differs most obviously is that it is an integrity model: it focuses on ensuring that the integrity of information is being maintained by preventing corruption. At the core of the model is a multilevel approach to integrity designed to prevent unauthorized subjects from modifying objects. Access is controlled to ensure that objects maintain their current state of integrity as subjects interact with them. Instead of the confidentiality levels used by Bell–LaPadula, Biba assigns integrity levels to subjects and objects depending on how trustworthy they are considered to be. Like Bell–LaPadula, Biba considers the same modes of access but with different results. *Figure 2.5* compares the BLP and Biba models.

Property	BLP Model	Biba Model
ss-property	A subject cannot read/access an object of a higher classification (no read up)	A subject cannot observe an object of a lower integrity level
*-property	A subject can only save an object at the same or higher classification (no write down)	A subject cannot modify an object of a higher integrity level
Invocation property	Not Used	A subject cannot send logical service requests to an object of a higher integrity

Source –

Hare, C., Policy development, in Information Security Management Handbook, 6th edn., Tipton, H.F. and Krause, M., Eds., Auerbach Publications. New York 2007. 47&

Figure 2.5 - **BLP and Biba Model Properties**

In the simple integrity property (*Figure 2.6* and *Figure 2.7*), a given subject has the ability to read information from different types of objects with differing levels of integrity or accuracy. In this case, less accurate information than what the subject would expect could result in corruption, so the subject must be prevented from reading from less accurate objects but can read from objects that are more accurate than the subject needs.

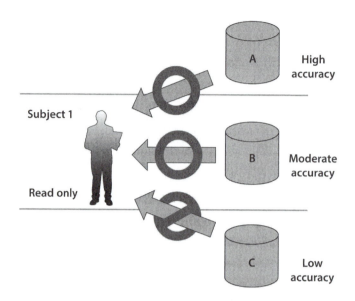

Figure 2.6 - **The simple integrity property according to Biba. In this example, Subject 1 has information that is moderately accurate and can read from a set of objects with varying degrees of accuracy. In order to prevent corruption, the subject may be able to read information with the same or higher level of accuracy but not information that is less accurate because that may compromise the integrity of the information it already possesses.**

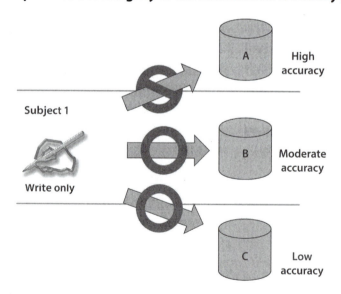

Figure 2.7 - **The simple integrity property according to Biba. In this example, Subject 1 has information that is moderately accurate and can write to a set of objects with varying degrees of accuracy. In order to prevent corruption, the subject may be able to write information with the same or lower level of accuracy but not information that is more accurate because that may compromise the integrity of the information in the more accurate object (Object A).**

For example, consider a subject that wishes to add two numbers together. The subject needs information that is reasonably accurate to two decimal places and has different values to choose from. Some of these values are accurate to more than two decimal places. Some are less accurate. To prevent corruption, the subject must only use information that is at least as accurate as two decimal places; information that is only accurate to one decimal place must not be used or corruption may occur.

In the * integrity property, a given subject has the ability to write information to different types of objects with differing levels of integrity or accuracy. In this case, the subject must be prevented from corrupting objects that are more accurate than it is. The subject should then be allowed to write to objects that are less accurate but not to objects that are more accurate. To allow otherwise may result in corruption. Biba also addresses the problem of one subject getting a more privileged subject to work on his or her behalf. In the invocation property, Biba considers a situation where corruption may occur because a less trustworthy subject was allowed to take advantage of the capabilities of a more trustworthy subject by invoking his or her powers. According to Biba, this must be prevented or corruption could occur.

Clark–Wilson Integrity Model[11]

As it turns out, Biba only addresses one of three key integrity goals. The Clark–Wilson model improves on Biba by focusing on integrity at the transaction level and addressing three major goals of integrity in a commercial environment. In addition to preventing changes by unauthorized subjects, Clark and Wilson realized that high-integrity systems would also have to prevent undesirable changes by authorized subjects and to ensure that the system continued to behave consistently. They also recognized that it would need to ensure that there is constant mediation between every subject and every object if such integrity was going to be maintained.

To address the second goal of integrity, Clark and Wilson realized that they needed a way to prevent authorized subjects from making changes that were not desirable. This required that transactions by authorized subjects be evaluated by another party before they were committed on the model system. This provided separation of duties where the powers of the authorized subject were limited by another subject given the power to evaluate and complete the transaction. This also had the effect of ensuring external consistency (or consistency between the model system and the real world) because the evaluating subject would have the power to ensure that the transaction matched what was expected in reality.

11 http://www.cs.clemson.edu/course/cpsc420/material/Policies/Integrity%20Policies.pdf

To address internal consistency (or consistency within the model system itself), Clark and Wilson recommended a strict definition of well-formed transactions. In other words, the set of steps within any transaction would need to be carefully designed and enforced. Any deviation from that expected path would result in a failure of the transaction to ensure that the model system's integrity was not compromised.

To control all subject and object interactions, Clark–Wilson establishes a system of subject–program–object bindings such that the subject no longer has direct access to the object. Instead, this is done through a program with access to the object. This program arbitrates all access and ensures that every interaction between subject and object follows a defined set of rules. The program provides for subject authentication and identification and limits all access to objects under its control.

Lipner Model

Lipner combines elements of Bell–LaPadula and Biba together with the idea of job functions or roles in a novel way to protect both confidentiality and integrity. The Lipner implementation, published in 1982, describes two ways of implementing integrity. One uses the Bell–LaPadula confidentiality model, and the other uses both the Bell–LaPadula model and the Biba integrity model together. Both methods assign security levels and functional categories to subjects and objects. For subjects, this translates into a person's clearance level and job function (e.g., user, operator, applications programmer, or systems programmer). For objects, the sensitivity of the data or program and its functions (e.g., test data, production data, application program, or system program) are defined according to its classification.

Lipner's first method, using only Bell–LaPadula model, assigns subjects to one of two sensitivity levels—system manager and anyone else—and to one of four job categories. Objects (i.e., file types) are assigned specific classification levels and categories. Most of the subjects and objects are assigned the same level; therefore, categories become the most significant integrity (i.e., access control) mechanism. The applications programmers, systems programmers, and users are confined to their own domains according to their assigned categories, thus preventing unauthorized users from modifying data (the first integrity goal).

Lipner's second method combines Biba's integrity model with Bell–LaPadula. This combination of models helps to prevent the contamination of high-integrity data by low-integrity data or programs. The assignment of levels and categories to subjects and objects remains the same as for Lipner's first method.

Integrity levels are used to avoid the unauthorized modification of system programs; integrity categories are used to separate domains that are based on functional areas (e.g., production or research and development). This method prevents unauthorized users from modifying data and prevents authorized users from making improper data modifications.

Lipner's methods were the first to separate objects into data and programs. The importance of this concept becomes clear when viewed in terms of implementing the Clark–Wilson integrity model; because programs allow users to manipulate data, it is necessary to control which programs a user may access and which objects a program can manipulate.

Brewer–Nash (Chinese Wall) Model

This model focuses on preventing conflict of interest when a given subject has access to objects with sensitive information associated with two competing parties. The principle is that users should not access the confidential information of both a client organization and one or more of its competitors. At the beginning, subjects may access either set of objects. Once, however, a subject accesses an object associated with one competitor, the subject is instantly prevented from accessing any objects on the opposite side. This is intended to prevent the subject from sharing information inappropriately between the two competitors, even if it is done unintentionally. It is called the Chinese Wall Model because, like the Great Wall of China, once on one side of the wall, a person cannot get to the other side. It is an unusual model in comparison with many of the others because the access control rules change based on subject behavior.

Graham–Denning Model

Graham–Denning is primarily concerned with how subjects and objects are created, how subjects are assigned rights or privileges, and how ownership of objects is managed. In other words, it is primarily concerned with how a model system controls subjects and objects at a very basic level where other models simply assumed such control.

The Graham–Denning access control model has three parts: a set of objects, a set of subjects, and a set of rights. The subjects are composed of two things: a process and a domain. The domain is the set of constraints controlling how subjects may access objects. Subjects may also be objects at specific times. The set of rights governs how subjects may manipulate the passive objects. This model describes eight primitive protection rights called commands that subjects can execute to have an effect on other subjects or objects. The model defines eight primitive protection rights:

1. **Create Object** – the ability to create a new object
2. **Create Subject** – the ability to create a new subject
3. **Delete Object** – the ability to delete an existing object
4. **Delete Subject** – the ability to delete an existing subject
5. **Read Access Right** – the ability to view current access privileges
6. **Grant Access Right** – the ability to grant access privileges
7. **Delete Access Right** – The ability to remove access privileges
8. **Transfer Access Right** – the ability to transfer access privileges from one subject or object to another subject or object

Harrison–Ruzzo–Ullman Model

This model is very similar to the Graham–Denning model, and it is composed of a set of generic rights and a finite set of commands. It is also concerned with situations in which a subject shall never gain particular privileges. To accomplish this, subjects are prevented from accessing programs or subroutines that can execute a particular command (to grant read access for example) where necessary.

Jurisdictional Implications

The information type and the flow of information should be identified along with jurisdiction when considering the healthcare regulatory environment and the laws and regulations that pertain to a specific organization. Healthcare jurisdiction can be complicated. For example, within the U.S. there are federal laws and regulations. But there are also state and county laws and regulations that may need to be considered. Another example is the EU Data Protection Directive that applies to countries of the European Economic Area (EEA), which includes all EU countries and the non-EU countries Iceland, Liechtenstein, and Norway.[12]

Data Subjects

When information is collected for the purpose of health or medical records, research, etc., the person the information relates to is referred to as the data subject. It is always important to avoid legal complications and ensure compliance with laws and regulations concerning data subjects and the collection, sharing, and processing of their information. For example, an organization should ensure the data subject or their legal representative is well aware of:

- The purpose of the information being collected.
- How the information will be used.
- If and to whom any of the information will be shared or disclosed.

---

12 http://ec.europa.eu/justice/data-protection/data-collection/data-transfer/index_en.htm

- The option for the individual or legal representative to opt out and the consequences for opting out.
- How long the organization will retain the information.

This list is not all-inclusive or applicable to all organizations. It is dependent on the organization and which laws and regulations apply to them. In addition, the collection of medical information should always be collected fairly and lawfully and processed only for the stated purpose during collection.

Data Owners/Controllers/Custodians/Processors

There are key roles that are often used within laws and regulations that one must consider when trying to understand the healthcare regulatory environment. Below is a list containing some key roles with a description that is by no means all-inclusive. Please note that different industries may use different terms.

Data Owners

Sometimes the term 'data owners' is referring to those within organizations that collect and define the metrics for the data. This is similar to the description of the term "information owner/steward" in the "Governance Structures" section of Domain Four when referring to information governance structures. Data owners may also refer to the data subject as referred to by the European Commission Directive - General for Justice, "Furthermore, persons or organizations which collect and manage your personal information must protect it from misuse and must respect certain rights of the data owners which are guaranteed by EU law."

Controllers

Controllers are also referred to as data controllers, depending on legislation or the nation. According to the European Commission Directive - General for Justice, "The people or bodies that collect and manage personal data are 'data controllers'. They must respect EU law when handling the data entrusted to them."[13] The rules outlined by the directive are:

- Personal Data must be processed legally and fairly;
- It must be collected for explicit and legitimate purposes and used accordingly;
- It must be adequate, relevant, and not excessive in relation to the purposes for which it is collected and/or further processed;
- It must be accurate, and updated where necessary;
- Data controllers must ensure that data subjects can rectify, remove, or block incorrect data about themselves;

---

13   http://ec.europa.eu/justice/data-protection/data-collection/index_en.htm

- Data that identifies individuals (personal data) must not be kept any longer than strictly necessary;
- Data controllers must protect personal data against accidental or unlawful destruction, loss, alteration, and disclosure, particularly when processing involves data transmission over networks. They shall implement the appropriate security measures;
- These protection measures must ensure a level of protection appropriate to the data.

Custodians

Custodians of data within the U.S. from the discovery of digital information perspective are the individuals or entities that are responsible for access control and maintain the protection of the information of the data. A similar description is used for the term *system owner* in the section on governance structures in Domain 4 when discussing information governance.

Processors

Processors are also referred to as data processors, depending on legislation or the nation and can easily be confused with a data controller. According to the Data Protection Commissioner of Ireland, "if you hold or process personal data, but do not exercise responsibility for or control over the personal data, then you are a 'data processor'". Some examples they give of data processors include payroll companies, accountants, and market research companies, all of which could hold or process personal information on behalf of someone else. In addition they state that, "It is possible for one company or person to be both a data controller and a data processor, in respect of distinct sets of personal data. For example, a payroll company would be the data controller in respect of the data about its own staff, but would be the data processor in respect of the staff payroll data it is processing for its client companies."[14]

Understand International Regulations and Controls

Upon completing this chapter, readers will have a better understanding of the major legal systems found throughout the world. This understanding is required for several reasons: Information systems security is an international phenomenon; crimes committed using information systems or targeted at information systems know no geographical boundaries. It is also important that healthcare professionals do not have false preconceptions of legal systems they are not familiar with (i.e., all common law countries have identical laws).

---

14 https://www.dataprotection.ie/docs/Are-you-a-Data-Controller-/43.htm

Major Legal Systems

As stated in the introduction, readers of this chapter will not be qualified to practice international law or serve on the bench of the world court for that matter just based on the content of this chapter. However, readers will hopefully have a better basic understanding of the major legal systems found throughout the world. It will soon be rare to find a professional in this field who, during the course of an investigation or breach, has not dealt with legal professionals from various countries or has been introduced to several different systems of law.

For the sake of this chapter, the major legal systems are categorized as:

- Common law
- Civil or code law
- Customary law
- Religious law
- Mixed law

This taxonomy is consistent with the current legal literature in this area. Maritime law is not addressed in this discussion, although it is an excellent example of the harmonization of international law.

Common Law

The legal system referred to as common law traces its roots back to England, or more precisely, the development of a customary law system of both the Anglo-Saxons in Northern France and the early residents of England. Due to England's rich history of colonization, the common law framework can be found in many parts of the world that were once colonies or territories of the British Empire (e.g., United States, Canada, United Kingdom, Australia, and New Zealand). The European continent has resisted the common law influence and is based primarily on a codified legal system, civil law. The common law system is based on the notion of legal precedents, past decisions, and societal traditions. The system is based on customs that predated any written laws or codification of laws in these societies. Prior to the twelfth century, customary law was unwritten and not unified in England; it was extremely diverse and was dependent on local norms and superstitions. During the twelfth century, the king of England created a unified legal system that was common to the country. This national system allowed for the development of a body of public policy principles.

A defining characteristic of common law systems is the adversarial approach to litigation and the findings of fact in legal fictions. It is assumed that adjudicated argumentation is a valid method for arriving at the truth of a matter. This approach led to the creation of barristers (lawyers) who take a very active role in the litigation process.

Another discriminating element of the common law system stems from its reliance on previous court rulings. Decisions by the courts are predicated on jurisprudence (case law), with only narrow interpretation of legislative law occurring. In this system, judges play a more passive role than in civil law systems and are not actively involved in the determination of facts. Although historically, common law was a non-codified legal system, this is no longer true; most, if not all, common law countries have developed statute laws and a codified system of laws related to criminal and commercial matters. Most descriptions of common law systems are quick to point out that the differences between civil and common law systems are becoming increasingly difficult to distinguish, with civil systems adopting a jurisprudence approach and common law systems increasingly relying on legislative statutes and regulations. Most common law systems consist of three branches of law: criminal law, tort law, and administrative law.

Criminal Law

Criminal law can be based on common law, statutory law, or a combination of both. Criminal law deals with behaviors or conduct that is seen as harmful to the public or society. In these cases, an individual has violated a governmental law designed to protect the public and, thus, the real victim is society. The government therefore prosecutes the transgressor on behalf of the public. Typically, the punishment meted out by the criminal courts involves some loss of personal freedom for the guilty party (e.g., incarceration, probation, death). However, monetary punishments in the way of fines or restitution to the court or victim are also common.

Tort Law

Tort law deals with civil wrongs (torts) against an individual or business entity. As the transgressions are not against the general public or society (in most cases), the law (government) provides for different remedies than in criminal cases. These remedies usually consist of money for the damages caused to the victim. These damages can be compensatory, punitive, or statutory. Interestingly enough, tort law can trace its origin to criminal law, and in some jurisdictions, offenses can fall into both the criminal and tort law categories (e.g., assault against an individual). Tort law can be divided into intentional torts, wrongs against a person or property, dignitary wrongs, economic wrongs, negligence, nuisance, and strict liability.

Administrative Law

Administrative law or, as it is known in some countries, regulatory law, is primarily an artifact of the Anglo-American common law legal system. However, some civil law systems have administrative courts to oversee social security law or grievances against the government itself (either national or local). This branch of common law is concerned with the governance of public bodies and the designation of power to administrative agencies, commissions, boards, administrative tribunals, or professional associations (e.g., Securities Exchange Committee, Labor Relations Boards, Law Societies, Medical Boards, School Boards). These agencies are often controlled by other government agencies, but they can come under the purview of the courts and are reviewed "under some principle of due process."

The objectives of administrative law include confining government power to its proper scope, curbing potential for abuse of power, ensuring that proper procedures are followed in the exercise of powers that affect the rights/interests of citizens, and ensuring performance of mandatory statutory duties. Punishments under administrative law consist of fines, inability to practice a profession (de-licensing), and, in some cases, incarceration.

Civil Law

Civil law traces its roots back to two beginnings. The first was the living law of the Roman Empire, which culminated with the compilation of the Code and Digest of Emperor Justinian. The second birth began as a result of Italian legal scholars and progressed through the codification of law in Europe, as exemplified with the Napoleonic Code of France and the French Civil Code of 1804.

The civil law system was, at one time, the most common legal system on the European continent. The system became regionalized over time with Germany, Norway, Sweden, Denmark, and Switzerland developing their own national systems, unique from the French Napoleonic system. Due to this nationalization, civil law can be subdivided into French civil law, German civil law, and Scandinavian civil law. Civil law is not confined to Europe alone. Many Asian countries have legal systems based on the German model of civil law.

The distinguishing feature of civil law is thought to be the codification of law and heavy reliance on legislation as the primary source of law, as opposed to jurisprudence. This is not accurate, as there are several countries that follow an uncodified civil law legal system (e.g., Scotland and South Africa). However, when civil law is contrasted against the common law system, other differences become apparent. Civil law emphasizes the abstract concepts of law and is influenced by the writings of legal scholars and academics, more so than common law systems. The common law doctrine of *stare decisis* (lower courts are compelled to follow decisions of higher courts) is absent from the civil law system. The role of judges in civil law systems is also different than in common law systems. In civil law legal systems, judges are distinct from lawyers and are not attorneys who have graduated through the ranks. Judges also play a more active role in determining the facts of the case and in some instances, direct the actual investigations.

2

Regulatory Environment

Customary Law

Custom or customary law systems are regionalized systems and reflect the society's norms and values based on programmatic wisdom and traditions. These countries have a rich history of traditions and customs that dictate acceptable behavior between the various members of society. These customs or norms over the years have become recognized as defining legitimate social contracts and have become part of the rule of law. It is rare to find a country whose rule of law is based solely on customary law. Most countries that have a strong law of custom also prescribe to another legal system, such as civil or common law (e.g., many African countries). This combination of legal systems is referred to as a mixed legal system and will be discussed in the "Mixed law" section. Punishment under customary law systems focuses on restitution to the victim by means of some kind of fine.

Religious Law

In a manner of speaking, all laws have been influenced by religion. The earliest societal rules of conduct that dictated the behavior of the people reflected the predominant religious teachings on morality. Over the years, many countries have attempted to separate the spiritual and secular lives of its citizens (e.g., First Amendment of the United States). Other countries not necessarily under the direct influence of Judaism or Christianity have made no such cultural or societal distinction. Although there are technically several religious law systems, we will confine this chapter to a very brief discussion of Muslim law. This system was chosen because the Islamic faith is practiced by a large portion of the world's population. Muslim societies, such as those found in North Africa and the Middle East, follow Islamic laws, or Sharia. Although Sharia has been the dominant system defining the rule of law, there is increasing pressure to adopt or, at the very least, incorporate more secular legal thinking and ideas (see "Mixed law" section).

Traditional Islamic law is separated into rules of worship and rules of human interaction and is guided by the Qur'arn and the "way," or Sunnah—the manner in which the prophet Muhammad lived his life. Sharia covers all aspects of a person's life, from religious practices, dietary choices, dress code, marriage/family life, and commerce to domestic justice and sexual behavior. Law is not considered a man-made entity; it is decreed by divine will. Lawmakers and law scholars do not create laws; they attempt to discover the truth of law. Jurists and clerics play a central role in this system and have a high degree of authority within the society. Like the civilian systems, Sharia has been codified, but it still remains open to interpretation and modification.

Mixed Law

With the new global economy (trade pacts such as the North American Free Trade Agreement (NAFTA), the creation of the European Union, etc.), the introduction or blending of two or more systems of law is now becoming more common. Mixed law by definition is the convergence of two or more legal systems, usually civil law and common law but increasingly customary, religious, and civil or common law. The interaction of these legal systems can be the result of historical, economic, or political pressures. Examples of mixed systems can be found in Europe with Holland, in North America with Quebec and Louisiana, in Africa with South Africa, and in the United Kingdom with Scotland.

Liability

Another integral part of a healthcare professional's job function is to understand issues related to liability, negligence, and due care. In the world's more increasingly litigious culture, these concepts become especially important, as we are seeing examples of shareholder lawsuits and third-party liability claims against organizations suffering information technology attacks and breaches. When organizations are weighing the costs versus the benefits of certain actions, inactions, or security controls, the ability to demonstrate reasonable corporate behavior and overall due diligence is an essential factor.

In law (i.e., tort), liability refers to being legally responsible. Sanctions in cases dealing with liability include both civil and criminal penalties. Liability and negligence are somewhat associated, as negligence is often used to establish liability. Negligence is simply acting without care or the failure to act as a reasonable and prudent person would under similar circumstances. The exact definition of a reasonable and prudent person is somewhat more complicated, as the courts usually engage in legal fiction by prescribing qualities that this person has without reference to any real person. The "reasonable person" yardstick is determined by the circumstances in question and is usually the center of heated debate during the litigation process.

Due care and due diligence are other terms that have found their way into issues of corporate governance. According to Sheridan, due care can be thought of as the requirement that officers and other executives with fiduciary responsibilities meet certain requirements to protect the company's assets. These requirements include the safety and protection of technology and information systems that fall under the term *corporate assets*.[15]

---

15 Another way of understanding these terms is to think of due care as doing the right thing and due diligence as evaluating the results of due care measures to ensure that they are performing as intended.

2

Regulatory Environment

89

Due diligence is a much more ethereal concept and is often judged against a continually moving benchmark. What used to constitute due diligence last year may not this year or the next. The dynamic nature requires a commitment to an ongoing risk analysis and risk management process and a good understanding of generally accepted business and information security practices, within the applicable industry, as well as international standards, and increasingly as dictated by legislation or regulations. The increase in government scrutiny of information system practices has resulted in the majority of companies allocating their security budgets to be compliant with the various current and pending regulatory requirements.

Computer Crime

As a healthcare professional, the HCISPP focuses his or her concerns on risks that arise not only from errors and omissions but also from behavior that is both malicious and intentional. The fact that computer systems have become the target for criminals should come as no surprise. The very features that make technology, information systems, and the Internet attractive to businesses also make them very attractive to criminals, both petty and professional or organized. As more of the new currency (e.g., personal information, bank account numbers, credit card information) moves online, the likelihood, impacts, and, correspondingly, risk that private citizens, companies, and governments will become victims of computer crime increases.

Although engaging in a comprehensive examination and discussion of computer crime is well beyond the scope of this chapter, it is important that conceptually pertinent elements are covered, at least cursorily. The phenomena of computer crime, or cybercrime, as it is often called, although a relatively recent concept compared to other, more traditional crimes, has plagued society for several years. Some of the so-called new computer crimes are actually more traditional criminal activities that have benefited from the new technological advances, such as the Internet, color scanners and copiers, etc. Computer crimes are often divided into three categories.

Computer as a Tool

This category involves computers merely allowing criminals to become more efficient at practicing their criminal tradecraft, more able to target victims, or more easily able to share contraband. Examples of these types of crimes are fraud, counterfeit, theft, and child pornography. With our society's increasing dependence on technology, the characteristics of what constitutes evidence have drastically changed. Some estimates indicate that currently 80% of all criminal investigations include evidence that is digital in nature. Here again, this is no surprise: we have become dependent on email, smart phones, electronic calendars, etc.

Computers as Incidental

This is a very broad category because it is so generic and encompasses all but very few types of criminal behavior.

Computers as the Target

This category involves criminal activities that have their origins in technology and have no analogous real-world equivalents. These crimes target information systems and the underlying architecture and represent some of the largest issues for information security. These activities denote concepts that legal systems have not had experience dealing with and have not effectively embodied into the statutes, regulations, etc. Within the classification of computer-targeted crime, several subcategories of activities exist. Examples of such directed activities include:

- Viruses
- Digital identity theft
- Computer hacking

Although this list is not at all exhaustive, it does capture some of the uniqueness of this type of criminal behavior. Just as the criminal activity seems unique, the type of offender seems to be exclusive as well. It is fair to say that individuals are attracted to specific types of crime for various reasons (e.g., personal choice, aptitude, social learning). Rather than trying to label offenders, for the sake of this discussion, it is more pragmatic to simply state that computer criminals have developed a distinctive tradecraft and that the various subclasses of computer crime require specific skills, knowledge, abilities, and access to technology.

The computer as incidental is a direct artifact of a wired society. Contrary to popular belief, all people have a digital "footprint" that is very extensive and rather intrusive. Online activities, whether Internet based or cell phone, are logged and recorded—often these are archived and open for anyone to look at without any court orders being required (e.g., news group postings or social network archives). Computers and computing technology (e.g., cell phones, smart phones) are often a repository of digital information related to activities, conversations, preferences, and so on. This type of information is often of interest during an investigation, including the more routine non-technology-related cases, such as murders, kidnappings, drug trafficking, custody disputes, etc.

A word of caution is necessary: although the media has tended to portray the threat of cybercrime as existing almost exclusively from the outside, external to a company, reality paints a much different picture. The greatest risk of cybercrime comes from the inside, namely, criminal insiders.

The HCISPP has to be particularly sensitive to the phenomena of the criminals or dangerous insiders, as these individuals usually operate under the radar, inside of our primarily outward/external facing security controls, thus significantly increasing the impact of their crimes while leaving few, if any, audit trails to follow.

International Cooperation

The biggest hindrance to effectively dealing with computer crime is the fact that this activity is truly international in scope and thus requires an international solution, as opposed to a domestic one based on archaic concepts of borders and jurisdictions. The concept of geographical borders is meaningless in the realm of cyber space; we are truly seeing the manifestation of a global village. The World Wide Web is exactly that - worldwide; criminals in one country can victimize individuals clear across the world with a keystroke, website, spam attack, phishing scam, etc. Previous attempts based on domestic solutions (e.g., the introduction of criminal statutes, regulations) designed to stop activities that utilized the ubiquitous nature of the Internet and distributed information systems (e.g., online gambling, adult pornography) were inadequate and completely unsuccessful. The framers of these solutions failed to take into account the global reach of technology; the owners of these sites simply moved their operations to countries whose governments condoned, tolerated, or turned a blind eye to the activities. The desired effect of stopping or at the very least deterring the activity did not occur. In some cases, the activity thrived due to the unprecedented media exposure.

International responses to computer crime have been met with mixed results. The Council of Europe (CoE) Cybercrime Convention is a prime example of a multilateral attempt to draft an international response to criminal behaviors targeted at technology and the Internet. Thirty countries, including Canada, the United States, and Japan, ratified the convention that came into effect July 1, 2004, (although states or countries have varying dates of entry into force and have yet to enact the convention despite signing the ratification). The Cybercrime Convention consists of 49 articles, and in summary it requires parties to:

- Establish laws against cybercrime and offenses related to child pornography.
- Ensure that their law enforcement officials have the necessary procedural authorities to investigate and prosecute cybercrime offenses effectively.
- Provide international cooperation to other parties in the fight against computer-related crime.

One of the Cybercrime Convention's stated objectives is to assist international enforcement efforts by creating a framework for the domestication and cooperation between ratifying states. This objective directly addresses one of the most difficult problems faced when dealing with computer crime: jurisdictional disputes. Issues related to establishment of jurisdiction, extradition of accused, and the lack of domestication have hamstrung many past investigations. The ultimate success of the convention is still unknown, but it is definitely a step in the right direction.

Licensing and Intellectual Property

Information Technology Laws and Regulations

Although no one expects an HCISPP to be a legal expert on all areas of technology-related law, (as with the various legal systems) a working knowledge of legal concepts directly related to information technology is required to fully understand the context, issues, and risks inherent with information systems. Two general categories of information technology law have the largest impact on information systems: intellectual property and privacy regulations. This section only provides a brief summary of these concepts. Readers wishing to delve deeper into this area are strongly encouraged to refer to the relevant legislation and regulations in their respective countries.

Intellectual Property Laws

Intellectual property laws are designed to protect both tangible and intangible items and property. Although there are various rationales behind the state-based creation of protection for this type of property, the general goal of intellectual property law is to protect property from those wishing to copy or use it, without due compensation to the inventor or creator. The notion is that copying or using someone else's ideas entails far less work than what is required for the original development. According to the World Intellectual Property Organization (WIPO):

> *Intellectual property is divided into two categories: Industrial property, which includes inventions (patents), trademarks, industrial designs, and geographical indications of source; and Copyright, which includes literary and artistic works such as novels, poems and plays, films, musical works, artistic works such as drawings, paintings, photographs and sculptures, and architectural designs.*

2

Regulatory Environment

Patent

Simply put, a patent grants the owner a legally enforceable right to exclude others from practicing the invention covered for a specific time (usually 20 years). A patent is the "strongest form of intellectual property protection." A patent protects novel, useful, and nonobvious inventions. The granting of a patent requires the formal application to a government entity. Once a patent is granted, it is published in the public domain to stimulate other innovations. Once a patent expires, the protection ends and the invention enters the public domain. WIPO, an agency of the United Nations, looks after the filing and processing of international patent applications.

Trademark

Trademark laws are designed to protect the goodwill a merchant or vendor invests in its products. Trademark law creates exclusive rights to the owner of markings that the public uses to identify various vendor or merchant products or goods. A trademark consists of any word, name, symbol, color, sound, product shape, device, or combination of these that is used to identify goods and distinguish them from those made or sold by others. The trademark must be distinctive and cannot mislead or deceive consumers or violate public order or morality. Trademarks are registered with a government registrar. International harmonization of trademark laws began in 1883 with the Paris Convention, which prompted the Madrid Agreement of 1891. In addition to patents, WIPO also oversees international trademark law efforts, including international registration.

Copyright

A copyright covers the expression of ideas rather than the ideas themselves; it usually protects artistic property such as writing, recordings, databases, and computer programs. In most countries, once the work or property is completed or is in a tangible form, the copyright protection is automatically assumed. Copyright protection is weaker than patent protection, but the duration of protection is considerably longer (e.g., a minimum of 50 years after the creator's death or 70 years under U.S. copyright protection). Although individual countries may have slight variations in their domestic copyright laws, as long as the country is a member of the international Berne Convention, the protection afforded will be at least at a minimum level, as dictated by the convention; unfortunately, not all countries are members.

Trade Secret

The final area covered in this section is trade secrets. Trade secret refers to proprietary business or technical information, processes, designs, practices, etc., that are confidential and critical to the business (e.g., Coca-Cola's formula). The trade secret may provide a competitive advantage or, at the very least, allow the company to compete equally in the marketplace. To be categorized as a trade secret, it must not be generally known and must provide some economic benefit to the company. Additionally, there must be some form of reasonable steps taken to protect its secrecy. A trade secret dispute is unique because the actual contents of the trade secret need not be disclosed. Legal protection for trade secrets depends upon the jurisdiction. In some countries, it is assumed under unfair business legislation, and in others, specific laws have been drafted related to confidential information. In some jurisdictions, legal protection for trade secrets is practically perpetual and does not carry an expiry date, as is the case with patents. Trade secrets are often at the heart of industrial and economic espionage cases and are the proverbial crown jewels of some companies.

Licensing Issues

The issue of illegal software and piracy is such a large problem that it warrants some discussion. More than one company has been embarrassed publicly, sued civilly, or criminally prosecuted for failing to control the use of illegal software or violating software licensing agreements. With high-speed Internet access readily available to most employees, the ability—if not the temptation—to download and use pirated software has greatly increased. According to a recent (2006) study by the Business Software Alliance (BSA) and International Data Corporation (IDC), prevalence and frequency of illegal software is exceedingly high - the weighted average was 35% worldwide. However, the median piracy rate was 62%. The same study found that for every two dollars' worth of legal software purchased, one dollar's worth of software was pirated. Though not all countries recognize the forms of intellectual property protection previously discussed, the work of several international organizations and industrialized countries seems somewhat successful in curbing the official sanctioning of intellectual property rights violations (e.g., software piracy).

There are four categories of software licensing: freeware, shareware, commercial, and academic. Within these categories, there are specific types of agreements. Master agreements and end-user licensing agreements (EULAs) are the most prevalent, though most jurisdictions have refused to enforce the shrink-wrap agreements that were commonplace at one time. Master agreements set out the general overall conditions of use along with any restrictions, whereas the EULA specifies more granular conditions and restrictions. The EULA is often a "click through" or radio button that the end user must click on to begin the install, indicating that he or she understands the conditions and limitations and agrees to comply.

Various third parties have developed license metering software to ensure and enforce compliance with software licensing agreements. Some of these applications can produce an audit report and either disable software attempting to run in violation of an agreement (e.g., exceeding the number of devices running software concurrently) or produce an automated alert. The use of carefully controlled software libraries is also a recommended solution. Ignorance is no excuse when it comes to compliance with licensing conditions and restrictions. The onus is clearly on the organization to enforce compliance and police the use of software or face the possibility of legal sanctions, such as criminal prosecution or civil penalties.

Import/Export

Some software such as encryption software may be illegal to import or export. Many software vendors are familiar with restrictions for their software, but the prudent information security professional will ensure all software complies with local laws. Other considerations include United Nation sanctions, which may prohibit technology of certain types or from certain countries being imported into a country.

Trans-Border Data Flow

As information moves from one server to another or from one cloud to another, the location of the data and the hosting organization begins to matter. Information developed in one country, transmitted through another, and finally stored in a third may be subject to three different jurisdictions and three different legal systems. In some situations even if information is stored in one country, if the organization who owns the server is a member of a different country, the latter may be able to gain jurisdiction over the information.

Treaties

Healthcare organizations operate in environments where laws, regulations, and compliance requirements must be met. Healthcare professionals must understand the laws and regulations of the country and industry they are working in. An organization's governance and risk management processes must take into account these requirements from an implementation perspective and a risk perspective. These laws and regulations often offer specific actions that must be met for compliance or, in some cases, what must be met for a "safe harbor" provision. A safe harbor is typically a set of "good faith" conditions, which if met may temporarily or indefinitely protect an organization from the penalties of a new law or regulation.

For example, the State of Texas in the United States requires that entities adhere to HIPAA and the Texas Medical Records Privacy Act (TMRPA). HIPAA and TMRPA mandate the use of specific actions, standards, and requirements for entities that possess PHI and ensure it is not disclosed to improper individuals. The State of Texas is taking the requirements from HIPAA and TMRPA to use as the baseline for its new certification program.[16] Therefore, when entities get certified, they adopt the standards required by HIPAA and TMRPA as their own. In doing so, they not only meet the requirements of the law, but they can also provide proof to external parties that they are making a good faith effort to comply with the requirements of the law.

Requirements stemming from legal or regulatory requirements are best addressed by ensuring an organization's policies and procedures; standards and guidance are consistent with any laws or regulations that may govern it. Furthermore it is advisable specific laws and their requirements are sited in an organization's governance program and information security training program. As a general rule, laws and regulations represent a "moral minimum" that must be adhered to and should never be considered wholly adequate for an organization without a thorough review. Additional requirements and specificity can be added to complement the requirements of law and regulation, but they should never conflict with them. For example, a law may require sensitive financial information to be encrypted, and an organization's policy could state that in accordance with the law all financial information will be encrypted. Furthermore, the agency may specify a standard strength and brand of encryption software to use.

Regulations

With an industry as crucial as healthcare, some countries feel it is necessary to also have regulatory bodies that provide oversight of the healthcare industry. For example, within the U.S. the Department of Health and Human Services (HHS) has been entrusted with the mission to protect the health and to provide essential human services to all Americans.[17] It can become very complicated when healthcare regulations are created and enforced at the state, county, and local level. For example, the Center for Medicare and Medicaid Services

---

16 http://www.phiprivacy.net/texas-to-launch-nations-first-privacy-and-security-certification-safe-harbor/

17 http://www.hhs.gov/about/

is responsible for both programs, Medicare and Medicaid. One is a federal program and the latter is offered at the state level and can have different regulations between states. In addition to these government regulators, there are private regulators such as the American Medical Association (AMA) and the Joint Commission (JCAHO)[18] that hospitals and physicians use for certification purposes. Industry specific laws add to this complexity.

Industry Specific Laws

The regulatory environment of healthcare is highly complex and varies significantly around the world with the existence of treaties and regulations specific to each country. Adding to the complexity are industry specific laws that exist. The few that are discussed below are not all-inclusive. They represent a sample of very sensitive types of healthcare information to familiarize and inform the healthcare practitioner of the existence of such laws. It is best for the healthcare practitioners to work with legal and/or compliance departments within their organization to identify the industry specific laws that apply to them.

Mental Health

Mental health laws have not been enacted in many countries. A study conducted by The World Health Organization in 2011 found that 60% of countries in the world had a dedicated mental health policy.[19] Mental health generally consists of psychological and developmental disorders. Laws may focus on different aspects. For example, in the U.S., HIPAA Privacy Rule addresses the disclosure of an individual's information to family, friends, and others involved in a patient's care. If an individual is incapacitated or unable to make decisions, a healthcare provider can communicate only critical information pertinent to the care of the patient, which is based on professional judgment. In addition, HIPAA specifically addresses psychotherapy notes in its regulations. As stated on the Health and Human Services website, psychotherapy notes are not only the personal information of a patient, but they are also the notes of a professional therapist. "Therefore, with few exceptions, the Privacy Rule requires a covered entity to obtain a patient's authorization prior to a disclosure of psychotherapy notes for any reason, including a disclosure for treatment purposes to a healthcare provider other than the originator of the notes."[20] The Mental Capacity Act 2005 is legislation that addresses individuals who lack the capacity to make certain decisions for themselves in the U.K.[21]

18   http://www.jointcommission.org/

19   http://www.who.int/gho/mental_health/policy_financing/policy_health_plan/en/

20   http://www.hhs.gov/ocr/privacy/hipaa/understanding/special/mhguidance.html

21   http://www.justice.gov.uk/protecting-the-vulnerable/mental-capacity-act

Substance Abuse

Substance abuse includes drug and alcohol addictions. The sensitive nature and stigma associated with these disorders has made it necessary to create additional laws and regulations in some countries. For example, in the U.S., Section 543 of the Public Health Services Act is used in addition to the HIPAA Privacy Rule to protect the confidentiality of information in connection with a substance abuse program or activity defined in the law.[22] In addition, drug and alcohol abuse services can originate in many different environments outside of the office of a general practitioner, such as a clinic, treatment center, or rehabilitation hospitals.

Pregnancy

Healthcare information laws regarding pregnancy in the U.S. are mainly focused on minors. HIPAA offers privacy protection options for minors concerning confidentiality in the manner that the information is communicated and whether a minor's parent is considered an individual to disclose the pregnancy information to.[23] In addition, sharing the information of a pregnancy is not always a positive in the work environment due to the perception and subsequent treatment. The Pregnancy Discrimination Act was enacted in the U.S. to address this concern.[24] The EU has had the Pregnant Workers Directive since 1992 to protect the safety of pregnant workers and those that have recently given birth and is supplemented by the Parental Leave Directive.[25] Although these laws exist, there is still concern regarding the discrimination of pregnant workers across the EU countries.[26]

HIV

HIV information is highly sensitive, and laws have been enacted regarding the disclosure of it from the perspective of a HIV-positive patient to the discrimination of it. In the U.S., attempts have been made to repeal states law that allow for criminal prosecution of a HIV-positive individual who did not reveal his or her status to partners regardless of whether there was risk of transmission or not.[27]

---

22 http://www.gpo.gov/fdsys/pkg/USCODE-2010-title42/pdf/USCODE-2010-title42-chap6A-subchapIII-A-partD-sec290dd-2.pdf

23 http://www.gpo.gov/fdsys/pkg/CFR-2011-title45-vol1/pdf/CFR-2011-title45-vol1-sec164-522.pdf

24 http://www.eeoc.gov/facts/fs-preg.html

25 http://europa.eu/legislation_summaries/employment_and_social_policy/health_hygiene_safety_at_work/c10914_en.htm

26 http://ec.europa.eu/justice/gender-equality/files/your_rights/discrimination__pregnancy_maternity_parenthood_final_en.pdf

27 http://www.theguardian.com/world/2013/dec/10/us-house-hiv-bill-discrimination

2

Regulatory Environment

The HCISPP should be aware of state and federal laws that pertain to criminal prosecution of HIV disclosure. Within the U.K., an HIV-positive individual is considered to be disabled. This allows the individual to be covered under the Equality Act 2010 and protects them from discrimination.[28]

Legislative

HIPAA

Health legislation can happen on many levels as long as the legislating body has the authority to create and enact laws. For example, health laws in the U.S. can be created at multiple levels. For example, The Health Insurance Portability and Accountability Act of 1996 (HIPAA),[29] Title II the Administrative Simplification provisions require the Department of Health and Human Services (HHS) to adopt national standards for electronic health care transactions and national identifiers for providers, health plans, and employers. It is a federal law that was enacted and has been furthered by the requirements of the Affordable Care Act of 2010:

- Operating rules for each of the HIPAA covered transactions
- A unique, standard Health Plan Identifier (HPID)
- A standard and operating rules for electronic funds transfer (EFT) and electronic remittance advice (ERA) and claims attachments

In addition, health plans will be required to certify their compliance. The Act provides for substantial penalties for failures to certify or comply with the new standards and operating rules. An example of state legislation was described in the section on Treaties.

Legislation can also occur at the international level; for example, the EU Data Privacy Directive only allows the processing of personal data under specific circumstances such as:

1. When processing is necessary for compliance with a legal action
2. When processing is required to protect the life of the subject
3. When the subject of the personal data has provided consent
4. When the processing is performed within the law and scope of "public interest"

---

28 http://www.nat.org.uk/Media%20library/Files/Communications%20and%20Media/Media%20Guidelines/Guidelines%20for%20Reporting%20HIV%202010/Guidelines%20for%20Reporting%20-%20by%20section/UK%20Law%20and%20HIV.pdf

29 http://www.gpo.gov/fdsys/pkg/PLAW-104publ191/html/PLAW-104publ191.htm

The four requirements listed above reflect only a small portion of the directive. The directive further states what rights the subjects have, such as objecting at any time to the processing of their personal data if the use is for direct marketing purposes. Recently, several Internet search companies and social media companies have been cited as not complying with this law. These organizations have been accused of using the personal data of the subject for direct marketing efforts without the subject's permission. The information security professionals working in a marketing firm in the European Union must understand the impact of these requirements on how information will be processed, stored, and transmitted in their organization.

HITECH

In the U.S., the HITECH Act strengthens the requirements of HIPAA. One of the most drastic changes is the requirement of breach reporting. HITECH ushered in an era of rapid electronic health record adoption, but it also brought in new requirements for security, privacy, and breach reporting. The scope of covered entities was also clarified to include business associates such as billing providers, health information exchanges, software companies, cloud computing providers, and in some cases banks.

The breach notification rules of HITECH are detailed and mandatory for covered entities. Covered entities must:

- Maintain a log of all breaches and submit the log to the U.S. Department of Health and Human Service.
- Notify individuals affected by a breach within 60 days.
- Breaches involving more than 500 individuals must be reported to the U.S. Department of Health and Human Services.
- Understand restrictions related to marketing activities using patient information.
- Use and disclose the minimum necessary subject data to conduct a particular function or task.
- Provide an electronic copy of a patient's health record upon request. The provider may charge a fee that covers his or her labor costs for producing the copy.
- Mail first class letters to patients who might be affected by the breach. If 10 or more letters are returned due to non-delivery, the covered entity must post a public notice on its home page and offer a toll free number for at least 90 days. In lieu of the website posting, an organization may choose to publish a breach notice in the local news media.

2

Regulatory Environment

■ Conduct a risk assessment after a breach to determine the harm caused. This is also known as the harm threshold. The risk assessment must determine if there is significant risk or harm to the individual as a result of the disclosure.

An important safe harbor provision exists in the HITECH act for encrypted information. If the information breached was encrypted with certified Federal Information Processing Standard 140-2 (FIPS 140-2) encryption, the breach does not have to be reported. Breaches do not have to be disclosed if the information was exposed to an authorized recipient and not further disclosed.

HITECH offers funding for federal auditors to review the security practices of covered entities in the U.S. Penalties may be assessed by the HHS Office of Civil Rights. Penalties for breaches can reach up to 1.5 million dollars per violation. These penalties are separate from any private, civil, or criminal actions. In addition to HHS fines, some healthcare organizations have also been fined for privacy breaches by the U.S. Federal Trade Commission for breaches of patient information. Recent court judgments have determined the Federal Trade Commission and HHS may both fine organizations for the same breach.[30]

Compare Internal Practices against New Policies and Procedures

Imagine the day-to-day operation of an organization without any policies. Individuals would have to make decisions about what is right or wrong for the company based upon their personal values or their own past experience. While many small companies and startups operate in this fashion, this could potentially create as many values as there are people in the organization. Policies establish the framework for the security program that ensures that everyone has a common set of expectations and communicates the management's goals and objectives.

Procedures, standards, guidelines, and baselines (illustrated in *Figure* 2.8) are components that support the implementation of the security policy. A policy without mechanisms supporting its implementation is analogous to an organization having a business strategy without action plans to execute the strategy. Policies communicate the management's expectations, which are fulfilled through the execution of procedures and adherence to standards, baselines, and guidelines.

---

30 http://causeofaction.org/assets/uploads/2013/09/LabMD-Answer-9-17-2013-Final.pdf

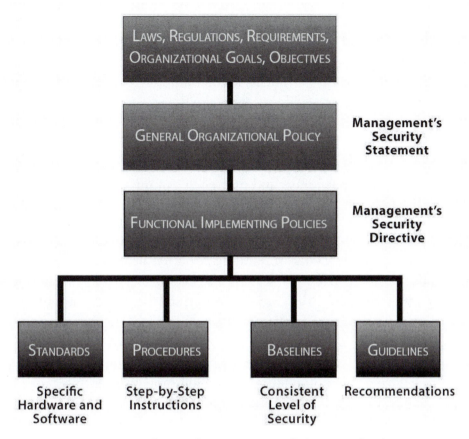

Figure 2.8 - **Relationships among policies, standards, procedures, baselines, and guidelines**

Security officers and their teams have typically been charged with the responsibility of creating the security policies. The policies must be written and communicated appropriately to ensure that they can be understood by the end users. Policies that are poorly written or written at too high of an education level (common industry practice is to focus the content for general users at the sixth- to eighth-grade reading level) will not be understood.

While security officers may be responsible for the development of the security policies, the effort should be collaborative to ensure that the business issues are addressed. The security officers will get better corporate support by including other areas in policy development. This helps build buy-in by these areas as they take on a greater ownership of the final product and reduces rework later should they need to provide vital input. Consider including areas such as HR, legal, compliance, various IT areas, and specific business area representatives who represent critical business units. When policies are developed solely within the IT department and then distributed without business input, they are likely to miss important business considerations.

Once policy documents have been created, the basis for ensuring compliance is established. Depending on the organization, additional documentation may be necessary to support policy. This support may come in the form of additional controls described in standards, baselines, or procedures to help personnel with compliance. An important step after documentation is to make the most current version of the documents readily accessible to those who are expected to follow them. Many organizations place the documents on their intranets or in shared file folders to facilitate their accessibility. Such placement of these documents plus awareness actions, training (if needed), checklists, forms, and sample documents can make awareness and ultimately compliance more effective.

Policies (Information Security and Privacy)

Policies form the foundation of an organization's expectations for its employees. Information security policy is crucial in ensuring an organization conveys the significance of information security and also is able to enforce information security should the need arise. Writing policies does not have to be a mystery, and there are several guidelines for creating good security policies practiced in the industry including the following:

- *Formally define a policy creation and policy maintenance practice:* A clearly defined process for initiating, creating, reviewing, recommending, approving, and distributing policies communicates the roles and responsibilities of all parties. Tools to help include process flows, flowcharts, and written documentation.
- *Policies should survive for up to five years:* Even though they should be reviewed and approved at least annually, policies should survive for at least two but up to five years.
- *Do not be too specific in policy statements:* Policies are high-level statements defining the security objectives of the organization. The underlying methods and technologies for implementing the controls that support the policies may change. These should be in other related documents such as procedures, standards, guidelines, and baselines. By doing this, the policy statements will need less frequent change, and the executive management or a board of directors that must review and approve policy annually does not need to review that information. This avoids frequent updates, keeps policy concise, and reduces frequent redistribution to the organization, which can lead to confusion.
- *Use forceful, directive wording:* Compliance with policies is expected. As such, statements including such words as *must, will,* and *shall* communicate this requirement. Weak directive words, such as *should, may,* or *can,* must not be used in policies as they would suggest an option of not following them. This latter type of wording fits better in guidelines or areas where there are options.

- *Technical implementation details do not belong in a policy:* Policies must be technology-independent. Technology controls may change over time as an organization's risk profile changes and new vulnerabilities are found.

- *Keep each policy as short as possible:* Policies published online should be limited in length to two or three pages maximum per policy. The intent for the policies is for the end user to understand and not to create long documents for the sake of documentation.

- *Provide references in policy to the supporting documents:* If the implementation of the policy is placed online, then providing hyperlinks in policy to the related procedures, standards, guidelines, and baselines is an effective method for ensuring that the appropriate procedures are followed. Some of the internal security procedures would not be appropriate for general knowledge, such as the procedure for monitoring intrusions or reviewing log files, and these need to be accessible by the security department and properly secured from general distribution.

- *Thoroughly review before publishing:* Proofreading of policies by multiple individuals allows errors to be caught that may not be readily seen by the author.

- *Conduct management review and sign-off:* Senior management must endorse the policies if they are to be effectively accepted by all management levels and subsequently the end users of the organization.

- *Employees should acknowledge policies:* All users should sign an acknowledgement that they have read and understand the policies. While this does not ensure that they have read or understand the policies, it will help to protect the organization if a user's behavior violates the policy. Typically this may be part of an information security awareness or training program.

- *Do not use technical jargon in policy language:* Policies are targeted to nontechnical users. Technical language is acceptable in technical documentation but not in high-level security policies.

- *Review incidents and adjust policies:* Review the security incidents that have occurred. These may indicate the need for a new policy, a revision to an existing policy, or the need to redistribute the current policy to reinforce compliance.

- *Periodically review policies:* Set a regular review schedule and ensure it is followed. The formalized review process will provide a mechanism to ensure that the security policies remain in alignment with business objectives. Time is not the only action that should trigger a review. Changes in mission, systems, interconnections, and business strategy should all necessitate a policy review.

2

Regulatory Environment

■ *Define policy exception rules:* A policy exception defines situations where a policy might not be enforced and requires that procedures document the exception and any special alternatives or monitoring that might be put in place to track the exception.

■ *Develop sanctions for noncompliance:* Effective policies have consistent sanctions as deterrents and enable action when the policies are not followed. These sanctions may include "disciplinary action up to and including termination." Stronger language can also be added to warn of prosecution for serious offenses.

Policies provide the foundation for a comprehensive and effective security program. The policies define various roles and responsibilities in the organization and assign the necessary authority for security activities and compliance. By somebody communicating the company policies as directives, accountability and personal responsibility for adhering to the security practices are established. The policies can be utilized for determining or interpreting conflicts that may arise. The policies also define the elements, scope, and functions of the security management framework.

Types of Security Policies

Security policies may consist of different types, depending upon the specific need for the policy. The different security policies will work together to meet the objectives of a comprehensive security program. Different policy types include the following:

■ *Organizational or Program policy* – This policy is issued by a senior management individual or group who creates the authority and scope for the security program. The purpose of the program is described, and the assigned responsibility is defined for carrying out the information security mission. The goals of confidentiality, integrity, and availability are addressed in the policy. Specific areas of security focus may be stressed, such as the protection of confidential information for a health insurance company. The policy should be clear as to the facilities, hardware, software, information, and personnel that are in scope for the security program. In most cases, the scope will be the entire organization. In larger organizations however, the security program may be limited in scope to a division or geographic location. The organization policy sets out the high-level authority to define the appropriate sanctions for failure to comply with the policy.

- **Functional, Issue-Specific policies –** While the organizational security policies are broad in scope, the functional or issue-specific policies address areas of particular security concern requiring clarification. The issue-specific policies may be focused on the different domains of security and address areas such as access control, segregation of duties (SOD), principles, and so forth. They may also address specific technical areas of existing and emerging technologies, such as use of the Internet, email, and corporate communication systems, wireless access, or remote system access. For example, an acceptable use policy may define the responsibilities of the end user for using the corporate computer systems for business purposes only or may allow the person some incidental personal use, provided the restriction of ensuring that usage is free from viruses, spyware, the downloading of inappropriate pictures or software, or the sending of chain letters through email. These policies will depend upon the business needs and the tolerance for risk. They contain the statement of the issue, the statement of the organization's position on the issue, the applicability of the issue, the compliance requirements, and the sanctions for not following the policy.

- **System-Specific policies –** Areas where it is desired to have clearer direction or greater control for a specific technical or operational area may have more detailed policies. These policies may be targeted for a specific application or platform. For example, a system-specific policy may address which departments are permitted to input or modify information in the check-writing application for the disbursement of accounts payable payments.

The more detailed and issue-specific a policy is, the higher the likelihood that the policy will require more frequent changes. Typically, high-level organizational security policies are broad statements, establish corporate security philosophy, and can survive for several years, while those focused on the use of technology will change much more frequently as technology matures and new technology is added to the environment. Even if an organization is not currently utilizing a technology, policies can explicitly strengthen the message that the technology is not to be used and is prohibited. For example, a policy regarding removable media such as USB storage devices or one regarding the use of wireless devices or camera phones would reinforce management's intentions concerning these technologies.

Standards

Whereas policies define what an organization needs, standards take this a step further and define the specific requirements. Standards provide the agreements that provide interoperability within the organization through the use of common protocols. Adherence to standards is typically mandatory in most organizations.

Standards provide a more technical perspective. They lay out the hardware and software mechanisms, which the organization may have selected for controlling security risks. Standards are prevalent in many facets of daily life, such as the size of the tires on automobiles, specifications of the height, color, and format of a STOP sign, and the RJ45 plug on the end of an Ethernet cable. Standards provide consistency in implementation as well as permit interoperability while reducing confusion. An organization may set several specific security standards. For example, when selecting a control for remote-access identification and authentication, an organization could decide to utilize log-in IDs and passwords, strong authentication through a security token, or a virtual private network (VPN) solution over the Internet. The standard would be specific to the authentication tool or mechanism implemented.

A standard might state, "Remote connectivity requires multifactor tokens". The standard might even establish the specific solution that the organization has standardized on for a control such as the antivirus product.

Standards can improve the operation of the security controls and increase efficiency by requiring consistency across the organization. It is more costly to support multiple software packages that do essentially the same thing. Imagine if each user was told to go to the local computer store and purchase his or her favorite antivirus product. Some users would ask the salesperson's opinion, some would buy the least expensive, and others might get the most expensive, assuming this would provide the greatest protection. Without a consistent standard for antivirus products, the organization might not get the level of protection required. Individual products may not consistently get virus signatures updated, and the organization would never know for sure if a workstation was protected. Additionally, each of these different products would have different installation, update, and licensing considerations, contributing to complex management. It makes sense to have consistent products chosen for the organization versus leaving the product choice to every individual or department.

Determination of which standards best meet the organization's security needs is driven by the security policies agreed upon by management. The standards provide the specification for the technology to effectively enable the organization to be successful in meeting the requirements set by policy. If, in the example of remote access, the organization was restricting information over the Internet or had many users in rural areas with limited Internet access, then the VPN standard over the Internet may not be a plausible solution. Conversely, for end users transmitting large amounts of information, the dial-up solution may be impractical. The policy defines the boundaries within which the standards must operate.

Standards may also refer to those guidelines established by a standards organization and accepted by management. Standards creators include organizations such as the United States' National Institute of Standards and Technology (NIST), International Organization for Standardization (ISO), Institute of Electronics and Electrical Engineers (IEEE), American National Standards Institute (ANSI), the United States' National Security Agency (NSA), and others.

Baselines

Baselines can describe the best way to implement a security configuration or standard of a software or environment to ensure that it is consistent throughout the organization. Different software packages, hardware platforms, and networks have different ways to ensure they are configured securely. Products and secure environments may have many different options and settings that can be configured to provide the best security protection. An analysis of the available configuration settings and their subsequent settings forms the basis for a consistent implementation of a standard. For example, turning off the remote desktop service may be specified in the hardening baseline document for servers. A procedure would describe how to turn off the service. Exceptions to the baseline may need to be documented in the event that the baseline cannot be followed in a particular department or environment, along with the business justification. Baselines are the specific rules describing how to implement the best security controls in support of policy and standards.

Testing of the current security controls on a periodic basis ensures that the baselines have been implemented as documented. The baselines themselves should be reviewed periodically to make sure that they are sufficient to address emerging threats and vulnerabilities. In large environments with multiple individuals performing systems administration and responding to urgent requests, there is an increased risk that one of the baseline configurations may not be implemented properly. Internal testing identifies these vulnerabilities and provides a mechanism to review why the control was or was not properly implemented. Failures in training, adherence to baselines and associated procedures, change control, documentation, or skills of the individual performing the changes may be identified through the testing.

2

Regulatory Environment

Procedures (Information Security and Privacy)

Procedures are step-by-step instructions to support compliance with the policies and standards. The procedure may provide step-by-step instructions for how to best implement the policy and who does what to accomplish various security tasks. The procedure provides clarity and a common understanding of the prescribed operations required to effectively support the policies on a consistent basis. Develop procedures with the input of each of the areas that might be impacted. This reduces the risk that important steps, communication, or required deliverables will be left out.

Companies must be able to provide assurance that they have exercised due diligence in the support and enforcement of company policies. This means that the company has made an effort to comply with the policies and has communicated these expectations to the workforce. Documenting procedures communicated to the users, business partners, and anyone utilizing the systems, as appropriate, minimizes the legal liability of the corporation.

The documentation of procedures is more than an exercise. The process itself can create a common understanding among the developers regarding the methods used to accomplish the task. Individuals from different organizational units may be very familiar with their work area, but not as familiar with the impact of a procedure on another department. This is a common problem where organizations sometimes appear as a large multidisciplinary mass, and the individuals working in different departments only understand their portion of the organization and may not understand the other parts of the organization. The exercise of writing down a single, consistent procedure has the added effect of establishing agreement among impacted parties. Many times at the beginning of the process, individuals will think they understand the process and realize that departments were executing different, individual processes to accomplish a task.

Guidelines

Guidelines are discretionary or optional recommendations that can be used to enable individuals who make judgments with respect to security actions. Guidelines provide implementation recommendations or suggested steps for complying with the implementation of policy, standard, or how best to implement a configuration baseline.

Guidelines are also the recommendations, best practices, and templates documented in the frameworks created by other organizations such as the Control Objectives for Information and Related Technology (COBIT), the Capability Maturity Model (CMM), and ISO27000 (formally known as ISO17799 or BS7799). Ultimately, any standard procedure or policy that is not mandatory for an organization or individual may be viewed as a guideline. Guidelines are by definition optional; however, some standards or policies may make them mandatory.

Documentation

Each of these documents can be closely related to the others and may be developed as the result of new regulations, external industry standards, new threats and vulnerabilities, emerging technologies, upgraded hardware and software platforms, or risk assessments. Often, organizations will combine the information into single documents for ease of management. Policies must not be combined with other documentation. It is also best to keep standards as stand-alone documents. This is to ensure only the appropriate level of management must be involved in changing a policy or a standard. Management must review and approve policy and, by keeping them concise, will make the review job easier and less confusing. Management, especially executive management or a board of directors, is not typically interested in procedures, guidelines, and technical configuration baselines. Policies as described in this chapter should be designed for less frequent change than the supporting processes, standards, or guidelines making it often less necessary to distribute and communicate policy changes. At a minimum, even if policy is not changed, it should be reviewed and approved on an annual basis.

Policy Analogy

A useful analogy to help remember the differences between policies, standards, guidelines, and procedures is to think of a company that builds cabinets and has a "hammer" policy. The different components may be as follows:

- **Policy** - *"All boards must be nailed together using company-issued hammers to ensure end-product consistency and worker safety."*

  Notice that the policy provides the flexibility that permits the company to define the hammer type as changes in technology or safety issues warrant. In this example, the purpose ("ensure end-product consistency") is also communicated to the employees.

- **Standard** - *"Eleven-inch fiberglass hammers will be used. Only hardened-steel nails will be used with the hammers. Automatic hammers are to be used for repetitive jobs only that are > 1 hour."* A standard may establish the maximum automatic power hammer settings or even the model of the hammer.

  Standards are the technical specifics that clarify the expectations that make sense for the current environment and represent management's decision.

- **Guideline** – *"To avoid splitting the wood, a pilot hole may be drilled first."*

The guideline is only a suggestion or recommendation and may not apply in all cases or in the analogy with all types of wood. The guideline is not a requirement, but rather it is a suggested practice to minimize wood splitting.

■ **Procedure** – "(1) Position nail in upright position on board. (2) Strike nail with full swing of hammer. (3) Repeat until nail is flush with board."

The procedure describes the process for using the hammer and the nail to get the best results and be successful. Following this procedure, with the appropriate standard hammers, and practicing guidelines where appropriate will keep the employee compliant with the policy.

Understand Compliance Frameworks

A compliance framework can help organizations navigate the laws and regulations. Multiple frameworks have been created to support security, auditing, and risk assessment including implemented security controls. The following frameworks have each gained a degree of acceptance within the auditing or information security and privacy community and assist with information security, privacy, and auditing.

ISO 27000 (Formally Known as ISO17799/BS7799)

The International Organization for Standardization (ISO) is the world's largest developer and publisher of international standards. ISO is a nongovernment organization of the national standards institutes of 157 countries, one member per country, with a Central Secretariat in Geneva, Switzerland, that coordinates the system. Its mission is to form a bridge between the public and private sectors, enabling consensus to be reached on solutions that meet both the requirements of business and the broader needs of society. The 27000 series of standards addresses information security practices.

The security standards 27001 and 27002 are universally recognized as the standards for sound security practices. Both standards were inspired by the earlier British Standard 7799 (BS7799). The first part of BS7799 inspired the publication of ISO/IEC 17799, which was renumbered as ISO/IEC 27002 in 2005. In turn, the second part of BS7799 strongly influenced the development of ISO/IEC 27001. Although they share common origins, these standards approach information security management in very different ways.

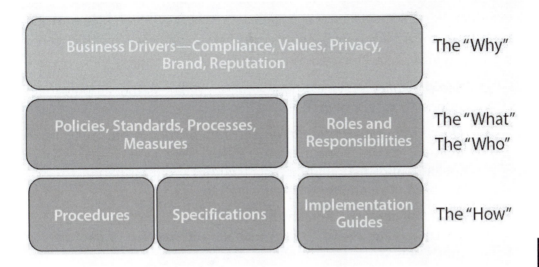

Figure 2.9 - **A generic Information Security Management System**
It starts with key business drivers and determines how the organization will
respond to them and how responsibility will be shared within the organization.

ISO/IEC 27001:2005 is focused on the standardization and certification of an organization's Information Security Management System (ISMS). An ISMS (*Figure 2.9*) is defined as the governance structure supporting an information security program. It addresses the tone at the top, roles and responsibilities, and maps business drivers to the implementation of appropriate controls vis-à-vis the risk management process. The following illustrates the elements common to a generic ISMS:

ISO/IEC 27001:2005 provides instructions on how to apply the ISMS concept and to construct, run, sustain, and advance information security management. The core of the standard is focused on five key areas:

1. General requirements of the ISMS
2. Management responsibility
3. Internal ISMS audits
4. Management review of the ISMS
5. ISMS improvement

ISO/IEC 27002 is often used in tandem with 27001. Rather than focus on security governance, it provides a "Code of Practice for Information Security Management," which lists security control objectives and recommends a range of specific security controls according to industry best practice. Unlike 27001, this standard is more of a guideline than a standard, leaving it up to the organization to decide what level of control is appropriate, given the risk tolerance of the specific environment under the scope of the ISMS. The recommended control objectives are the "how"—they demonstrate the implementation of operational controls. A well-rounded information security program will likely include services that address each of these control objectives. ISO/IEC 27002 includes the following 11 focus areas:

1. **Security Policy** provides management guidance and support for information security.

2. **Organization and Information Security** provides a formal and defined security mechanism within an organization that includes information processing facilities and information assets accessed or maintained by third parties.

3. **Asset Management** protects the organization's assets by ensuring valuable data assets are identified and receive appropriate protection.

4. **Human Resources Security** minimizes the risks of human error, theft, and misuse of resources, provides information security threats and concerns to users, and disseminates information to support the corporate security policy.

5. **Physical and Environmental Security** prevents unauthorized physical access, damage, and interference to facilities and data.

6. **Communications and Operations Management** ensures the proper and secure operation of data processing facilities by protecting software, communications, data, and the supporting infrastructure, as well as ensuring proper data exchange between organizations.

7. **Access Control** limits access to data, mobile communications, telecommunications, and network services, as well as detects unauthorized activities.

8. **Information Systems Acquisitions, Development, and Maintenance** implements security controls into operations and development systems to ensure the security of application systems software and data.

9. **Information Security Incident Management** implements procedures to detect and respond to information security incidents.

10. **Business Continuity Management** mitigates an incident's impact on critical business systems.

11. **Compliance** ensures adherence to criminal and civil laws and statutory, regulatory, or contractual obligations, complies with organizational security policies and standards, and provides for a comprehensive audit process.

Each of these control objectives also includes numerous clauses describing specific controls along with recommendations on how they should be implemented in a typical enterprise.

Both standards can be used to guide security architecture and design. The big difference lies with certification. An organization's ISMS may be certified by a licensed third-party assessor under ISO/IEC 27001, but its control practices cannot be so certified. The certification process allows the assessors to capture the essential elements of the organization's ISMS and publish their findings in a form of a statement of applicability. This document is intended not only to highlight the ISMS but also to allow different organizations to compare their ISMSs. For this reason, ISO/IEC 27001 certification is commonly used by service organizations that use it to share with current and potential customers.

U.S. NIST SP 800–66, 800-111, and the Meaningful Use Testing Standards

In the U.S., the National Institute of Standards and Technology provided the SP 800 series to address the statutory responsibility under the Federal Information Security Management Act (FISMA) of 2002 to "develop standards and guidelines, including minimum requirements for the adequate information security for all agency operations and assets…"

800-66[31]

In 2008, NIST implemented the SP 800-66 Revision 1 *"An Introductory Resource Guide for Implementing the Health Insurance Portability Accountability Act (HIPAA) Security Rule"*. The guide is designed to familiarize healthcare organizations and professionals with the security standards included in the HIPAA Security Rule along with its structure and organization. *Figure 2.10, HIPAA Components,* illustrates the structure of the security rule and the supporting regulations and standards.

---

31 http://csrc.nist.gov/publications/nistpubs/800-66-Rev1/SP-800-66-Revision1.pdf

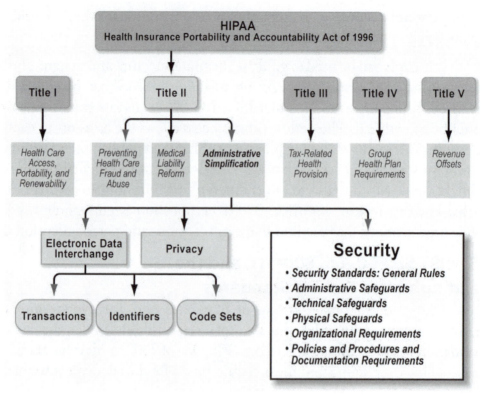

Figure 2.10 - **HIPAA Components**

800-111[32]

NIST SP 800-66 lists HIPAA-related storage security needs. For example, Section 4.14 of NIST SP 800-66 describes the need to encrypt and decrypt electronic protected health information (EPHI). NIST SP 800-111, *Guide to Storage Encryption Technologies for End User Devices*, describes the basics of storage security to prevent the disclosure of information that is sensitive, such as PII or EPHI. It assists organizations with planning, implementing, and maintaining storage encryption solutions. Although the documentation doesn't require previous experience with encryption technologies, experience with information security is assumed. It is important for the HCISPP to note that this guidance covers data at rest but not data in transit. When one is securing sensitive information, it is important to think of both states of data. Data in transit is discussed in NIST SP 800-52, *Guidelines for the Selection and Use of Transport Layer Security (TLS) Implementations*; NIST SP 800-77, *Guide to IPSEC VPNs*; or NIST SP 800-113 *Guide to SSL VPNs*.

---

32 http://csrc.nist.gov/publications/nistpubs/800-111/SP800-111.pdf

Meaningful Use Testing Standards[33]

"The American Recovery and Reinvestment Act of 2009 emphasizes the need for the U.S. to move toward the use of electronic health records. To encourage a more widespread adoption of interoperable health information technology, the legislation calls for the Office of the National Coordinator (ONC) for Health IT, in consultation with NIST, to recognize a program for the voluntary certification of health information technology as being in compliance with applicable certification criteria to meet defined meaningful use requirements. In collaboration with ONC, NIST developed the necessary functional and conformance testing requirements, test cases, and test tools in support of the health IT certification program."[34] Meaningful use focuses on the entire electronic health record system, not just the security. Several areas exist for security, but session security is largely ignored.

Common Criteria

Although ITSEC provided some international harmonization, it was not universally adopted, and vendors continued to have to develop their products with multiple criteria in mind. The publication of the Common Criteria as the ISO/IEC 15408 standard provided the first truly international product evaluation criteria. It has largely superseded all other criteria, although there continue to be products in general use that were certified under TCSEC, ITSEC, and other criteria. It takes a very similar approach to ITSEC by providing a flexible set of functional and assurance requirements, and like ITSEC, it is not very proscriptive as TCSEC had been. Instead, it is focused on standardizing the general approach to product evaluation and providing mutual recognition of such evaluations all over the world.

While flexibility can be desirable, it does make it difficult for vendors to develop products to a common set of requirements or for consumers to evaluate two or more products against a predefined common baseline. To help with this, common criteria introduced protection profiles (PP). These are a common set of functional and assurance requirements for a category of vendor products deployed in a particular type of environment. For example, the "Software based Personal Firewall for Home Internet Use" PP provides functional and assurance requirements that should be common to all such firewall systems. This could then be used as the basis for vendor development and subsequent product evaluation.

---

33   http://healthcare.nist.gov/use_testing/index.html

34   http://healthcare.nist.gov/use_testing/index.html

In many cases, however, these PP may not be specific enough or may not cover the specific situation required by the consumers, so they may still choose to develop their own ST. A ST is the specific functional and assurance requirements that the author of the ST wants a given product to fulfill. The vendor product (referred to as a ToE) is then examined against this specific ST by a third-party evaluation lab using a common evaluation methodology (CEM).

The result of that evaluation is a report that outlines whether the ToE met the requirements identified by the PP or ST (whichever one was used). It also assigns the evaluation an Evaluation Assurance Level (EAL) as shown in *Figure 2.11*, Standard EAL Packages. The EAL level is intended to provide the consumers or the vendors with some idea of how confident they should be in the results of the evaluation, based on how much information was available to the evaluation lab and how carefully the system was examined. The EALs are as follows:

- **EAL 1:** The product is functionally tested; this is sought when some assurance in accurate operation is necessary, but the threats to security are not seen as serious.
- **EAL 2:** Structurally tested; this is sought when developers or users need a low to moderate level of independently guaranteed security.
- **EAL 3:** Methodically tested and checked; this is sought when there is a need for a moderate level of independently ensured security.
- **EAL 4:** Methodically designed, tested, and reviewed; this is sought when developers or users require a moderate to high level of independently ensured security.
- **EAL 5:** Semi-formally designed and tested; this is sought when the requirement is for a high level of independently ensured security.
- **EAL 6:** Semi-formally verified, designed, and tested; this is sought when developing specialized TOEs for high-risk situations.
- **EAL 7:** Formally verified, designed, and tested; this is sought when developing a security TOE for applications in extremely high-risk situations.

EALs are frequently misunderstood to provide a simple means to compare security products with similar levels. In fact, products may be very different even if they are assigned the same EAL level because functionality may have little in common.

Short Name	Long Name	Level of Confidence
EAL1	Functionally tested	Lowest
EAL 2	Structurally tested	
EAL3	Methodically tested and checked	
EAL4	Methodically designed, tested, and reviewed	Medium
EAL5	Semi-formally designed and tested	
EAL6	Semi-formally verified design and tested	

Source:

Herrman, D.S. The common criteria for IT security evaluation, in Information Security Management Handbook, 6th edn., Tipton, H.F. and Krause, M. Eds., Auerbach Publications, New York, 2007, 1496.

Figure 2.11 – **Standard EAL Packages**

IG Toolkit

The U.K. Department of Health created the Information Governance (IG) Toolkit that is now hosted by the Health and Social Care Information Centre. The toolkit is used by all health and social care service providers, commissioners, and suppliers to perform required self-assessments of their compliance with numerous information governance regulations and guidelines related to personal information. The following list of information governance is included in the IG toolkit:[35]

- The Data Protection Act 1998
- The common law duty of confidentiality
- The Confidentiality NHS Code of Practice
- The NHS Care Record Guarantee for England
- The Social Care Record Guarantee for England
- The international information security standard: ISO/IEC 27002: 2005
- The Information Security NHS Code of Practice
- The Records Management NHS Code of Practice
- The Freedom of Information Act 2000
- The Human Rights Act article 8
- The Code of Practice for the Management of Confidential Information

The self-assessments performed by organizations may differ by organization type, but all must assess the following areas:

---

35 https://www.igt.hscic.gov.uk/about.
aspx?tk=417481545636676&cb=03%3a40%3a32&clnav=YES&lnv=5

- Management structures and responsibilities (e.g. assigning responsibility for carrying out the IG assessment, providing staff training, etc.)
- Confidentiality and data protection
- Information security

Generally Accepted Privacy Principles (GAPP)[36]

Volunteers from the U.S. and Canada collaborated on a taskforce to develop the GAPP. The participating organizations were the American Institute of CPAs (AICPA) and the Canadian Institute of Chartered Accountants (CICA). The task force reviewed current local, national, and international privacy regulatory requirements and best practices to provide principles that could enable CPAs to provide appropriate guidance to their clients regarding privacy. The GAPP consists of one overall privacy objective supported by 10 principles. Although it was created for CPAs and CAs, the GAPP can be used by any organization to develop a privacy program. According to the GAPP, the overall privacy principle is "Personal information is collected, used, retained, disclosed, and disposed of in conformity with the commitments in the entity's privacy notice and with criteria set forth in Generally Accepted Privacy Principles issued by the AICPA and CICA."[37] The 10 principles are listed below and described with measurable criteria in the documentation.

1. Management
2. Notice
3. Choice and consent
4. Collection
5. Use, retention, and disposal
6. Access
7. Disclosure to third parties
8. Security for privacy
9. Quality
10. Monitoring and enforcement

---

36 http://www.aicpa.org/InterestAreas/InformationTechnology/Resources/Privacy/GenerallyAcceptedPrivacyPrinciples/Pages/default.aspx

37 http://www.aicpa.org/InterestAreas/InformationTechnology/Resources/Privacy/GenerallyAcceptedPrivacyPrinciples/DownloadableDocuments/GAPP_PRAC_%200909.pdf

Understand Response for Risk-Based Decision

Risk-based decisions are made after a risk assessment has been conducted. Once risks and their impact to the organization are determined, it is up to the stakeholders to make a risk-based decision as to accept the risk or to implement controls that can help to lessen the risk to an acceptable level. Different types of risk treatments can be used and are discussed in section on *Risk Treatment* in domain 4. An important thing to note is that when organizations decide to lessen the impact of a risk by implementing controls and choose to continue to use the data, they are essentially accepting the risk. The only way to ensure that there is no risk is to not use the data. The possible risk treatments discussed in domain 4 are:

- Risk Mitigation/Remediation
- Risk Transfer
- Risk Acceptance
- Risk Avoidance

Compensating Controls

When lessening risk, the controls discussed above are called compensating controls. Controls are discussed in detail in the *Controls* section of domain 4 and include compensating controls. Also see the section later in this domain on *Residual Risk Tolerance*, which describes residual risk tolerance and its relation to compensating controls.

Control Variance Documentation

Domain 4 discusses the risk management process and exceptions. Controls protecting healthcare information are susceptible to exceptions and variances just as the controls identified in the risk management process. Variances should be treated from a risk management perspective and the same objectives apply.

- The most important thing to note with any exception is to be sure that they are well documented. Ensure the documentation describes the exception in detail, including the duration the exception will be allowed, the party requesting the exception, and, most important, all the risk the exception introduces.
- Ensure senior management and stakeholders are aware of the exception and that the appropriate parties have agreed to allow it.
- Acceptance of risk introduced by the variance needs to be documented.
- Resources should be identified and compared to the amount of variance. Large variances that can be mitigated through low amounts of resources should be prioritized for action.

Residual Risk Tolerance

Domain 4 discusses residual risk and how the elimination of all risk in a given area is virtually impossible while still allowing functionality. The domain describes residual risk as the acceptable level of risk determined by the organization left after compensating controls have been applied. The organization, through its risk management process, should have determined its acceptable level of risk. Some important takeaways are:

- Compensating controls can also be temporary solutions to accommodate a short-term change or support the evolution of a new application, business development, or major project.
- Implementing compensating controls are not the only choices an organization has to address risk.
- Allowing a system to continue to operate while implementing controls or not means that the residual risk is being accepted by default.

Understand and Comply with Code of Ethics/ Conduct in a Health Information Environment

The consideration of computer ethics fundamentally emerged with the birth of computers. There was concern right away that computers would be used inappropriately to the detriment of society, or that they would replace humans in many jobs, resulting in widespread job loss. To fully grasp the issues involved with computer ethics, one must consider the history. The following provides a brief overview of some significant events.

Consideration of computer ethics is recognized to have begun with the work of MIT professor Norbert Wiener during World War II in the early 1940s, when he helped to develop antiaircraft cannons that are capable of shooting down fast warplanes. This work resulted in Wiener and his colleagues creating a new field of research that Wiener called cybernetics, the science of information feedback systems. The concepts of cybernetics, combined with the developing computer technologies, led Wiener to make some ethical conclusions about the technology called information and communication technology (ICT), in which Wiener predicted social and ethical consequences. Wiener published the book The Human Use of Human Beings in 1950, which described a comprehensive foundation that is still the basis for computer ethics research and analysis.

In the mid-1960s, Donn B. Parker, at the time with SRI International in Menlo Park, California, began examining unethical and illegal uses of computers and documenting examples of computer crime and other unethical computerized activities. He published "Rules of Ethics in Information Processing" in Communications of the ACM in 1968 and headed the development of the first Code of Professional Conduct for the Association for Computing Machinery, which was adopted by the ACM in 1973.

During the late 1960s, Joseph Weizenbaum, a computer scientist at MIT in Boston, created a computer program that he called ELIZA that he scripted to provide a crude imitation of "a Rogerian psychotherapist engaged in an initial interview with a patient." People had strong reactions to his program, some psychiatrists fearing it showed that computers would perform automated psychotherapy. Weizenbaum wrote *Computer Power and Human Reason* in 1976, in which he expressed his concerns about the growing tendency to see humans as mere machines. His book, MIT courses, and many speeches inspired many computer ethics thoughts and projects.

Walter Maner is credited with coining the phrase "computer ethics" in the mid-1970s when discussing the ethical problems and issues created by computer technology, and he taught a course on the subject at Old Dominion University. From the late 1970s into the mid-1980s, Maner's work created much interest in university-level computer ethics courses. In 1978, Maner published the Starter Kit in Computer Ethics, which contained curriculum materials and advice for developing computer ethics courses. Many university courses were put in place because of Maner's work.

In the 1980s, social and ethical consequences of information technology, such as computer-enabled crime, computer failure disasters, privacy invasion using computer databases, and software ownership lawsuits, were being widely discussed in America and Europe. James Moor of Dartmouth College published "What Is Computer Ethics?" in Computers and Ethics, and Deborah Johnson of Rensselaer Polytechnic Institute published Computer Ethics, the first textbook in the field in the mid-1980s. Other significant books about computer ethics were published within the psychology and sociology field, such as Sherry Turkle's The Second Self, about the impact of computing on the human psyche, and Judith Perrolle's Computers and Social Change: Information, Property and Power, about a sociological approach to computing and human values.

Maner Terrell Bynum held the first international multidisciplinary conference on computer ethics in 1991. For the first time, philosophers, computer professionals, sociologists, psychologists, lawyers, business leaders, news reporters, and government officials assembled to discuss computer ethics. During the 1990s, new university courses, research centers, conferences, journals, articles, and textbooks appeared, and organizations like Computer

Professionals for Social Responsibility, the Electronic Frontier Foundation, and the Association for Computing Machinery-Special Interest Group on Computers and Society (ACM-SIGCAS) launched projects addressing computing and professional responsibility. Developments in Europe and Australia included new computer ethics research centers in England, Poland, Holland, and Italy. In the U.K., Simon Rogerson, of De Montfort University, led the ETHICOMP series of conferences and established the Centre for Computing and Social Responsibility.

Several organizations and groups have defined the computer ethics their members should observe and practice. In fact, most professional organizations have adopted a code of ethics, a large percentage of which address how to handle information. To provide the ethics of all professional organizations related to computer use would fill a large book. The following are provided to give you an opportunity to compare similarities between the codes and, most interestingly, to note the differences (and sometimes contradictions) in the codes followed by the various diverse groups.

Organizational Code of Ethics

Peter S. Tippett has written extensively on computer ethics. He provided the following action plan to help corporate information security leaders to instill a culture of ethical computer use within organizations:

1. Develop a corporate guide to computer ethics for the organization.

2. Develop a computer ethics policy to supplement the computer security policy.

3. Add information about computer ethics to the employee handbook.

4. Find out whether the organization has a business ethics policy and expand it to include computer ethics.

5. Learn more about computer ethics and spread what is learned.

6. Help to foster awareness of computer ethics by participating in the computer ethics campaign.

7. Make sure the organization has an email privacy policy.

8. Make sure employees know what the email policy is.

Fritz H. Grupe, Timothy Garcia-Jay, and William Kuechler identified the following selected ethical bases for IT decision making:

- **Golden Rule** — Treat others as you wish to be treated. Do not implement systems that you would not wish to be subjected to yourself. Is your company using unlicensed software although your company itself sells software?

- **Kant's Categorical Imperative** — If an action is not right for everyone, it is not right for anyone. Does management monitor call center employees' seat time but not its own?

- **Descartes' Rule of Change (also called the slippery slope)** — If an action is not repeatable at all times, it is not right at any time. Should your website link to another site, "framing" the page, so users think it was created and belongs to someone else?

- **Utilitarian Principle (also called universalism)** — Take the action that achieves the most good. Put a value on outcomes and strive to achieve the best results. This principle seeks to analyze and maximize the IT of the covered population within acknowledged resource constraints. Should customers using an organization's website be asked to opt in or opt out of the possible sale of their personal data to other companies?

- **Risk Aversion principle** — Incur least harm or cost. When there are alternatives that have varying degrees of harm and gain, choose the one that causes the least damage. If a manager reports that a subordinate criticized him in an email to other employees, who would do the search and see the results of the search?

- **Avoid Harm** — Avoid malfeasance or "do no harm." This basis implies a proactive obligation of companies to protect their customers and clients from systems with known harm. Does a company have a privacy policy that protects rather than exploits customers?

- **No Free Lunch Rule** — Assume that all property and information belong to someone. This principle is primarily applicable to intellectual property that should not be taken without just compensation. Has a company used unlicensed software or hired a group of IT workers from a competitor?

- **Legalism** — Is it against the law? Moral actions may not be legal and vice versa. Might Web advertising exaggerate the features and benefits of products? Are websites collecting information illegally on minors?

- **Professionalism** — Is an action contrary to codes of ethics? Do the professional codes cover a case, and do they suggest the path to follow? When presenting technological alternatives to managers who do not know the right questions to ask, do consultants tell them all they need to know to make informed choices?

2

Regulatory Environment

- ***Evidentiary Guidance*** — Is there hard data to support or deny the value of taking an action? This is not a traditional "ethics" value, but one that is a significant factor related to IT's policy decisions about the impact of systems on individuals and groups. This value involves probabilistic reasoning where outcomes can be predicted based on hard evidence based on research. Does management assume it knows PC users are satisfied with IT's service, or has data been collected to determine what they really think?

- ***Client/Customer/Patient Choice*** — Let the people affected decide. In some circumstances, employees and customers have a right to self-determination through the informed consent process. This principle acknowledges a right to self-determination in deciding what is "harmful" or "beneficial" for their personal circumstances. Are your workers subjected to monitoring in places where they assume that they have privacy?

- ***Equity*** — Will the costs and benefits be equitably distributed? Adherence to this principle obligates a company to provide similarly situated persons with the same access to data and systems. This can imply a proactive duty to inform and make services, data, and systems available to all those who share a similar circumstance. Has IT made intentionally inaccurate projections as to project costs?

- ***Competition*** — This principle derives from the marketplace where consumers and institutions can select among competing companies, based on all considerations such as degree of privacy, cost, and quality. It recognizes that to be financially viable in the market, it is necessary to have data about what competitors are doing and understand and acknowledge the competitive implications of IT decisions. When presenting a build or buy proposition to management, is it fully aware of the risk involved?

- ***Compassion/Last Chance*** — Religious and philosophical traditions promote the need to find ways to assist the most vulnerable parties. Refusing to take unfair advantage of users or others who do not have technical knowledge is recognized in several professional codes of ethics. Do all workers have an equal opportunity to benefit from the organization's investment in IT?

- ***Impartiality/Objectivity*** — Are decisions biased in favor of one group or another? Is there an even playing field? IT personnel should avoid potential or apparent conflicts of interest. Do any IT employees have a vested interest in the companies that they deal with?

- *Openness/Full Disclosure* — Are persons affected by this system aware of its existence, aware of what data are being collected, and knowledgeable about how it will be used? Do they have access to the same information? Is it possible for a website visitor to determine what cookies are used, and what is done with any information they might collect?
- *Confidentiality* — IT is obligated to determine whether data it collects on individuals can be adequately protected to avoid disclosure to parties whose need to know is not proven. Have they reduced security features to hold expenses to a minimum?
- *Trustworthiness and Honesty* — Does IT stand behind ethical principles to the point where it is accountable for the actions it takes? Has IT management ever posted or circulated a professional code of ethics with an expression of support for seeing that its employees act professionally?[38]

(ISC)² Code of Ethics

The following is an excerpt from the (ISC)² Code of Ethics preamble and canons, by which all associates, credential holders, and HCISPPs must abide. Compliance with the preamble and canons is mandatory to maintain certification. HCISPPs should resolve conflicts between the canons in the order of the canons. The canons are not equal, and conflicts between them are not intended to create ethical binds.

Code of Ethics Preamble

Safety of the commonwealth, duty to our principals, and to each other requires that we adhere, and be seen to adhere, to the highest ethical standards of behavior. Therefore, strict adherence to this Code is a condition of certification.

Code of Ethics Canons

Protect society, the commonwealth, and the infrastructure.

- Promote and preserve public trust and confidence in information and systems.
- Promote the understanding and acceptance of prudent information security measures.
- Preserve and strengthen the integrity of the public infrastructure.
- Discourage unsafe practice.

---

38 CISSP chapter 9 page 1210

Act honorably, honestly, justly, responsibly, and legally.

- Tell the truth; make all stakeholders aware of your actions on a timely basis.
- Observe all contracts and agreements, express or implied.
- Treat all constituents fairly. In resolving conflicts, consider public safety and duties to principals, individuals, and the profession in that order.
- Give prudent advice; avoid raising unnecessary alarm or giving unwarranted comfort. Take care to be truthful, objective, cautious, and within your competence.
- When resolving differing laws in different jurisdictions, give preference to the laws of the jurisdiction in which you render your service.

Provide diligent and competent service to principals.

- Preserve the value of their systems, applications, and information.
- Respect their trust and the privileges that they grant you.
- Avoid conflicts of interest or the appearance thereof.
- Render only those services for which you are fully competent and qualified.

Advance and protect the profession.

- Sponsor for professional advancement those best qualified. All other things equal, prefer those who are certified and who adhere to these canons. Avoid professional association with those whose practices or reputation might diminish the profession.
- Take care not to injure the reputation of other professionals through malice or indifference.
- Maintain your competence; keep your skills and knowledge current. Give generously of your time and knowledge in training others.

Support Organization's Code of Ethics

In 1998, Michael Davis described a professional ethics code as a "contract between professionals." According to this explanation, a profession is a group of persons who want to cooperate in serving the same ideal better than they could if they did not cooperate. Information security professionals, for example, are typically thought to serve the ideal of ensuring the confidentiality, integrity, and availability of information and the security of the technology that supports the information use. A code of ethics would then specify how professionals should pursue their common ideals so that each may do his or her best to reach the goals at a minimum cost while appropriately addressing the issues involved. The code helps to protect professionals from certain stresses and pressures (such as the pressure to cut corners with information security to save money) by making it reasonably likely that most other members of the profession will not take advantage of the resulting conduct of such pressures. An ethics code also protects members of a profession from certain consequences of competition and encourages cooperation and support among the professionals.

Considering this, an occupation does not need society's recognition to be a profession. Indeed, it only needs the actions and activities among its members to cooperate to serve a certain ideal. Once an occupation becomes recognized as a profession, society historically has found reason to give the occupation special privileges (e.g., the sole right to do certain kinds of work) to support serving the ideal in question (in this case, information security) in the way the profession serves society.

If one can understand a code of ethics as a contract between professionals, it can be explained why each information security professional should not depend upon only his or her private conscience when determining how to practice the profession, and why he or she must take into account what a community of information security professionals has to say about what other information security professionals should do. What others expect of information security professionals is part of what each should take into account in choosing what to do within professional activities, especially if the expectation is reasonable. The ethics code provides a guide to what information security professionals may reasonably expect of one another, basically setting forth the rules of the game. Just as athletes need to know the rules of football to know what to do to score, computer professionals also need to know computer ethics to know, for example, whether they should choose information security and risk reduction actions based completely and solely upon the wishes of an employer or, instead, also consider information security leading practices and legal requirements when making recommendations and decisions.

A code of ethics should also provide a guide to what computer professionals may expect other members of our profession to help each other do. Keep in mind that people are not merely members of this or that profession. Each individual has responsibilities beyond the profession and, as such, must face his or her own conscience, along with the criticism, blame, and punishment of others as a result of actions. These issues cannot be escaped just by making a decision because their profession told them to.

HCISPPs must take their professional code of ethics and apply it appropriately to their own unique environments. To assist with this, Donn B. Parker describes the following five ethical principles that apply to processing information in the workplace and also provides examples of how they would be applied.

1. ***Informed consent.*** Try to make sure that the people affected by a decision are aware of your planned actions and that they either agree with your decision or disagree, but understand your intentions. Example: An employee gives a copy of a program that she wrote for her employer to a friend and does not tell her employer about it.

2. ***Higher ethic in the worst case.*** Think carefully about your possible alternative actions and select the beneficial necessary ones that will cause the least, or no, harm under the worst circumstances. Example: A manager secretly monitors an employee's email, which may violate his privacy, but the manager has reason to believe that the employee may be involved in a serious theft of trade secrets.

3. ***Change of scale test.*** Consider that an action you may take on a small scale, or by you alone, could result in significant harm if carried out on a larger scale or by many others. Examples: A teacher lets a friend try out, just once, a database that he bought to see if the friend wants to buy a copy, too. The teacher does not let an entire classroom of his students use the database for a class assignment without first getting permission from the vendor. A computer user thinks it's okay to use a small amount of her employer's computer services for personal business because the others' use is unaffected.

4. ***Owners' conservation of ownership.*** As a person who owns or is responsible for information, always make sure that the information is reasonably protected and that ownership of it, and rights to it, are clear to users. Example: A vendor, who sells a commercial electronic bulletin board service with no proprietary notice at log-on, loses control of the service to a group of hackers who take it over, misuse it, and offend customers.

5. ***Users' conservation of ownership.*** As a person who uses information, always assume others own it and their interests must be protected unless you explicitly know that you are free to use it in any way that you wish. Example: Hacker discovers a commercial electronic bulletin board with no proprietary notice at logon and informs his friends, who take control of it, misuse it, and then uses it to offend other customers.

The following articles and documents contain more information about the healthcare regulatory environment. They are freely available on the Internet.

More to Know

» Identity Theft Assistance Center: http://www.identitytheftassistance. org/pageview.php?cateid=47#JavelinStrategyResearchReport Global Compendium of data privacy laws: http://www.bakerlaw.com/files/ Uploads/Documents/Data%20Breach%20documents/International-Compendium-of-Data-Privacy-Laws.pdf

» U.K. health laws and regulations: http://ico.org.uk/for_organisations/ sector_guides/health
IG Toolkit: https://www.igt.hscic.gov.uk/about. aspx?tk=416028318855193&cb=19%3a57%3a21&clnav=YES&lnv=5

» U.S. health laws and regulations: http://www.hhs.gov/regulations/

» EU health laws and regulations: http://www.healthdatanavigator.eu/ data-management/data-protection

2

Regulatory Environment

Summary

The healthcare regulatory environment is complex, and compliance with healthcare information is a core activity for any healthcare organization that drives information security spending, policy, hiring, and ultimately impact. Organizations have survived or failed due to how they approach healthcare compliance to healthcare regulations. Throughout this chapter the following concepts have been addressed:

- Identification of applicable regulations related to the healthcare information industry.
- General understanding of international regulation and controls related to the healthcare information industry.
  - Major legal systems
  - Liability and computer crimes
  - Treaties, regulations, and industry specific laws.
- Ability to compare internal practices against new policies and procedures.
- Describe compliance frameworks.
  - ISO 27000
  - U.S. NIST
  - Common Criteria
  - IG toolkit
  - GAPP
- Identify different responses for risk-based decisions.
  - Compensating controls
  - Control variance documentation
  - Residual risk tolerance
- Understand and comply with code of ethics/conduct in a healthcare information environment.

It should be apparent that the domain of regulatory environment covers a very large range of knowledge, skills, and abilities. The intent of this domain is to provide concepts based on a fairly high level summary of the issues, topics, and processes that need to be a part of the repertoire of healthcare professionals. It is unreasonable to expect an individual to have a deep expertise in all the areas that were discussed. However, it is very reasonable to expect a professional to have enough general knowledge to understand the issues and potential pitfalls and to know how to search out the appropriate expertise.

The regulatory environment domain highlights the international nature of today's business environment and the necessity to have global cooperation to have truly effective healthcare information assurance and security. Cross-border commerce requires the understanding of various legal systems, legislation, and regulations. Today, no business and, in a sense, no network is an island; our business practices and stewardship of data and information may fall under the purview of several different regulations and laws, both foreign and domestic. Understanding compliance requirements, effectively assessing our abilities to comply, making the appropriate changes, and maintaining this compliance and due diligence on a go-forward basis are now integral parts of healthcare corporate governance.

Historically, the focus has been on detecting attacks against information systems or infrastructures and, once detected, how to properly determine the who, what, when, where, why, and how with the objective of minimizing the impact and returning to a production state as quickly as possible. With the increased public and governmental focus on the protected health information and with the passing in several countries of privacy laws and regulations, the focus is now shifting to preventative and proactive approaches, e.g., policies, and encryption. It is no longer reasonable to have a strictly reactive healthcare information security posture; businesses must demonstrate that they have put sufficient forethought into how to prevent system compromises or the unauthorized access to or disclosure of data and, if these are detected, how to disclose the incident to affected parties, e.g., the public.

In the dynamic field of healthcare information security and assurance, knowledge is one of the greatest resources. The domain of regulatory environment does not exist in a vacuum. It is but one piece of the larger mosaic collectively referred to as healthcare information security. To be truly effective, a holistic, multidisciplinary approach that weaves all the foundations (domains) together is necessary.

2

Regulatory Environment

Domain 2 – *Review Questions*

1. An organization needs to use data flow modeling to develop a system that will boot securely, perform routine checks to ensure the system is still secure, and perform security checks based on certain activities. Which data flow model **BEST** describes this approach?

   A. State Machine Model

   B. Multilevel Lattice Model

   C. Noninterference Model

   D. Information flow Model

2. The Bell-LaPadula security model allows _____.

   A. Objects to read information from subjects at a similar classification level or at lower levels, but they are barred from reading any information from objects classified at a higher level of confidentiality.

   B. Subjects to read information from objects at a higher classification levels, but they are barred from reading any information from objects classified at a lower level of confidentiality.

   C. Subjects to read information from objects at a similar classification level or at lower levels, but they are barred from reading any information from objects classified at a higher level of confidentiality.

   D. Subjects to read information from objects at a similar classification level or at higher levels, but they are barred from reading any information from objects classified at a lower level of confidentiality

3. To avoid disclosure according to the ""* property", _____.

    A. The subject would be able to write information to objects at a similar classification level or lower levels but would be barred from writing any information to objects classified at a higher level of confidentiality.

    B. The object would be able to write information to subjects at a similar classification level or higher levels but would be barred from writing any information to subjects classified at a lower level of confidentiality.

    C. The object would be able to write information to subjects at a similar classification level or lower levels but would be barred from writing any information to objects classified at a higher level of confidentiality.

    D. The subject would be able to write information to objects at a similar classification level or higher levels but would be barred from writing any information to objects classified at a lower level of confidentiality.

4. The Biba simple integrity model ensures _____.

    A. The subject is prevented from reading from more accurate objects but can read from objects that are less accurate than the subject needs.

    B. The object is prevented from reading from less accurate subjects but can read from subjects that are more accurate than the object needs.

    C. The object is prevented from reading from more accurate subjects but can read from subjects that are less accurate than the object needs.

    D. The subject is prevented from reading from less accurate objects but can read from objects that are more accurate than the subject needs.

5. Which of the following models focuses on preventing conflict of interest when a given subject has access to objects with sensitive information associated with two competing parties?

    A. Clark-Wilson

    B. Brewer-Nash

    C. Biba

    D. Bell-LaPadula

2

Regulatory Environment

6. Which of the following is designed to protect the goodwill a merchant or vendor invests in its products by creating exclusive rights to the owner of markings that the public uses to identify various vendor or merchant products or goods?

   A. Copyright

   B. Criminal Law

   C. Due Diligence

   D. Trademark

7. An organization wishes to use 1,500 patient health records for research. The organization operates in the United States and is subject to HIPAA. The organization has decided to remove eighteen personal identifiers from each record to de-identity the information in accordance with HIPAA. The act of removing the information in accordance with the law is **BEST** described as _____.

   A. Safe Harbor

   B. Expert Determination

   C. Risk Transference

   D. Risk Avoidance

8. A nurse working the floor is approached by an individual claiming to be a psychotherapy patient's mother. The person requests access to the patients psychotherapy notes. According to HIPAA which of the following responses **BEST** describes what the nurse can disclose?

   A. Once the individual is verified as the patient's mother, the nurse may disclose critical psychotherapy information pertinent to the care of the patient.

   B. Nothing The nurse may not disclose any information related to the psychotherapy information to anyone except the patient or the creator of the notes.

   C. Once the individual is verified as the patient's mother, the nurse must ask the mother to complete a non-disclosure agreement. After the agreement is completed, the nurse may provide the information.

   D. Nothing. The nurse may not disclose any information related to the psychotherapy to anyone including the patient or the creator of the notes.

9. The U.S. Affordable Care Act requires _____.

A. Operating rules for each of the HIPAA covered transactions; a unique, standard Health Plan Identifier (HPID); and a standard and operating rules for electronic funds transfer (EFT) and electronic remittance advice (ERA) and PHI processing when performed within the law and scope of "public interest."

B. Operating rules for each of the HIPAA covered transactions; a unique, standard Health Plan Identifier (HPID); and a standard and operating rules for electronic funds transfer (EFT) and electronic remittance advice (ERA) and claims attachments.

C. PHI processing when performed within the law and scope of "public interest" and a standard and operating rules for electronic funds transfer (EFT) and electronic remittance advice (ERA) and claims attachments.

D. Operating rules for each of the HIPAA covered transactions; PHI processing when performed within the law and scope of "public interest"; and a standard and operating rules for electronic funds transfer (EFT) and electronic remittance advice (ERA) and claims attachments.

10. An information security assessment has determined numerous controls are not in place to help protect an organization's information system. The organization's leader states they will differ acceptance of any risk but refuses to shut down or limit the operation of the affected systems. Can the leader do this?

A. Yes because she is the leader of the organization, and it is her decision to make.

B. Yes, major risk management frameworks such as ISO and NIST support not accepting risk while allowing system operation.

C. No, the organizational leader is not the ultimate authority for risk acceptance decisions.

D. No, it is not possible to be aware of risks due to system operation and not accept them by default if a system is running.

2

Regulatory Environment

Domain 3

Privacy and Security in Health Care

PRIVACY AND SECURITY work hand-in-hand to provide protection for the data of individuals, but they also provide protections for the healthcare organization and its employees. Everyone—except the attackers—benefits when policies, procedures, processes, and safeguards are implemented correctly, understood by stakeholders, and maintained. This chapter will explore security safeguards and how they are used to protect healthcare data. The HCISPP also will walk away with an understanding of key privacy concepts and frameworks and their application in the healthcare arena.

While the United States has specific laws and regulations to address healthcare information, privacy and security laws and regulations in other countries tend to include health-related information in with other individually identifiable information. That is why this chapter will make several specific references to the U.S. Health Insurance Portability and Accountability Act (HIPAA) Security and Privacy rules while reflecting international elements where possible.

TOPICS

- Security Objectives and Attributes
  - Confidentiality
  - Integrity
  - Availability
- General Security Definitions and Concepts
  - Access Control
  - Data Encryption
  - Training and Awareness
  - Logging and Monitoring
  - Vulnerability Management
  - Systems Recovery
  - Segregation of Duties
  - Least Privilege (Need to Know)
  - Business Continuity
  - Data Retention and Destruction
- General Privacy Principles
  - Consent/Choice
  - Limited Collection/Legitimate Purpose/Purpose Specification
  - Disclosure Limitation/Transfer to Third Parties/Trans-border Concerns
  - Access Limitation
  - Security
  - Accuracy, Completeness, Quality
  - Management, Designation of Privacy Officer, Supervisor Re-authority, Processing Authorization, Accountability
  - Transparency, Openness
  - Proportionality, Use and Retention, Use Limitation
  - Access, Individual Participation
  - Notice, Purpose Specification
  - Additional Measures for Breach Notification
- Privacy and Security
  - Dependency
  - Integration
- Sensitive Data and Handling Implications
  - Personal and Health Information Protected by Law
  - Sensitivity Mitigation (e.g., de-identification, annonymization)
  - Categories of Sensitive Data (e.g., mental health)
- Security and Privacy Terminology Specific to Healthcare

OBJECTIVES

HCISPP candidates should be able to understand:

- Security objectives / attributes
- General security definitions and concepts
- General privacy definitions and concepts
- The relationship between privacy and security
- The disparate nature of sensitive data and handling implications
- Security and privacy terminology specific to healthcare

Understand Security Objectives/Attributes

It is important for the HCISPP candidate to understand the expectations individuals have in regard to the security of their sensitive healthcare information. Simply put, before focusing on the "how" of information security, the HCISPP must first look at the "why". Users of computer systems storing healthcare data and the people to whom the data belongs have an expectation that the information will be protected at rest, in use, and in transit. The charge of the HCISPP is to protect that information. Simply put, the individuals will want their information to be:

- Secure from unauthorized use and disclosure
- Protected from defacement or tampering
- Accessible when it is needed by them or by providers of health care services

These basic needs form the three pillars of information security: Confidentiality, Integrity, and Availability. This is known as the "CIA triad" and is shown in *Figure 3.1*. Each individual aspect of the model has equal importance for the HCISPP and needs to be addressed as part of the overall design of information security controls. Every security control is designed to meet one or more aspects of the CIA triad.

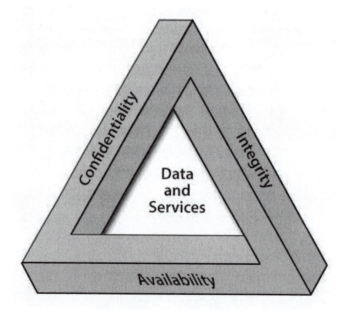

*Figure 3.1 - **CIA Triad***

Confidentiality

The purpose of confidentiality is to limit information access to only those people who are authorized and to prevent access by anyone else. When there is an unintentional release of information, confidentiality is sacrificed. To avoid this, security controls must be deployed to ensure protected information is not disclosed to unauthorized parties. Confidentiality is not a new concept to healthcare professionals. They have long honored the principles associated with physician-patient privilege. The modern version of the Hippocratic Oath to which many physicians pledge discusses the concept of the patient's right to privacy. The oath states, "I will respect the privacy of my patients, for their problems are not disclosed to me that the world may know."[1]

In the latter part of the 20th century, focus began to be placed on the privacy and security of individually identifiable information. As detailed in Domain 2, Regulatory Environment, laws and regulations continue to be created and modified to govern the protection of individuals' sensitive data. In the United States, this was first codified in the Privacy Act of 1974 "that governs the collection, maintenance, use, and dissemination of personally identifiable information about individuals that is maintained in systems of records by federal agencies" and later in the Health Insurance Portability and Accountability Act (HIPAA) of 1996 that focused on the security and privacy of protected health information (PHI). Confidentiality continues to be challenged by the introduction of new technologies and advances in existing technology capabilities. The European Union Data Protection Directive of 1995 (updated in 2012) contains provisions to govern the use and transfer of data for citizens of member countries.[2] It is often looked to as a model for personal data privacy. Canada has the Personal Information Protection and Electronic Documents Act (PIPEDA), and Great Britain has the Data Protection Act.

Attacks on confidentiality can target the storage media containing sensitive information or the transmission medium that carries information. While there have been some well-publicized breaches resulting from attackers hacking into a poorly secured healthcare provider's computer systems, the majority of the reported breaches over the past few years have resulted from the theft of unencrypted computers, hard drives, and backup tapes due to poor physical security or media disposal practices. An area of equal or greater concern should be the exposure of sensitive healthcare information as it travels across both private and public networks, primarily the Internet. Not all healthcare provider systems are designed with the same focus on security. This could be due to a lack of security understanding within their development staff, poor IT security governance practices, or because of cost constraints.

---

1   "Hippocratic Oath (modern version) Johns Hopkins Sheridan Libraries

2   European Commission news release dated January 25, 2013

Integrity

Integrity actually has two purposes.

The first, information integrity, provides assurance that data quality remains whole, unaltered, and uncorrupted. Incorrect information in the healthcare arena could have dire consequences. Imagine if prescription information was altered so that a dosage was entered incorrectly or altered to be many times what was originally prescribed.

The second, authentication integrity, ensures that the sender of a communication can be validated and not impersonated without detection. This concept is also known as "non-repudiation," meaning the sender cannot deny he or she sent the message, and the receiver can also have confidence that the sender is who he or she claims to be. Non-repudiation will be discussed further in regards to digital signatures.

Modern methods of validating data integrity in electronic files and messages involve the use of mathematical hash algorithms to generate a message summary (message digest) that acts as a digital fingerprint of the sender's original data that can be compared against the result of the recipient's calculated hash of the same data. If the results differ even by a single bit, the data is viewed as having been tampered with and discarded. For the secondary purpose of authentication integrity to validate the creator of a file or sender of a message, a digital signature that is created by the sender's private key can be used to allow the recipient to use a copy of the sender's public key to validate the authenticity of the file creator or message source.

Digital signatures and hashes do not protect the data from being viewed; they only ensure that it has arrived intact and unaltered and that the sender can be validated. Digital signatures also provide for the principle of non-repudiation, meaning that through validation of the digital signature, the sender of a message cannot deny being the originator of the message because only the holder of the private key could have signed the communication.

In terms of protecting the integrity of health information, a potential compromise can have many ramifications, but the single greatest threat is to patient safety from incomplete, corrupt, or deliberately altered records. The source of the integrity loss could be attributed to deliberate alteration of the data contents, destruction of critical files by malware or media corruption, and even unintentional human error. In addition to the digital signatures and hashing security controls, the use of anti-virus/anti-spyware software on desktop computer systems and network servers can be used to mitigate the risk of integrity compromises. System edits and limiting the data that can be entered into particular fields (e.g., drop-down menus) can help to prevent human error as a challenge to data integrity. Electronic PHI that is improperly altered or destroyed can result in clinical quality problems for a covered entity, including patient safety issues.

Availability

The purpose of the final pillar of the CIA triad, *availability*, focuses on providing uninterrupted system and data access even amidst system attacks and/or a catastrophic event, such as an electrical blackout, flood, or earthquake. The concepts of continuity of operations, system high availability, and data redundancy have become a focus in both commercial and government sectors, which now understand that confidentiality and integrity of organizational data becomes a moot point if the systems hosting the data are inaccessible or the disks storing the information become corrupted or damaged. Availability becomes more important as electronic systems and medical devices become more prevalent in healthcare.

This focus on continuous system availability has resulted in an increased focus on Business Continuity and Disaster Recovery planning and solutions. Methods such as Redundant Array of Independent Disk (RAID) technologies and server clustering can provide redundancy and high availability of disk and server resources within a site, but for true failover capability, a facility recovery method needs to be part of the solution. An organization needs to determine the appropriate recovery investments, such as a hot site, warm site, or cold site alternative, based on the critical nature of the information being protected, the necessary speed of recovery required, and the available financial resources available to invest in facility recovery.

One statistic to consider regarding availability is that, according to information from the Centers for Disease Control, as of 2013, only 78-percent of "office-based" U.S. physicians were using an Electronic Health Record system. That means there are still a large number of paper records or records stored in rudimentary systems.[3]

Understand General Security Definitions and Concepts

Access Control, which primarily protects the confidentiality of data, refers to the method by which systems validate that a user or process (referred to as a subject) is a known entity within a security domain and determines whether the entity should be granted admission to the resources (referred to as objects) protected within that security domain. These resources could be logical (files, databases, printers) or physical (access to secure facilities), and the access control is provided through a combination of administrative controls (policies), technical controls (access control lists, authentication mechanisms), and physical controls (card readers, cipher locks, biometric scanners). Access controls determine the operations that the subjects will be allowed to perform on the objects they are attempting to access.

---

3   Hsiao, Chun-Ju, PhD and Hing, Esther, MPH

Access Control involves four main phases or mechanisms: Identification, Authentication, Authorization, and Accountability.

- During **Identification**, the unverified entity (known as a subject) presents a unique identifier (username) or label to the system that can be checked against an internal list of authorized entities. If a match is found for the label, the subject is successfully identified.

- During the next phase, **Authentication**, the subject's purported identity is validated by one or more credentials from the three main categories of authentication factors: something the subject knows (password or passphrase), something the subject has (smartcard, token, or certificate), or something the subject is (a biometric such as a fingerprint or retina scan). For the best security, multi-factor authentication should be used, meaning that a combination of authentication factors would need to be successfully verified before the entity would be validated. In healthcare treatment settings, the level and complexity of access controls needs to be balanced against ease-of-access to information for providing care.

- During the **Authorization** phase, the authenticated entity is matched against the list of access control entries associated with an information asset where access has been requested. Depending on the access control model in use, either an access control list or a matrix will determine the level of access that can be granted to the subject. This authorization can be granted to an individual user or process, to a group of users, or to multiple systems.

- The final phase of the Access Control process is the **Accountability** phase. In this phase, actions taken on a system are logged to ensure that they can be attributed to a single authenticated entity so that they can be held accountable for its actions within the security domain. Because this information is used for system auditing, this is also sometimes referred to as the **Auditability** phase.

The four main access control models discussed in this chapter are mandatory access control, discretionary access control, role-based access control, and rule-based access control.

1. ***Mandatory Access Control (MAC)*** – is the most restrictive of the models and is typically found in military or government intelligence agencies with stringent security and secrecy requirements. In this model, both subjects and objects are assigned security labels that indicate the level of confidentiality assigned. Permissions are granted based on matching the subject's label to the object's label. In this model, the subject must have a label of equal or greater level to the label of the object in order

for access to be granted. In one variation of Mandatory Access Control called lattice-based access control, this is accomplished through the use of an access control matrix to determine the level of access each subject has to each and every object. The object's attributes are stored in an access control list and are compared against the subject's attributes stored in a capabilities table.

2. ***Discretionary Access Control (DAC)*** – is the least restrictive model and is popular in commercial environments because of its use in UNIX and Microsoft Windows operating systems. It is based on the concept of object ownership and the premise that access to objects should be at the discretion of the object's owner. In this model, the owners have complete control of their objects and can selectively grant other subjects access to their objects. A major weakness in this model is that it relies on security being set by untrained users and that can lead to incorrect permissions being granted. Another weakness is that the security attributes are stored within the operating system, which can leave the data vulnerable to an attack if the operating system is not currently loaded or can be bypassed with an alternative. An attacker using a system disk could boot the system into an alternate operating system and gain access to the files because the access control lists restricting them will not be present in the alternate operating system. Discretionary Access Control should be integrated with local encryption controls so that the data can be protected regardless of whether the operating system is loaded.

3. ***Role Based Access Control (RBAC)*** – also referred to as Non-discretionary Access Control, is enforced by a central authority within an organization that assigns permissions to particular roles within the organization. When an employee is placed in a job that is linked to that pre-defined role, he or she is automatically granted the access designated for the role. When the employee's job assignment changes, the role is removed and the access is revoked. Because access is no longer at the discretion of an individual owner and is linked to the needs of a pre-defined role, the risk of incorrect permissions being granted is reduced. The roles must be managed to ensure that they stay current; otherwise, the number of non-role permissions will continue to increase.

4. ***Rule Based Access Control*** – is a variation of Role Based Access Control. It integrates a set of rules to govern the assignment of roles. Whereas the assignment of a role is done manually by a centralized authority in the standard Role Based Access

Control Model, in Rule Based Access Control the pre-defined set of rules created by a data custodian to govern access to resource objects is checked when a user attempts access to the object and can dynamically assign the subject a role based on those rules. This model is more flexible than the classic Role Based Access Control and is often used to manage access across multiple systems for a subject.

Access Control Models	Characteristics
Mandatory Access Control	■ Most restrictive of the models ■ Relies on labels to match subject's security clearance level (user) to the classification of the object (resource) ■ Centralized authority
Discretionary Access Control	■ Least restrictive of the models ■ Access to a resource should be determined by the owner ■ Decentralized authority ■ Permissions assigned to an individual
Role-Based Access Control	■ Links a user to a pre-defined role based on function ■ Centralized management ■ Permissions assigned at a group level ■ Centralized authority
Rule-Based Access Control	■ Rules govern the assignment of roles ■ Can dynamically assign rules ■ More flexible than Role-Based Access Control

Table 3.1 – **Access Control Methods**

Data Encryption

Encryption primarily protects the confidentiality and integrity of the data. It is the process of taking a message or file in its original form, referred to as "plaintext," meaning it is plainly readable by people, and converting it into a form called "ciphertext" that is unreadable to anyone who has not been provided with a means to convert it back to the original plaintext form. It relies on the use of a mathematical encryption algorithm along with a series of bits, called the key, to transform plaintext into ciphertext that is unreadable to unauthorized personnel. The reverse operation to convert ciphertext back into plaintext using the key is called decryption. Encryption and decryption are functions of a process called cryptography. Some laws and regulations, such as the HIPAA rules, provide safe harbor against a breach if the data was appropriately encrypted. Covered entities will want to know if their encryption solutions comply with the National Institute for Standards and Technology (NIST) special publications 800-111 Guide to Storage Encryption for End-User Devices, 800-52 Guidelines for the Selection and Use of Transport Layer Security (TLS) Implementation and 800-77 Guide to IPsec, VPNs and 800-113 Guide to SSL VPNs.

Cryptography can provide various forms of information security that support the CIA triad. It can provide encryption functions to ensure the confidentiality of data, hash functions to protect the integrity of the data, availability of the data to only users with the correct key, and digital signature functions to ensure both the authenticity of the sender and accountability of the sender for non-repudiation purposes to prove that he or she was the source of the transmission. To provide these capabilities, cryptography provides three categories of algorithms: hash algorithms, symmetric encryption algorithms, and asymmetric encryption algorithms.

Hash algorithms are used to provide integrity to provide a unique digital "fingerprint" of the data called a "hash" that can be used to ensure that the received file or message has arrived intact without a single bit being altered from the original source file or message. The hash itself provides no encryption of the message or file, but it is used to compare the source and destination payload to ensure that they match exactly. Hashing is extremely effective at preventing "man-in-the-middle attacks" as the man-in-the-middle will alter information as it flows through him. Hashes are also used to validate the integrity of downloaded content from the Internet. The most common hash algorithms are Message Digest 5 (MD5) used in commercial organizations and Secure Hash Algorithm (SHA 1, 2 and 3) used in government and military organizations. While still used, MD5 should be considered "broken" as a flaw was found in 1996 and in 2004, which led to many organizations replacing the algorithm with SHA-2.

Symmetric encryption, also called *private key encryption*, is primarily used for bulk data encryption because it provides extremely fast computing algorithms that result in much quicker encryption and decryption processes than what asymmetric encryption algorithms can provide. Symmetric encryption uses the same private key to encrypt and decrypt the data. This presents two interesting challenges: anyone who has a copy of the shared key can decrypt any of the messages encrypted with that single key, and secure distribution of the private key requires planning and coordination. Because of these challenges and the risk that the key might be intercepted in transit, transfer of the recipient's copy of the key must be done in what is called an "out of band" method, meaning a

149

different channel than the one being used to transmit the ciphertext. This may even mean manual transmission via a courier if secure distribution via electronic means is unavailable. Some examples of symmetric encryption algorithms are Data Encryption Standard (DES), Triple DES, and Advanced Encryption Standard (AES). Both DES and Triple DES are now obsolete due to increases in computing power that enabled them to be broken within a short period of time, and AES has been the federal government's encryption standard since 2002.

Asymmetric Encryption Algorithms, also called ***public key encryption algorithms***, were designed to overcome the problem of secure key distribution inherent in symmetric key encryption. Instead of using a single key for both encryption and decryption, asymmetric encryption uses two mathematically related keys in the encryption process. A ***private key*** is generated as a single instance and associated with a single individual, but the associated ***public key*** is made available to anyone who wants a copy. In a secure transmission, the sender would obtain a copy of the recipient's public key, which could then be used to encrypt the message before transmission to the recipient. As it travelled across the network, the contents of the message would be encoded as ciphertext. The recipient would then use the only copy of the private key (his or her private key) to decrypt the message back into plaintext. Because the public key was only used to encrypt and only the private key could be used by its owner to decrypt the message, this provided a means of secure communication where the encryption key could be made publicly available because only the authorized user had possession of the single private key used in decryption. When a private key is used for creating a digital signature to provide authenticity and non-repudiation functions, the reverse operation would take place. The senders would create a digital signature using their private key to validate that the message was created by them and sent from their account, and the recipient would obtain a copy of the sender's public key to decrypt the digital signature to prove that the message source was authentic. Because only the sender had access to the private key, the message could only have been signed by them, but anyone wanting to validate the sender could obtain a copy of the sender's public key to do so. Examples of asymmetric encryption algorithms are RSA (short for its developers Rivest, Shamir, and Adleman) and Elliptic Curve Cryptography.

Encryption can be provided either by hardware- or software-based means. One method of hardware-based encryption is **USB device encryption** that automatically encrypts all data copied onto a flash drive, refuses connection to a computer until a secure password has been supplied, and automatically destroys the data if a set amount of bad logons occur. Another method is a ***Trusted Platform Module (TPM),*** which is an embedded chip on the computer's motherboard that provides cryptographic functions. A TPM conducts all its operations within the hardware so it is impervious to a software-based attack and can prohibit a computer from starting if an alteration to the files is detected, or it can require a password to be supplied if the hard drive is transferred to another computer. Software-based encryption, although not as secure as the hardware alternatives, can be built into an operating system, as in the case of the Windows Encrypted File System and Microsoft BitLocker, or it can be applied as an application such as Pretty Good Privacy (PGP) and CheckPoint's PointSec PC. Encryption can be applied to one or many files on either a single partition or as a whole-disk encryption method. After the theft of an unencrypted Veterans Administration laptop in 2006, the U.S. Office of Management and Budget mandated that all federal laptops and portable devices containing sensitive information be encrypted with whole disk encryption to avoid additional breaches from unprotected mobile devices.

Training and Awareness

It is a well-known tenet of information security that the defense-in-depth model is only as strong as its weakest link. If individuals are unaware of what to do or do not understand their role in information security protections, the human element can be the weakest link. The best awareness programs help individuals understand how to weave information security practices into their lives and their job functions. Security is seen as part of the job rather than an "extra" consideration.

Regardless of the complexity of security controls that have been implemented across the organization, an employee that is compromised through social engineering can provide a backdoor into the internal network that will be difficult to detect, such as a password compromise or the introduction of malware. People can be the weakest link in security chain, mainly because they are not aware of the implications their actions have on the overall security of the organization. Once attackers have successfully breached the internal network, they are masquerading under the context of a valid user or process. Conversely, with knowledge and training, people can be strong links in the chain because they can watch for suspicious activity, report unusual occurrences, and understand the value of the data. One of the key education points is to teach individuals how to avoid social engineering. Attackers prey on the natural tendency for human beings to be helpful, or they convince people they will gain something by giving up information.

The overall security posture of an organization can be drastically improved when the weakest link in the security chain is given the proper attention. The best mitigation is to provide security awareness training to educate employees of the risks and the best practices needed to avoid a compromise. This education needs to become part of an organizational culture and not a yearly compliance requirement.

3

Privacy and Security in Health Care

The methods of delivery need to be addressed creatively to stop the information from becoming "white noise" to employees. Some examples of the various mediums that can be effective in maintaining the focus on adhering to established security procedures are posters with security tips in commonly traversed areas, websites with security best practices posted on the main page, and emails containing a security "Tip of the day." Finally, having approachable security professionals who are willing to take the time to explain the "why" behind the security policies can go a long way toward instituting a security aware organization.

Effective security awareness provides the benefit of improving management's ability to hold employees accountable for their activities. Although all employees need some level of education in the basic concepts of security, specialized training must be developed differently for the different groups of employees that make up the organization. Specifically, customized security awareness training should be targeted at senior management, data custodians, and users. There is one other consideration: Regulatory auditors often want to understand not only the policies, procedures, and standards an entity has related to information security but also how that information is communicated via an organizational awareness program. Additionally, training individuals on the proper handling of sensitive information provides the organization with a defensible position in the event of a breach- the person acting in violation of the organization's training, policies, and procedures. Therefore the focus should be on the individual who committed the breach more so than the organization.

CASE STUDY

Even with all that is known about the protections offered by encryption, it is amazing how many breach situations could have been prevented with encryption technologies. The up-front investment could save millions of dollars in regulatory fines and remediation costs. There are countless examples of healthcare entities or their business associates reporting theft or loss of unencrypted devices or media. A third-party vendor of Tricare, the U.S. military health program, lost unencrypted backup tapes with records for close to 5 million individuals.[4] In Alberta, Canada, a laptop was reported stolen by an employee of Medicentres Family Health Care Clinics. The theft exposed health information, including diagnosis codes, for more than 600,000 individuals.[5]

---

4   McGee, Marianne Kolbasuk

5   CBC News

Logging and Monitoring

In addition to implementing security controls, such as encryption and access control to protect sensitive healthcare data, the HCISPP needs to also monitor the environment. It is one thing to apply controls, but it is another to validate their effectiveness and ongoing status.

Systems should be monitored to detect any deviation from established access control policies and record all successful and unsuccessful authentication processes, credential assertion, user management, rights usage, and access attempts. Additionally, monitoring can indicate the status of controls to ensure they are in line with policies and expectations. This last point is typically overlooked and represents a significant potential to mask or hide unauthorized activities. For example, if the control activities are monitored, yet the status of controls is not, attackers can disable various controls, grant themselves access, and then re-enable the controls without detection. The logging and monitoring of the activities will then not raise any suspicion because they are now valid operations, thanks to the attacker.

Systems and activity logs are electronic records of any activity that has occurred within a system or application. They provide the documented record of what has happened and can be extremely useful when investigating an operational or security incident. Logs and their contents are important to security management and maintenance of an effective access control solution. A log can include:

- User IDs used on systems, services, or applications.
- Dates and times for logon and logoff.
- System identities, such as IP address, host name, or media access control (MAC) address. It may also be possible to determine the network location of a device through local area network (LAN) logging, wireless access point identification, or remote-access system identification, if applicable.
- Logging of both successful and rejected authentication and access attempts. Knowing when and where people are utilizing their rights can be very helpful to determine if those rights are necessary for a job role or function. It is also helpful to know where access rights are denied to have a better understanding of what a user is trying to do. This can help determine if you have a user who does not have adequate rights to perform his or her job.

3

Privacy and Security in Health Care

Audit logs should be retained for a specified period, as defined by organizational need and (potentially) regulatory requirements. In the latter case, this is preordained and not open to interpretation. However, there are cases where no legal or regulatory demands exist. If this is the case, the retention time will probably be defined by organizational policy and the size of available storage. The security of the logs is critical. If a log can be altered to erase unauthorized activity, there is little chance for discovery, and if discovered, there may be no evidence. Logs must also be protected from unauthorized reading as well as writing, as they can contain sensitive information such as passwords (for instance, when users accidentally type the password into a user ID prompt). Log security is also critical if the logs are needed as evidence in a legal or disciplinary proceeding. If logs are not secure and can be proven as such before, during, and after an event, the logs may not be accepted as valid legal evidence due to the potential for tampering. The fundamental approach to logs is that they must be an accurate reflection of system activity and, as such, must be secured and maintained for an appropriate period of time in order to provide a reference point for future investigative activity.

Periodic log review is necessary to evaluate the impact of a given event. Typically, system logs are voluminous, making it difficult to isolate and identify a given event for identification and investigation. To preserve potential evidence, many organizations will make a copy of the log (preserving the original) and use suitable utilities and tools to perform automated interrogation and analysis of the log data. There are several tools available that can be very helpful in analyzing a log file to assist administrators in identifying and isolating activity. Once again, separation of duties plays an important role in reviewing logs. Logs should never be initially reviewed or analyzed by the "subject" of the logs. For example, a system administrator should not perform the log review for a system he or she manages. Otherwise, it may be possible for the person to "overlook" evidence of his or her unauthorized activity or intentionally manipulate the logs to eliminate that evidence. Therefore, it is necessary to separate those being monitored from those performing the review.

Vulnerability Management

Vulnerabilities are the points at which assets are susceptible to a threat and are often attributed to unintended design flaws in the implementation of a hardware device, software application, or a system. They can originate from people, processes, or technology. They are not the attack itself but are instead an exploitable weakness that **could be** used to launch an attack. There are various types of vulnerability categories that have their own challenges when attempting to mitigate risk:

- *Physical vulnerabilities* include things like unlocked or unmonitored doors or windows or easily guessed door lock combinations. Physical vulnerabilities can be challenging to manage in some healthcare environments such as hospitals where so many people come and go at various times for different reasons.

- *Natural vulnerabilities* can include facilities built in natural disaster areas subject to earthquakes, brushfires, tornados, or hurricanes or those that have inadequate fire-suppression systems.

- *Hardware/Software vulnerabilities* include inadequately patched operating systems and applications and computers left unlocked or configured without password-protected screensavers that auto-lock after a specific idle time threshold.

- *Media/Communications vulnerabilities* include unshielded data circuits that are easily degraded from noise or electromagnetic interference, unencrypted communication protocols, or delicate cabling such as fiber-optic cable that is easily exposed to breakage.

- *Human vulnerabilities* including apathetic and unobservant security guards and poor security awareness of users leading to password compromises through social engineering attacks.

The HCISPP cannot prevent every vulnerability from being introduced into the environment, but rather he or she can try to prevent compromises through mitigation of the vulnerabilities. Solid risk management practices can be used to meet this goal when designing your security infrastructure.

With the frequency of new bugs and vulnerabilities being discovered within applications and operating systems, effective *patch management* is a necessity to minimize the risk of compromise. In addition, systems administrative personnel must test patches prior to deployment to verify that the cure is not worse than the symptom because many patches have had unexpected impacts on other system components. Timely and comprehensive deployment of patches is required to minimize the window of opportunity that an intruder has to exploit system vulnerabilities. Mature organizations use multiple environments such as test and stage to test patches prior to promotion and production.

A process called *system hardening* provides a preventative vulnerability management mechanism to reduce the attack surface of computers, servers, and network appliances. This can be accomplished by closing network ports, disabling system services, and removing unnecessary software. The more functions that a system performs, the more difficult it will be to harden it while allowing all the functions to perform effectively. To facilitate system hardening, one can apply security templates to meet security baselines or compliance levels.

3

Privacy and Security in Health Care

System Recovery

IT professionals know that the time will come when systems have to be restarted to recover from an operational outage or to execute legitimate code changes. Procedures must be documented and executed in an appropriate manner so that the system cannot be compromised during recovery or reboot. The field of disaster recovery is dedicated to documenting, testing, and practicing the restoration of services and system recovery.

Segregation of Duties

When a single user is trusted with complete control of a process or application, in addition to the threat of unchecked system errors, there is also a potential for fraudulent activity within that system. These threats can be mitigated by instituting a segregation of duties model for personnel that separate two or more aspects of a process into discrete functions that can be isolated from one another. This method, also referred to as *separation of duties*, provides an internal control that mandates that the completion of an operation involving sensitive information requires the involvement of more than one individual. This prevents the chance that an improper execution of this process can be conducted without another employee facilitating its completion.

Within IT operations, an example of this practice could be granting one person the right to back up the system and another person the corresponding right to restore the system data. This segregation of duties approach could prevent a single individual from backing up sensitive data from a system protected by local security (access control lists) and restoring it to another system without local security so that the data can be accessed without restrictions. In financial institutions, this is a common practice to prevent fraud or embezzlement by separating multiple system roles from one another so that no single individual has all the keys necessary to complete a transaction. Within a hospital, the person in procurement who orders supplies should not also be the same person who can approve payment for the supplies.

The concept of segregation of duties relies on the fact that it would require deliberate cooperation between people performing these complimentary functions, an act referred to as collusion. Any chance of successfully breaching the system through collusion increases the chance of being caught. Still, the possibility of fraud, embezzlement, or a security breach still exists if segregation of duties is the only operations security control in place. That is why the additional practices of **job rotation** and **mandatory vacations** are used in conjunction with segregation of duties to provide a defense-in-depth approach to operations security.

Job rotation is a practice of periodically moving employees between positions with different job responsibilities both within and between departments so that no employee is performing functions that cannot be audited by another employee. Because the employees may come from different backgrounds with different views, a new person performing the job function may notice irregularities in the work done by the previous employee that could expose fraudulent activity. In addition to the benefits in exposing fraud and preventing collusion, job rotation can minimize employee burnout as well as improve skills redundancy in an organization. Organizations must be careful to revoke rights and access for the prior function when rotating a job. Malicious actors will try and cover their tracks or continue the fraud while in a new position if they still have access to information and systems of the old one.

Mandatory vacations, as the name implies, is a security control where the employees are required to take a vacation so that their functions can be audited. This practice provides detective controls as well as serving as a deterrent to fraud because employees know that whatever activities they are engaged in will be exposed when they are removed from their workplace.

Least Privilege (Need to Know)

Least privilege is a security measure that dictates that users and system services should only be given the amount of privileges absolutely necessary for them to perform their duties. Under the U.S. HIPAA laws, the term is referred to as "minimum necessary."

When successfully administered, least privilege can help reduce attack surfaces by eliminating unnecessary access, privileges, and permissions. One challenge to successful implementation comes from personnel who make the mistake of confusing privilege level with status because they consider themselves "power users" or "administrators" deserving of advanced administrative access. Depending on the level of political status of the individual within the organization, he or she can exert enormous pressure to be granted an access level commensurate with his or her authority. This can provide pressure, which can lead to assigning them a higher level of privilege than they should be afforded to perform their duties. Additional logging and monitoring beyond the reach of the administrator should be considered in these situations.

System administrators need to take special precautions when exercising least privilege to avoid having their privileged account from being accessed by a rogue process in the event of a malware infection. Separate accounts need to be created on systems supporting it, a limited user account, and an administrative account. During basic computer operations such as word processing, email, and Internet access, the limited user account would be used. The administrative account would only be used when performing administrative tasks via the "Run As" logon to the chosen administrative tool. "Run As" in Windows allows an administrator to open a separate virtual environment session from within the current logon environment that can be run at an escalated level of privilege. In Unix and Linux operating systems, this is also known as "sudo." This grants a higher level of privilege only to that process in a protected mode of operation while isolating every other running process and keeping them running at the level of privilege of the limited user account. If the user is infected by a virus or Trojan horse introduced by email or accessing the Internet, the malware will be restricted to the limited-user level of privilege and not be able to leverage the higher level of access.

Need to Know is a similar concept to Least Privilege except that it relates to a data classification structure where access to individuals is granted not only based on their level of security clearance but also their requirement for access to perform their job functions.

Business Continuity

The ability to resume business following a natural or man-made disaster is critical in health care. Not only might a healthcare entity experience a disaster, but often it is also a critical component of handling emergency situations during a disaster, such as a hurricane or fire. Healthcare providers, such as hospitals or skilled nursing care facilities, have to plan for patient safety in the event of a disaster. For example, considerations need to be made as to the procedures for moving critically ill patients. In fact, this even comes into play when a hospital is moving into a new facility outside of a disaster situation.

The number one concern for any business continuity and disaster recovery program is human safety. The HIPAA Security Rule recognizes the importance of contingency planning and demonstrates that by requiring covered entities to develop and maintain a data backup plan, a disaster recovery plan, and an emergency mode operations plan.

Special Publication 800-34 from the National Institute for Standards and Technology provides a seven-step process for business continuity:[6]

1. **Develop the contingency planning policy statement.** This provides the authority to carry out the program activities, states senior management support for the policy and program, and contains statements to demonstrate compliance with relevant regulatory requirements.

---

6   Swanson, Marianne, Bowen, Pauline, Wohl Phillips, Amy, Gallup, Dean, Lynes, David

2. **Conduct the business impact analysis (BIA).** The BIA identifies the critical processes as well as the resources and systems needed to support those processes. The BIA provides information on the impact of a disruption and how quickly business must resume. Senior management must be involved in this process because they have a more global view of the organization and its mission than each functional manager does. The BIA must be periodically refreshed to ensure that it stays current as business changes occur.

   Two important considerations are the *Recovery Time Objective (RTO)* and *Recovery Point Objective (RPO)*. All applications, like all organization functions, need to be classified as to their time sensitivity for recovery. For applications, this is commonly referred to as the RTO or Maximum Tolerable Downtime (MTD). This is the amount of time the organization can function without that application before a significant impact occurs. With regard to the actual data, decisions need to be made about how current data needs to be to function in recovery mode. This is commonly referred to as the RPO. Backup policies and procedures for electronic data and hard copy data need to comply with the RPO established by the organization.

3. **Identify preventive controls.** Part of planning is to identify those investments in controls that can help to avoid or reduce the impact of a major business disruption. Some of the considerations include the environmental and physical controls in place at the data center. There are many considerations that go into the selection of a data center site, including the geographic location. For example, to reduce risk, one should locate a data center in a place that has a lower probability of severe weather. The primary data center and the backup recovery site should not be located too close in proximity. Environmental controls help to mitigate damage if a disaster strikes. Having appropriate fire suppression, water sensors in computer rooms, and redundant power are important considerations. Decisions also need to be made about where backup media should be stored for recovery.

4. **Create contingency strategies.** Planning is key to a successful business continuity program. The HCISPP needs to consider where the recovery of critical systems will occur, what resources are needed to support the recovery, and what investments need to be made.

3

Privacy and Security in Health Care

5.   **Develop an information system contingency plan.** NIST 800-34 provides guidance on the sections the plan needs to include:

A.   ***Supporting Information*** – Included in this section are items such as a plan scope, a description of the systems, assumptions made within the plan, and roles and responsibilities.

B.   ***Activation and Notification*** – This section considers how key individuals will be notified to execute on the plan, as well as how communication will happen with employees, customers, key vendors, and other constituents. For key individuals, the plan should contain their contact information and detail who is responsible for reaching out to them, though the actual contact information may be included in the appendix.

C.   ***Recovery Phase*** – This section outlines how recovery will occur, such as the sequence of system recovery. Recovery teams needs to consider the dependencies for each system. For example, System B is dependent on a feed from System A. In large, complex environments, there may be multiple underlying plans that contain step-by-step instructions for each system. It should be noted that recovery may result in work-arounds, such as the execution of manual processes until a system is fully recovered or in the event a system cannot be recovered.

D.   ***Reconstitution Phase*** – This portion of the plan addresses what needs to occur once a disaster situation is declared as closed. During this phase, validation needs to occur to demonstrate that systems have returned to an operational state. Cleanup needs to occur at the alternate recovery site to prevent unnecessary data exposure. Stakeholders, including employees, need to be notified that there will be a return to normal operations and what they need to do. This is an opportunity to note where documentation needs to be updated based on activities that occurred during the event.

E.   ***Appendices*** – Any additional detail needed to support the plan should be included here. This can include things like employee and vendor contact lists.

It is important to note that copies of the plan must be stored in locations accessible by an entity or organization if they cannot access their systems.

6. **Ensure plan testing, training, and exercises**. The plan must be periodically tested to ensure that it is viable and can be executed as documented. This is an opportunity to make individuals aware of their responsibilities and to practice them in preparation for an actual event. Exercises can range in complexity and scope. A tabletop exercise is a chance for key stakeholders to review the plan and discuss the execution. A simulation provides an opportunity to actually recover the people, processes, and technology called for in the plan.

7. **Ensure plan maintenance.** The plan must be updated as the environment changes. People, process, and technology changes prompt the need for plan updates.

3

Privacy and Security in Health Care

CASE STUDY

In the aftermath of disasters, such as Hurricane Katrina and the subsequent flooding that occurred, New Orleans hospitals had to simultaneously care for existing patients and those affected by the disaster while also trying to maintain operations in dire circumstances (e.g. power loss, lack of clean water). There were many questions about the level of preparation the hospitals exhibited in advance of Katrina. In fact, according to a report released by the Urban Institute, by the time some hospitals made a decision to evacuate, they faced other problems, such as overwhelming traffic jams.[7]

Backup Strategies

An organization must prepare for a recovery situation by ensuring that it is continually backing up its data—especially data that is critical for the organization. Organizations need to develop a backup strategy. The strategy should address the following:

- What data is being backed up? The highest priority needs to be given to the most critical data.
- Where will the backups occur (on-site or remote)?
- How often will backups occur?
- Who is responsible for performing the backup?
- Who is responsible for monitoring backups to ensure they successfully execute?
- Are there places where data is stored that may not fall under your traditional backup strategy? For example, do an organization's executives maintain paper files at their homes? Is any of the critical data stored by third-party vendors?

Backup types generally come in three flavors: full, incremental, and differential.

- *A Full Backup* is the most time-consuming type of backup and uses the most storage space. It occurs less frequently than other backup types. For example, an organization may execute a full backup on a weekly basis.
- *Incremental Backup* backs up only those files that have been created or changed since the last incremental backup. If today is March 7 and the last incremental backup was on March 6, today's backup will capture all changes since the incremental backup occurred on March 6.

---

7   Gray, Bradford H. and Hebert, Kathy

- *A Differential Backup* backs up only those files that have been created or changed since the last full backup. If today is March 7 and your last full backup was on March 3, the differential backup will capture all changes since March 3.

Alternate Site Strategies

Organizational needs for recovery and the investment an organization is willing to make will determine the recovery strategies selected for the technology environment:

- *Dual Data Center* – Used for applications that cannot afford downtime without negatively impacting the organization. The applications are split between two geographically dispersed data centers and either load balanced between the two centers or hot swapped between the two centers. The surviving data center must have enough headroom to carry the full production load in either case.

- *Hot Site* – This site, which could be an internal or external solution, is standby ready with all the technology and equipment necessary to run the applications positioned there. The recovery environments must be kept as close to identical as possible with the production environment to avoid problems with O/S levels, hardware differences, capacity differences, etc., from preventing or delaying recovery. Hot site vendors tend to have the most commonly used hardware and software products to attract the largest number of customers to utilize the site. Unique equipment or software would generally need to be provided by the organization either at time of disaster or stored there ahead of time.

- *Warm Site* – A leased or rented facility that is usually partially configured with some equipment but not the actual computers. It will generally have all the cooling, cabling, and networks in place to accommodate the recovery, but the actual servers, mainframe, etc., equipment are delivered to the site at time of disaster.

- *Cold Site* – A cold site is a shell or empty data center space with no technology on the floor. All technology must be purchased or acquired at the time of disaster.

- *Mobile Site* – Another option available is the "mobile site," meaning the data center of an organization is housed in a mobile trailer or possibly a standard sea cargo shipping container. Should disaster strike, an organization can simply load up the cargo container data center and move it to another location that has the power, resources, and connectivity required to continue operations.

163

Data Retention and Destruction

Data retention and destruction is the act of storing and destroying data in accordance with a records management framework that meets legal, regulatory, and business requirements. Data that is retained must be appropriately protected. When it is no longer needed and must be destroyed, appropriate procedures need to be followed to minimize the risk of unnecessary data exposure.

In healthcare, data is often stored both in paper and electronic form, as well as on media such as prescription bottles or laboratory samples. The U.S. Department of Health and Human Services Office for Civil Rights provides the following guidance:

- Protected health information in paper form must be destroyed so that it cannot be reconstructed. Techniques such as fine cross-cut shredding and pulping ensure that it is no longer in a form that can be deciphered.
- For information on media like a prescription bottle, the bottles can be placed in opaque bags and stored in secured areas until an authorized Business Associate can execute appropriate destruction.
- For electronic protected health information, there are several methods; clearing, purging, or destruction can be employed.[8]

General Privacy Principles

The HCISPP should be familiar with general privacy concepts, as well as frameworks, laws, and regulations that help to define and provide guidance on the application of those concepts. This section will examine two frameworks, the Organization for Economic Cooperation and Development (OECD) Privacy Principles[9] and the Generally Accepted Privacy Principles[10] (GAPP), and three laws, the Canadian Personal Information Protection and Electronic Documents Act (PIPEDA), the U.K. Data Protection Act (DPA) of 1998, and the U.S. Health Insurance Portability and Accountability Act (HIPAA) Privacy and Security Rules. Unless otherwise noted, quotations come directly from the particular framework or law / regulation.

---

8   U.S. Department of Health and Human Services Office for Civil Rights: "Frequently Asked Questions About the Disposal of Protected Health Information"

9   Unless otherwise noted, quotations for OECD come from the OECD "Privacy Principles"

10   Unless otherwise noted, quotations for GAPP come from the AICPA and Chartered Accountants of Canada: "Generally Accepted Privacy Principles"

The OECD privacy framework, which was adopted in 1980, provides a foundation for the European Union's Privacy Directive. In recognition of the increasing emphasis on personal data privacy and the proliferation of technology that has made data sharing much easier, the OECD released a revised Guidelines on the *Protection of Privacy and Transborder Flows of Personal Data* in 2013. Another framework to consider is the Generally Accepted Privacy Principles (GAPP) developed jointly by the American Institute of Certified Public Accountants (AICPA) and the Canadian Institute of Chartered Accountants (CICA). The GAPP was developed to help organizations navigate the privacy landscape by providing them with some key principles and associated explanations culled from laws and regulations, as well as best practices.

Consent / Choice

This represents the right of the individuals to agree to the use of their data. In healthcare, that can mean things such as agreeing to release information to an insurance company.

OECD	The 2013 framework suggests there should be cooperative trans-border limits to the collection, storage, use, and disclosure of personal information, and it should be gathered through lawful means with the individual's consent.
GAPP	Defines this as a principle where "the entity should describe the choices available to the individual and obtains implicit or explicit consent with respect to collection, use and disclosure of personal information."
PIPEDA	The Act provides for individual protections requiring individual consent, but it also provides several far-reaching clauses, which grant collection, use, and disclosure without knowledge or consent of the individual.
DPA	Defines this as a principle where "personal data shall be processed fairly and lawfully and not processed under certain conditions set forth in the Act."
HIPAA	Distinguishes between consent and authorization. Consent is not required but can be obtained for use of protected health information to carry out treatment, payment, and healthcare operations. Authorization is required for disclosures of PHI that are typically not allowed under the HIPAA Privacy Rule, such as for information to be released to another individual. [11]

Limited Collection / Legitimate Purpose/ Purpose Specification

Data can be used in different ways for different purposes. Limited collection principles provide the individuals with protections against the data being used for purposes other than what was originally intended.

---

11 U.S. Department of Health and Human Services: "What is the difference between "consent" and "authorization" under the HIPAA Privacy Rule?"

OECD	"There should be limits to the collection of personal data and any such data should be obtained by lawful and fair means and, where appropriate, with the knowledge or consent of the data subject."
GAPP	Defines this as a principle where "the entity collects personal information only for the purposes identified in the notice."
PIPEDA	The Act defines this as a principle where "personal information shall be limited to that which is necessary for the purposes identified by the organization. Information shall be collected by fair and lawful means. The Act also empowers the 'Commissioner' to consent, under specific procedures, to the sharing of information for requested purposes."
DPA	Defines this as a principle where "personal data shall be obtained only for one or more specified and lawful purposes, and shall not be further processed in a manner incompatible with that purpose or those purposes."
HIPAA	The minimum necessary amount of protected health information is to be used for the treatment, payment, and healthcare operations. Other uses are prohibited or require authorization from the individual.

Disclosure Limitation / Transfer to Third Parties / Trans-border Concerns

Essentially, these principles ensure that individuals are aware when their data is disclosed to third parties. This becomes more complicated as data leaves national boundaries and crosses into countries whose laws and/or cultural attitudes toward privacy of information may vary greatly from the country in which the individual resides. This is especially relevant for citizens of the European Union. Because their privacy protections are often more restrictive than other countries, issues arise when data needs to leave the European Union.

OECD	"Personal data should not be disclosed, made available or otherwise used for purposes other than those specified in accordance with Paragraph 9 except: i) a) with the consent of the data subject; or ii) b) by the authority of law."
GAPP	"The entity discloses information to third parties only for the purposes identified in the notice and with the implicit or explicit consent of the individual."
PIPEDA	The Act empowers the "Commissioner" to disclose to foreign state, under specific procedures, the information requested.
DPA	"Personal data shall not be transferred to a country or territory outside the European Economic Area unless the country or territory ensures an adequate level of protection for the rights and freedoms of data subjects in relation to the processing of personal data."
HIPAA	If data is required by third parties to assist in payment, treatment, or healthcare operations, the Privacy Rule requires the execution of a Business Associate (BA) Agreement. The BA Agreement spells out provisions for appropriate uses and disclosures and requires administrative, technical, and physical safeguards.

Access Limitation (Individual Rights)

OECD	"An individual should have the right:
	
	a) to obtain from a data controller, or otherwise, confirmation of whether or not the data controller has data relating to him;
	b) to have communicated to him, data relating to him
	   i) within a reasonable time;
	   ii) at a charge, if any, that is not excessive;
	   iii) in a reasonable manner; and
	   iv) in a form that is readily intelligible to him;
	c) to be given reasons if a request made under subparagraphs (a) and (b) is denied, and to be able to challenge such denial; and
	d) to challenge data relating to him and, if the challenge is successful to have the data erased, rectified, completed or amended."

GAPP	"The entity provides individuals with access to their personal information for review and access."
PIPEDA	The Act empowers the "Commissioner" to set limits in writing and by agreement.
DPA	"Appropriate technical and organizational measures shall be taken against unauthorized or unlawful processing of personal data and against accidental loss or destruction of, or damage to, personal data."
HIPAA	HIPAA provides for a number of individual rights for individuals to whom the data belongs[12]: ■ **Access:** In general, individuals have the right to access their own PHI contained in what is known as the "designated record set" ■ **Amendment:** Individuals can request to have information corrected that they believe is inaccurate or incorrect ■ **Disclosure Accounting:** Individuals have the right to know if their PHI was released for purposes other than what was intended by law ■ **Restriction:** Individuals can request that their PHI not be released to certain entities or individuals ■ **Confidential Communication:** Individuals have the right to have their PHI communicated to them through an alternate means, particularly if the normal means could put an individual in danger

Security

Individuals need assurance that their data will be appropriately safeguarded. As explained earlier in this chapter, the tenets of Confidentiality, Integrity, and Availability must be advanced through the implementation of appropriate administrative, technical, and physical controls.

3

Privacy and Security in Health Care

---

12 U.S. Department of Health and Human Services: "Summary of the HIPAA Privacy Rule"

OECD	"Personal data should be protected by reasonable security safeguards against such risks as loss or unauthorized access, destruction, use, modification or disclosure of data."
GAPP	Defines this as a principle where "the entity protects personal information against unauthorized access (both physical and logical)."
PIPEDA	The Act defines this as a principle where "personal information shall be protected by security safeguards appropriate to the sensitivity of the data."
DPA	Does not address security or safeguards except through a reference to the Safeguarding Vulnerable Groups Act 2006.
HIPAA	Requires that appropriate administrative, physical, and technical safeguards be applied to protect health information.

Accuracy / Completeness / Quality

Individuals have the right to request corrections to amend errors. A mechanism needs to exist for them to dispute a denial of a correction request.

OECD	"Personal data should be relevant to the purposes for which they are to be used and, to the extent necessary for those purposes, should be accurate, complete and kept up-to-date."
GAPP	"The entity maintains accurate, complete, and relevant personal information for the purposes identified in the notice."
PIPEDA	"Personal information shall be as accurate, complete and up to date as is necessary for the purposes for which it is to be used."
DPA	"Personal data shall be accurate and where necessary kept up to date."
HIPAA	"The covered entity must permit an individual to request that the covered entity amend the protected health information maintained in the designated record set."

Management / Designation of a Privacy Officer / Supervisor Re-authorization

This principle recognizes the need for someone with the authority to carry out the responsibilities required to implement and maintain privacy principles and practices and ensure compliance with applicable laws and regulations.

OECD	The accountability principle discusses the need for proper designation of stakeholders and identification of a data controller. Laws need to hold officers and controllers accountable by penalty should a breach occur.
GAPP	"The entity defines, documents, communicates, and assigns accountability for its privacy policies and procedures."
PIPEDA	"An organization is responsible for personal information under its control."
DPA	Personal data is under the stewardship of the Data Controller, who responds to requests from a Commissioner, which is an appointed government position.
HIPAA	The HIPAA Privacy and Security Rules require designation of privacy and security officials. The privacy and security officials maintain policies and procedures. The privacy official responds to official complaints.

Transparency and Openness

Transparency and openness provide individuals with an understanding of how, when, and where their information will be collected and used.

OECD	"There should be a general policy of openness about developments, practices and policies with respect to personal data. Means should be readily available of establishing the existence and nature of personal data, and the main purposes of their use, as well as the identity and usual residence of the data controller."
GAPP	The framework addresses this principle conceptually only when discussing topics of consent and notice. Explains the difference between implicit and explicit consent and that in some cases, explicit consent from the individual is required.
PIPEDA	"An organization shall make readily available to individuals specific information about its policies and practices relating to the management of personal information."
DPA	"Personal data shall be processed fairly and lawfully."
HIPAA	Trust and transparency principles allow individuals to understand the information that is collected about them, as well as how that information will be used and shared. It helps individuals understand the choices available to them regarding their information. [13]

Notice and Purpose Specification

Notice and purpose specification provide individuals with information on how their data will be used. The notice should be made available to the individuals and written so they can understand its contents.

OECD	"The purposes for which personal data are collected should be specified not later than at the time of data collection and the subsequent use limited to the fulfillment of those purposes or such others as are not incompatible with those purposes and as are specified on each occasion of change of purpose."
GAPP	"The entity provides notice about its privacy policies and procedures and identifies the purposes for which personal information is collected, used, retained, and disclosed."
PIPEDA	According to a companion "Privacy Toolkit" provided to businesses by the Office of the Privacy Commissioner of Canada, "Information about these policies and practices should be made available in person, in writing, by telephone, in publications or on your organization's website. The information presented should be consistent, regardless of the format."[14]
DPA	An organization that will process personal information must provide notice to and register with the "Commissioner."
HIPAA	The covered entity must provide a Notice of Privacy Practices that "describes the ways in which the covered entity may use and disclose protected health information."[15] It also provides individuals with information on how to file a privacy complaint and helps them understand their individual rights under the Rule.

---

13 U.S. Department of Health and Human Services Office for Civil Rights: "The HIPAA Privacy Rule and Electronic Health Information Exchange in a Networked Environment: Openness and Transparency"

14 Office of the Privacy Commissioner of Canada: "A Guide for Businesses and Organizations: Privacy Toolkit: Canada's Personal Information Protection and Electronic Documents Act"

15 U.S. Department of Health and Human Services: "Summary of the HIPAA Privacy Rule"

3

Privacy and Security in Health Care

Additional Measures for Breach Notification

This principle recognizes the responsibility that organizations have to provide information when a data breach occurs. This may involve not only notifying the individual whose data was breached but also may require regulatory reporting. Organizations also must take action to mitigate the risk posed by the breach and investigate the cause of the breach.

OECD	This concept is introduced in the 2013 revised guidelines: "Provide notice, as appropriate, to privacy enforcement authorities or other relevant authorities where there has been a significant security breach affecting personal data. When the breach is likely to adversely affect data subjects, a data controller should notify affected data subjects."[16]
GAPP	Management criteria 1.2.7 in the framework guidance for practitioners state, "A documented privacy incident and breach management program has been implemented…" It goes on to explain key elements of the program that need to be included, such as escalation and the need to meet regulatory breach reporting timelines.
PIPEDA	As of this writing, the Act does not include specific breach notification provisions.[17] However, in 2007, the Canadian Privacy Commissioner released breach guidelines to complement existing privacy regulatory requirements.[18]
DPA	"Appropriate technical and organizational measures shall be taken against unauthorized or unlawful processing of personal data and against accidental loss or destruction of, or damage to, personal data."[19]
HIPAA	Breach notification requirements for HIPAA actually are contained within the HITECH regulation and the subsequent HIPAA Omnibus Rule. Covered entities and business associates must not only investigate and mitigate breach situations, but they also must provide notification to impacted individuals within 60 days of breach discovery, provide notification to HHS-OCR (for breaches involving data for more than 500 individuals, the information is published on the HHS-OCR website), and provide notification to the media in certain situations.

The Relationship between Privacy and Security

Dependency

For privacy principles to be effective, they rely on security controls to function effectively. Understanding the sensitivity classification of the data is an integral part of designing security controls that align to privacy objectives.

Remember, the CIA triad is a way to illustrate this. Throughout this Domain, the HCISPP candidate has learned about a number of privacy principles and security safeguards. Dependency can be explained as follows:

---

16 OECD Recommendation of the Council concerning Guidelines governing the Protection of Privacy and Transborder Flows of Personal Data (2013)

17 De Jesus, Ron

18 Office of the Privacy Commissioner of Canada news release from August 1, 2007

19 U.K. Information Commissioner's Office: "Data Protection Principles"

- Individuals expect that their sensitive health data will remain confidential and used only for the purposes intended. For this privacy principle to work, access controls must be in place to govern who can access the data and how much of it they are entitled to see and use.

- When health data is needed by third parties, privacy advances the concept that the transfer must be appropriate and protected from inappropriate changes. For integrity to remain intact, encryption technologies are deployed to not only ensure that data is protected in transit but also that the sender and recipient are correct.

- Individuals want to know that they, or their providers, can access data when needed for treatment and payment.

Integration

Privacy and security cannot be considered together only during controls design. The HCISPP must be aware of changes in technology that could impact privacy, such as system upgrades or the introduction of new technologies. The privacy of the data must be considered across the System Development Life-Cycle (SDLC).

The Nature of Sensitive Data and Handling Implications

Personal and Heath Information Protected by Law

As noted earlier in this chapter, as well as throughout Domain 2, Regulatory Environment, there are many laws and regulations for an HCISPP to consider. In the United States, the HIPAA Privacy and Security Rules govern the use, disclosure, and required safeguards for Protected Health Information at the national level. It is also a good idea to understand if there are specific privacy and security rules at a state level in the United States. Outside of the United States, many of the privacy and security rules in other countries were not developed specific to healthcare data, but rather, they include it under the same umbrella as other sensitive personal data. The European Union Privacy Directive has provided a model.

Sensitivity Mitigation

The overall objective for an HCISPP is to assess the risk associated with the confidentiality, integrity, and availability of health information and to determine the appropriate level of safeguards needed to bring the risk to an acceptable level. One way to reduce risk is to provide health information in ways that does not identify it to an individual when it does not need to be. This is known as de-identification.

There are valid reasons why healthcare data in a de-identified form still is useful, such as for research, so the laws and regulations provided methods for doing so even if there is a small amount of associated residual risk. Because de-identified data does not provide data about a known individual, it does not require the same level of security controls afforded to individually identifiable health information.

De-Identification

At face value, de-identification seems to be a simple concept. People who are not experienced with the regulatory requirements often think removing an individual's name or name and date of birth is enough. However, for information to meet the HIPAA regulatory standard, it requires certain steps to be taken. Under the HIPAA Privacy Rule, health information is considered de-identified if it does not identify an individual and if the covered entity has no reasonable basis to believe it can be used to identify an individual. The Privacy Rule provides two methods, Expert Determination and Safe Harbor. If followed correctly, these methods will allow health information to be considered de-identified.

Expert Determination

Essentially, expert determination requires an individual with appropriate knowledge and experience in statistical and scientific principles, such as a statistician, to apply those principles and demonstrate that the information could not be used alone or in combination with other reasonably available information to identify the individual to whom the information is about. The methods used to make this determination must be properly documented.

Safe Harbor

The Safe Harbor method requires that the following identifiers be removed: (NOTE: You may see Safe Harbor mentioned in other sections of this book relating to the same or different regulations. This instance of Safe Harbor is specific to de-identification.)

- Name
- All geographic subdivisions smaller than state. There are particular rules around ZIP codes to ensure that they cover a certain number of individuals. It is possible to use the first three digits of a ZIP code in de-identified data if the number of persons across all ZIP codes with those same digits exceeds 20,000. If a three-digit ZIP code is aggregated with others that have the same first three digits and the total number of individuals does not exceed 20,000, the digits must be changed to "000".

- All elements of dates (except year). For individuals older than 89 years of age, their data must be consolidated and not tied to a specific year.
- Telephone number
- Fax number
- Email address
- Social Security number
- Medical record number
- Health plan beneficiary number
- Account number
- Certificate / license number
- Vehicle identifiers and serial numbers, including license plate number
- Device identifiers and serial numbers
- Web Universal Resource Numbers (URLs)
- Internet Protocol (IP) addresses
- Biometric identifiers, including fingerprints and voiceprints
- Full facial photographs or comparable images
- Other unique identifying number, characteristic, or code[20]

Figure 3.2, adapted from information provided by the U.S Department of Health and Human Services, summarizes the differences between the two methods of de-identification.

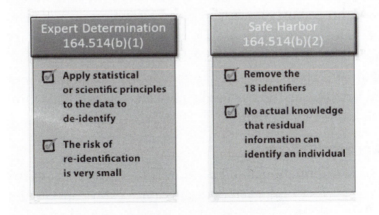

Figure 3.2 – **Methods of De-identification under HIPAA Privacy**

---

20 U.S. Department of Health and Human Services: "Guidance Regarding Methods for De-identification of Protected Health Information in Accordance with the Health Insurance Portability and Accountability Act (HIPAA) Privacy Rule"

CASE STUDY

Some may wonder why birth year has to be removed for individuals over age 89. Consider that one of the oldest living individuals in the United States is 114. For de-identification to work, organizations cannot tie the data back to an individual. If just birth year is listed and not birthdate, an attacker could still easily find out that there are only one or two people of that age. It would be relatively easy to figure out who they were, even if the attacker did not have much other information. To prevent the possibility of identification, one should exclude the specific birth year for individuals over age 89.

Limited Data Set

The HIPAA Privacy Rule does recognize that in certain situations, researchers will need information beyond what de-identified data can provide, so there are provisions for what is known as a limited data set. Although the limited data set excludes most of the identifiers, just as de-identified data does, it can include specific dates and some basic geographic information. The National Institutes of Health (NIH) defines a limited data set as follows: "Refers to PHI that excludes 16 categories of direct identifiers and may be used or disclosed, for purposes of research, public health, or healthcare operations, without obtaining either an individual's Authorization or a waiver or an alteration of Authorization for its use and disclosure, with a data use agreement." The NIH goes on to explain that the limited data set may include, "city; state; ZIP Code; elements of date; and other numbers, characteristics, or codes not listed as direct identifiers."[21] To release a limited data set, the Covered Entity must have a Data Use Agreement in place with the research entity.

Categories of Sensitive Data

In general, most information about an individual's health is sensitive, but there are certain categories of information that require extra considerations and / or safeguards. By their nature, many of the categories listed below are not always well understood or accepted by the public, so additional laws often govern how this information must be protected and when it can be shared.

---

21   National Institutes of Health: "Protecting Personal Health Information in Research: Understanding the HIPAA Privacy Rule"

Mental Health

HIPAA extended the medical information category to include mental health information from past, present, or future mental or physical health records.

The HIPAA Privacy rule provides additional protections to psychotherapy notes, which can contain highly personal information about an individual's condition and state of mind. Information needed to treat the patient, such as medications, or to pay for care must be included in the medical record instead of the psychotherapy notes. Because psychotherapy notes are not included in the medical record, very few entities have a need to use them. In general, the individual's authorization is required to release psychotherapy notes.[22]

Substance Abuse

U.S. federal laws and regulations protect the confidentiality of alcohol and drug abuse patient records maintained by programs that receive federal assistance. In general, program employees may not disclose to anyone outside the program that a patient attends the program nor can they identify a patient as an alcohol or drug abuser.

The U.S. laws covering the confidentiality of substance abuse information include not only the HIPAA Privacy Rule but also the Federal confidentiality regulations (42 CFR Part 2 or Part 2) that were enacted in the 1970s.[23]

Pregnancy

Although, pregnancy is generally an obvious condition, pregnant women are still entitled to certain privacy and health care rights. The HIPAA Portability rule prohibits considering pregnancy as a pre-existing condition. With the passage of the Affordable Care Act, pregnant women can now obtain individual health insurance plans, and employer-sponsored plans must cover maternity care.[24]

HIV

Although HIPAA now offers protections for individuals with conditions such as HIV, there are laws that pre-date HIPAA that recognized the need to protect the rights of individuals with HIV. For example, the Rehabilitation Act of 1973 and the Americans with Disabilities Act of 1990 offer protections such as access to health care from organizations that receive federal funding or by any government entity.

---

22 U.S. Department of Health and Human Services: "HIPAA Privacy Rule and Sharing Information Related to Mental Health"

23 U.S. Department of Health and Human Services: Substance Abuse and Mental Health Services Administration Center for Substance Abuse Treatment

24 HealthCare.gov: "What does Marketplace health insurance cover?"

3

Privacy and Security in Health Care

Although there are laws in place to protect the rights and prevent the discrimination of individuals with HIV, these also have to be balanced against public health obligations.[25] The HCISPP must understand how to safeguard sensitive information for the benefit of the individual while allowing it to be securely shared with entities that require the information, such as public health agencies.

CASE STUDY

The U.S. Department of Health and Human Services Office for Civil Rights opened a case as a result of a privacy complaint. A dental practice was not taking care to mask the way it identified patients with HIV. Dental practice employees were placing red "AIDS" stickers on the outside covers of paper medical files. That information was visible to other patients and employees who did not have a need to know that a patient had HIV.[26] The dental practice had to discontinue this procedure and apologize to the individual who filed the complaint. Of course, it is legitimate for the dentist to know if a patient has a condition such as HIV, but the matter needs to be handled with sensitivity to protect the patient's right to privacy. The American Dental Association provides its members with information on what should and should not be in a dental medical record and how the outside of the record can be used.[27] For example, it is acceptable to have a name on the outside of the folder but not information about a specific condition. The HCISPP should be on the lookout for situations like these that could lead to issues with confidentiality.

Genetic Privacy

With scientific advances making it possible for genetic information to be used for a variety of purposes, laws have been enacted to put some parameters around the use and protection of sensitive genetic information. For example, the United States has the Genetic Information Nondiscrimination Act (GINA) that went into effect in 2009. Its purpose is to prevent genetic discrimination. Under GINA, a health insurance company cannot use genetic information as a way to determine coverage eligibility, and an employer cannot use it for hiring or other employment decisions.[28] State and territory laws vary in terms of genetic privacy.

---

25 U.S. Department of Health and Human Services Health Information Technology and Quality Improvement.

26 U.S. Department of Health and Human Services: "All Case Examples"

27 American Dental Association

28 U.S. National Library of Medicine: "The Genetic Nondiscrimination Act (GINA)"

The most famous database for DNA information is the Combined DNA Index System (CODIS), which is managed by the U.S. Federal Bureau of Investigations (FBI). The DNA information contained in CODIS is used by forensic laboratories to verify DNA matches in criminal cases. Although it is used by law enforcement and not healthcare professionals, it is one example where sensitive health information is stored for a use other than care of the individual.

The HCISPP must have an understanding of the extra requirements afforded to special categories of sensitive health information. These should be accounted for in an entity's data classification and sensitivity program.

Security and Privacy Terminology Specific to Healthcare

Healthcare security and privacy has some terminology that may or may not have equivalent concepts in other industries. Some examples to be aware of include:

- *Minimum Necessary* – This is consistent with Least Privilege. It is a term specifically mentioned under the HIPAA Privacy and Security rules. The requirement is to use the least amount of information to carry out a particular function even if the function is permitted under the law.
- *Protected Health Information (PHI)* – This is individually identifiable health information and includes 18 identifiers.
- *Covered Entity* – An organization that directly handles Protected Health Information, including providers, payers, and healthcare clearinghouses.
- *Business Associate* – In the United States, third parties who will create, store, process, or transmit Protected Health Information are defined under the HIPAA rules as Business Associates.
- *Business Associate Agreement* – The Covered Entity must ensure that a Business Associate Agreement is executed with the Business Associate. This agreement contains provisions on appropriate use and disclosure of PHI and states that appropriate administrative, technical, and physical controls must be in place.
- *Electronic Health Record* – Electronic systems that store a patient's health information, such as the patient's history of diseases and medications. EHRs allow providers to easily track a patient's health information.

Summary

Security and privacy go hand-in-hand, and this is especially true in the sensitive area of health care. Individuals have the right to know how their information is being used and shared, as well as how it is protected. Each information security safeguard is designed to provide confidentiality, integrity, and availability (CIA). Some security safeguards, such as training and awareness, are considered to be administrative controls. Others, like encryption, are technical. The third category, physical controls, provides for things like facility security, visitor procedures, and environmental controls within the data center.

An individual's expectation of and right to privacy are encompassed by a variety of privacy principles. Information needs to be accurate, protected, used for its intended purpose, and made available to those who have a need to know, as well as to those to whom the information belongs. In the event protected health information is breached, organizations need to execute breach response plans that include an investigation, mitigation, and notification to appropriate parties. Laws and regulations continue to be updated and enacted to provide protections, and frameworks, such as the Organization for Economic Cooperation and Development (OECD) Privacy Principles and the Generally Accepted Privacy Principles (GAPP), provide a baseline from which an organization can develop its program.

The role of the HCISPP is to understand security controls and privacy principles and how they work together. It is imperative that security professionals stay on top of regulatory and industry changes, as well as understand the business functions that facilitate the need for appropriate access to information. Advances in healthcare and changes in technology will present challenges and opportunities from a security and privacy perspective. For example, the introduction of "big data"—the ability to quickly correlate large volumes of data from disparate sources—may contribute to better health outcomes, but it also presents a wealth of information to a potential attacker or can be misused by a well-intentioned employee who does not understand data use limitations. Medical technologies that can allow for enhanced treatment options or a better quality of life for the patient also carry with them the opportunity to be compromised. All of these factors demonstrate the need for security and privacy professionals who can design policies and controls to protect and govern the use of technologies, processes, and data.

3

Privacy and Security in Health Care

References

AICPA and Chartered Accountants of Canada, "Generally Accepted Privacy Principles: CPA and CA Practitioner Version", August 2009. Available from AICPA and Chartered Accountants of Canada, accessed on April 19, 2014.

"All Case Examples." Health Information Privacy. U.S. Department of Health and Human Services, n.d. Web. April 12, 2014.

American Dental Association Council on Dental Practice Division of Legal Affairs. "Dental Records", 2010. Available from American Dental Association, accessed April 12, 2014.

De Jesus, Ron. "Exploring Federal Privacy Breach Notification in Canada". *The Privacy Advisor*. April 1, 2013. International Association of Privacy Professionals (IAPP) The Privacy Advisor on the Web, accessed April 20, 2014.

European Commission. "Commission Proposes a Comprehensive Reform of Data Protection Rules to Increase Users' Control of Their Data and to Cut Costs for Businesses" European Commission news release, January 25, 2012. European Commission website: http://europa.eu/rapid/press-release_IP-12-46_en.htm?locale=en, accessed on April 25, 2014.

Gray, Bradford H., PhD and Hebert, Kathy, MD, MMM, MPH, The Urban Institute, "After Katrina: Hospitals in Hurricane Katrina: Challenges Facing Custodial Institutions in a Disaster", July 2006. Available from The Urban Institute, accessed April 24, 2014.

"HIPAA Privacy Rule and Sharing Information Related to Mental Health." Health Information Privacy. U.S. Department of Health and Human Services, n.d. Web. April 12, 2014.

"Hippocratic Oath, (Modern Version)", Guide to finding information about bioethics and related subjects, Johns Hopkins Sheridan Libraries, April 3, 2014. Web. April 15, 2014.

Hsiao, Chun-Ju, PhD and Hing, Esther, MPH, Centers for Disease Control, "Use and characteristics of electronic health record systems among office-based physician practices:

United States 2001-2013", January 2014. Available from Centers for Disease Control, accessed April 20, 2014.

"Laptop stolen with health information of 620,000 Albertans: Health officials recently informed of theft from last September". *CBC News*. January 22, 2014 (updated January 23, 2014). CBC News on the Web, accessed April 15, 2014.

McGee, Marianne Kolbasuk. "TRICARE Breach Lawsuits Consolidated: Case to be Handled in Washington U.S. District Court". *Healthcare Info Security*. July 10, 2012. Healthcare Info Security on the Web, accessed April 15, 2014.

National Institutes of Health, "Protecting Personal Health Information in Research: Understanding the HIPAA Privacy Rule", n.d. Available from the National Institutes of Health, accessed April 21, 2014.

OECD, "OECD Recommendation of the Council concerning Guidelines governing the Protection of Privacy and Transborder Flows of Personal Data (2013)", July 11, 2013. Available from OECD, accessed April 18, 2014.

Office of the Privacy Commissioner of Canada, "A Guide for Businesses and Organizations: Privacy Toolkit: Canada's Personal Information Protection and Electronic Documents Act", March 2014. Available from the Office of the Privacy Commissioner of Canada, accessed April 21, 2014.

Office of the Privacy Commissioner of Canada. "Privacy Commissioner Releases Privacy Breach Guidelines" Office of the Privacy Commissioner of Canada news release, August 1, 2007. Office of the Privacy Commissioner website: http://www.priv.gc.ca/media/nr-c/2007/nr-c_070801_e.asp, accessed on April 20, 2014.

"Summary of the HIPAA Privacy Rule." Health Information Privacy. U.S. Department of Health and Human Services, n.d. Web. April 12, 2014.

Swanson, Marianne, Bowen, Pauline, Wohl Phillips, Amy, Gallup, Dean and Lynes, David, National Institute of Standards and Technology, "Contingency Planning Guide for Federal Information Systems," May 2010.

"The Genetic Nondiscrimination Act (GINA)." Genetics Home Reference: Your Guide to Understanding Genetic Conditions. U.S. Library of National Medicine, April 7, 2014. Web. April 12, 2014.

3

Privacy and Security in Health Care

U.K. Information Commissioner's Office, "Data Protection Principles", n.d. Available from U.K. Information Commissioner's Office, accessed April 20, 2014.

U.K. Information Commissioner's Office, "Notification of data security breaches to the Information Commissioner's Office ICO): Data Protection Act (version 1)", July 23, 2012. Available from Information Commissioner's Office, accessed April 20, 2014.

U.S. Department of Health and Human Services Office for Civil Rights, "Guidance Regarding Methods for De-identification of Protected Health Information in Accordance with the Health Insurance Portability and Accountability Act (HIPAA Privacy Rule", November 26, 2012. Available from U.S. Department of Health and Human Services Office for Civil Rights, accessed April 13, 2014.

U.S. Department of Health and Human Services Office for Civil Rights, "Know the Rights that Protect Individuals with HIV and AIDS", n.d. Available from U.S. Department of Health and Human Services Office for Civil Rights, accessed April 12, 2014.

U.S. Department of Health and Human Services Office for Civil Rights, "Frequently Asked Questions About the Disposal of Protected Health Information", n.d. Available from U.S. Department of Health and Human Services Office for Civil Rights, accessed April 13, 2014.

U.S. Department of Health and Human Services Office for Civil Rights, "The HIPAA Privacy Rule and Electronic Health Information Exchange in a Networked Environment: Openness and Transparency", n.d. Available from U.S. Department of Health and Human Services Office for Civil Rights, accessed April 12, 2014.

U.S. Department of Health and Human Services Substance Abuse and Mental Health Services Administration Center for Substance Abuse Treatment, "The Confidentiality of Alcohol and Drug Abuse Patient Records Regulation and the HIPAA Privacy Rule: Implications for Alcohol and Substance Abuse Programs.", June 2004. Available from the U.S. Department of Health and Human Services Substance Abuse and Mental Health Services Administration Center for Substance Abuse Treatment, accessed April 12, 2014.

"What are the specific privacy and security needs of HIV/AIDS patients?" What are the specific privacy and security needs of HIV/AIDS patients?

U.S. Department of Health and Human Services Health Information Technology and Quality Improvement, n.d. Web. April 12, 2014.

"What does Marketplace health insurance cover?" Topics. Centers for Medicare and Medicaid Services, n.d. Web. April 25, 2014.

"What is the difference between 'consent' and 'authorization' under the HIPAA Privacy Rule?" HIPAA Frequent Questions. U.S. Department of Health and Human Services Office for Civil Rights, March 14, 2006. Web. April 13, 2014.

3

Privacy and Security in Health Care

Domain 3 – *Review Questions*

1. The pillars of information security consist of _____.
   A. Confidentiality, Integrity, and Availability.
   B. Privacy, Integrity, and Availability.
   C. Confidentiality, Privacy, and Availability.
   D. Confidentiality, Integrity, and Privacy.

2. A patient wants to ensure the email he received from his primary care specialist is actually from the person he expects and not an impostor. Which concept will **BEST** ensure the sender of the email is actually the primary care specialist?
   A. Availability
   B. Confidentiality
   C. Digital Signatures
   D. Hashing

3. During _____ the subject's purported identity is validated by one or more credentials from the three main categories of factors: something the subject knows (password or passphrase), something the subject has (smartcard, token, or certificate), or something the subject is (a biometric such as a fingerprint or retina scan).
   A. Identification
   B. Accountability
   C. Access Control
   D. Authentication

4. HIPAA provides safe harbor against a breach if _____.
   A. The data was collected more than five years ago.
   B. The data was breached by a third party doing work on behalf of the original provider.
   C. The organization didn't understand information security and privacy.
   D. The information was properly encrypted.

5. Public Key Infrastructure or PKI is a form of _____.

    A. Asymmetric encryption.

    B. Symmetric encryption.

    C. Hashing functions.

    D. Digital signatures.

6. Complete the following with the **BEST** answer: Sharing of login credentials _____.

    A. Should be encouraged because it greatly reduced administrative burdens.

    B. Should be used only for workstations where the users know and trust each other very well.

    C. Should be discouraged but tolerated as employee moral must be preserved.

    D. Should be discouraged because non-repudiation will be violated.

7. _____ are the points at which assets are susceptible to an exploit or attack and are often attributed to unintended design flaws in the implementation of a hardware device, software application, or a system.

    A. Threats

    B. Vulnerabilities

    C. Likelihoods

    D. Risks

8. Separation of duties is **BEST** used in situations where _____.

    A. There must be high level of certainty about who performed an action.

    B. Systems must be available for several days no matter the circumstances.

    C. An individual must not have access to modify a record without permission.

    D. A process requires checks and balances that force collusion.

3

Privacy and Security in Health Care

9. An organization works mostly with older patients and wants to perform research on its patient population. The organization is subject to HIPAA, and an HCISPP has informed them they will need to remove all date information for patients older than 89 years of age. What is the **BEST** reason the organization must do this?

   A. HIPAA provided an arbitrary age to limit the population of studies.

   B. After the age of 89, there are considerably fewer people alive to match information to, and therefore an attacker can easily guess the individual.

   C. The organization believes the HCISPP is an "expert" and therefore is relying on them for an expert determination.

   D. Research on patients over 89 years of age is covered by legislation other than HIPAA.

10. Least privilege is a form of _____.

    A. Minimum necessary.

    B. Non-repudiation.

    C. Rotation of duties.

    D. Mandatory vacations.

Domain 4

Information Governance and Risk Management

THE INFORMATION SECURITY Governance and Risk Management domain of the HealthCare Information Security and Privacy Professional (HCISPP)® Common Body of Knowledge (CBK)® addresses the framework and policies, concepts, principles, structures, and standards used to establish criteria for the protection of information assets to instill holistically the criteria and assess the effectiveness of implemented protection. It includes issues of governance, organizational behavior, and security awareness.

Information security and privacy management establishes the foundation of a comprehensive and proactive security and privacy program(s) to ensure the protection of an organization's information assets. Depending on the structure of the organization, the privacy program may be separate or included in the information security program. For the sake of not being redundant, future references of information security management will be inclusive of privacy. Today's environment of highly interconnected, interdependent systems necessitates the requirement to understand the linkage between information technology and meeting business objectives.

Information security management communicates the risks accepted by the organization due to currently implemented security controls and continually works to cost effectively enhance the controls to minimize the risk to the company's information assets. Security management encompasses the administrative, technical, and physical controls necessary to adequately protect the confidentiality, integrity, and availability of information assets. Controls are manifested through a foundation of policies, procedures, standards, baselines, and guidelines.

Information security management practices that are used to manage risk include tools such as risk assessment and risk analysis. Information assets are classified, and through risk assessment, the threats and vulnerabilities related to these assets are categorized, and the appropriate safeguards to mitigate risk of compromise can be identified and prioritized.

Risk management minimizes loss to information assets due to undesirable events through identification, measurement, and control. It encompasses the overall security review, risk analysis, selection and evaluation of safeguards, cost–benefit analysis, management decision, and safeguard identification and implementation, along with ongoing effectiveness review. Risk management provides a mechanism to the organization to ensure that executive management knows current risks, and informed decisions can be made to use one of the following risk management principles: risk avoidance, risk transfer, risk mitigation, or risk acceptance, all described in more detail later in this chapter.

Information security management is concerned with regulatory, customer, employee, and business partner requirements for managing data as they flow between the various parties to support the processing and business use of the information. Confidentiality,

4

integrity, and availability of the information must be maintained throughout the process.

The healthcare environment can be exceedingly complex due to escalating threats and the myriad ways in which information must be utilized to provide patient-centered care, improve clinical outcomes, and support business goals and objectives. These challenges exist for all types of healthcare organizations, whether a large insurance conglomerate or small physicians practice group, and the cost of ignoring information-related risk continues to grow. Organizations must formally establish and be actively engaged with their security and privacy programs to address these challenges and ensure appropriate levels of due diligence and due care are provided for the cost-effective protection of sensitive health-related information. The HCISPP must understand how organizations manage information risk through security and privacy governance, basic risk management methodology and lifecycles, and the principle risk activities they are likely to support.

TOPICS

- **Security and Privacy Governance**
  - Information Governance
  - Governance Structures

- **Risk Management Methodology**
  - Approach (e.g., qualitative, quantitative)
  - Information Asset Identification
  - Asset Valuation
  - Vulnerability
  - Exposure
  - Threats
  - Likelihood
  - Impact
  - Risk
  - Controls
  - Residual Risk
  - Risk Acceptance

- **Information Risk Management Lifecycles**
  - NIST
  - CMS
  - ISO

- **Participate in Risk Management Activities**
  - Remediation Action Plans
  - Risk Treatment (e.g., mitigation/remediation, transfer, acceptance, avoidance)
  - Communications
  - Exception Handling
  - Reporting and Metrics

OBJECTIVES

According to the (ISC)[2] Candidate Information Bulletin, a HCISPP candidate is expected to understand:

- The planning, organization, and roles of individuals in identifying and securing an organization's information assets.

- The development and use of policies stating management's views and position on particular topics and the use of guidelines, standards, and procedures to support the policies.

Understand Security and Privacy Governance

In addition to understanding the types of information that may be collected, stored, transmitted, and deleted within a healthcare organization, a healthcare professional needs an understanding of the governance surrounding the information and basic risk management methodologies used by the healthcare industry. This understanding assists with ensuring their organization is complying with laws and regulations while maintaining high standards of information handling.

Many countries have enacted laws to protect the privacy of patients and their information at varying degrees.[1] Examples include the European Data Protection Directive[2] and the U.S. Health Insurance Portability and Accountability Act (HIPAA)[3]. Domain 2 of the HCISPP common body of knowledge "Regulatory Environments" describes the legal and regulatory requirements regarding healthcare information in detail. The focus of this section will be the information governance that is necessary to support those regulatory environments. Privacy governance is a component that is addressed within information governance and in some organizations may have a separate management chain or office.

Privacy laws and regulations pose "confidentiality" challenges for the healthcare professional. Healthcare personal information is becoming more easily accessible and available. While valuable for the patient and medical industry, this information can also be an excruciating liability for an organization that runs afoul of information privacy regulations and laws.

For example, in the United States, any organization or individual involved in the processing, storing, or transmitting of an individual's protected health information is subject to HIPAA. The "Privacy Rule" of HIPAA provides substantial monetary and civil penalties for those who fail to comply with the requirement to protect patient health information.[4] Every year, organizations pay fines in the millions of U.S. dollars due to violations of patient privacy often due to negligence or willful abuse of the information.

---

1   http://www.oecd.org/els/health-systems/HealthPolicyBrief_OECD-Report-on-Health-Information-Infrastructure.pdf

2   http://www.legislation.gov.uk/ukpga/1998/29/contents

3   http://www.gpo.gov/fdsys/pkg/PLAW-104publ191/html/PLAW-104publ191.htm

4   HIPAA violations often amount to millions of dollars in fines. See the following website for information about specific fines: http://www.hhs.gov/ocr/privacy/index.html

Another example is the European Data Protection Directive. This directive only allows the processing of personal data under specific circumstances such as:

1. When processing is necessary for compliance with a legal action.

2. When processing is required to protect the life of the subject.

3. When the subject of the personal data has provided consent.

4. When the processing is performed within the law and scope of "public interest."

The four requirements listed above reflect only a small portion of the directive. The directive further states what rights the subject has, such as objecting at any time to the processing of his or her personal data if the use is for direct marketing purposes. Recently, several Internet search companies and social media companies have been cited as not complying with this law. These organizations have been accused of using the personal data of the subject for direct marketing efforts without the subject's permission. The HCISPPs working for a health-marketing firm in the European Union must understand the impact of these requirements on how information will be processed, stored, and transmitted in their organization.

Information Governance

The basic principles of security and privacy discussed in domain 3 "Privacy and Security in Healthcare" along with legal provisions, guidance, and best practices are the building blocks for information and privacy governance. They help to establish a consistent manner for the appropriate handling of patient, corporate, and personal information.

Information systems are often the focus of healthcare related information security concerns, but the focus should be on the information type irrespective of what form it is in. Information can be stored on computers or in file cabinets. In either case, the information may require specific handling instructions depending on its sensitivity. Within a healthcare organization, there is not only the personal information of patients and employees but also corporate information such as financials and accounting records. Depending on the role of the practitioners, they may encounter more than one type. Organizations must implement safeguards through information governance for all types of information. Although all types and forms of information should be considered by an organization's information governance framework, this section will primarily focus on personal health information.

Another important concept regarding information governance is ownership of the information. For example, perhaps the information technology department (IT) owns and maintains the computer that information is stored on, but the information is not owned by IT. The information is owned by the practice area. IT shouldn't be the one making decisions regarding the information's relevance to address the business area's needs; IT is focused on delivering technology. Moreover, the practice area should define the business requirements concerning its information. The practice area may need to consult IT to identify a solution that best fits its need if one isn't easily discernible. For example, consider a study observing cholesterol levels for patients on low-carb diets. IT doesn't know how often and for how long a patient's cholesterol and eating habits need to be documented or retained for the study. They would be defined by the practice area conducting the study. It is important to note that records retention may have time requirements based on laws or policies to consider outside of the business need for retention. Records retention and information system roles and responsibilities will be discussed further in the next section "Governance Structures."

When an organization evaluates the security and privacy needs of the information it interacts with, it is necessary for the organization to evaluate various policies and determine what is applicable. Depending on the role of the organization, it may need to consider international, country, or industry laws and standards. After identifying applicable policies, an organization will need to perform a risk assessment to determine the impact of non-compliance based on an organization-wide risk perspective that is discussed further in the section on "Understanding Basic Risk Management Methodology".

Governance Structures

There is no perfect structure for information governance within an organization. Governance structures are dependent on the adoption by the organization; one size does not fit all. However, there are specific components that should be present in any governance structure. Fundamentally, there should always be a legal component. They are best equipped to navigate the complex legislative language, discern an organization's legal obligations, and provide professional legal advice. Another is a compliance component. As with any other organization, policy is necessary to have enforceable process to ensure employees are adhering to the policy. Internal audit can fulfill this role, or independent assessments can be obtained through third-party sources. The other component is IT. It is essential to have someone who is able to implement technical solutions to the privacy and security requirements that are defined. Finally, senior management must be involved. Senior management buy-in is crucial for any initiative to be successful. They are generally the one(s) who champion the initiative and are able to get the money and dedicated resources to enable organizational change.

Organizations may have their information governance maintained within a records retention office. This office has varying degrees of the components discussed above and is generally held responsible for setting the policies and procedures for the creation, storage, maintenance, and destruction of records.

In addition to the components described, there are also common roles that are related to information and privacy governance that should be understood by the HCISPP.

Information System Owner

This can be IT as discussed in the example given in the "Information Governance" section, or it can be another department or even organization. It is the entity that is responsible for the operation and maintenance of the information system that the information is stored on.

Information Owner/Steward

This is generally the business area in an organization as discussed in the "Information Governance" section. They have the best understanding of the information and are generally responsible for classifying or categorizing it. The classification of information may involve a security or privacy expert who can assist with identifying what is PHI or sensitive. Ultimately, the information owner/steward is responsible for the information and safeguarding it.

Information System Security Officer (ISSO)

Not all information systems or organizations will have an ISSO. The role of an ISSO is to implement the appropriate security controls needed to meet the security requirements that ensure the confidentiality, integrity, and availability of the information. If an ISSO is not assigned to the information system, then ultimately the system owner and data steward are responsible.

End User

Any employee who creates, transmits, stores, or deletes an organization's information is an end user. Whether the information is handwritten or typed doesn't make a difference nor does emailing vs. standard postal mail. That employee is still interacting with the organization's information and needs to be cognizant of the policies and procedures and his or her role in information and privacy governance.

Although these roles are discussed, information security and privacy is every employee's responsibility. Whether he or she is an end user that needs to understand the policies and procedures or an employee whose job function directly involves creating or implementing those policies and procedures, the employee must understand his or her role in ensuring the protection of the organization's information.

Basic Risk Management Methodology

All organizations need a process that is consistent and continuous to manage risk. In addition, risk should also be managed with an organization-wide perspective to ensure that it is holistic when considering business and security requirements. An organization's process to manage risk is based on its risk management methodology. The methodology is the set of principles that provides a framework for processes and sub-processes (within any process). For example, U.S. NIST SP 800-39[5] provides a risk management process that many organizations align with in *Figure 4.1*. Their risk management process is based on 4 components.

1. **Framing Risk** – Produce the risk strategy, identify risk tolerance, assumptions, and constraints

2. **Assessing Risk** – Identify threats, vulnerabilities, impact, likelihood, and determine risk

3. **Responding to Risk** – Identify a consistent manner to respond to risk from an organization-wide perspective

4. **Monitoring Risk** – Continuously monitor the risk environment

The risk management process should be continuous and flexible to be able to adjust to the dynamic regulatory and threat environments impacting the organization. The figure depicts this by illustrating that information and communication flows both ways from all components.

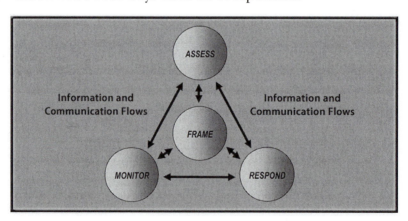

Figure 4.1 – **Risk Management Process**

A risk strategy is the approach or direction an organization will take towards risk management. For example, the U.S. NIST SP 800-39 refers to a risk management strategy as something that is produced to address "how organizations intend to

---

5   http://csrc.nist.gov/publications/nistpubs/800-39/SP800-39-final.pdf

assess risk, respond to risk, and monitor risk- making explicit and transparent the risk perceptions that organizations routinely use in making both investment and operational decisions."[6] Establishing a risk tolerance is one component within the risk strategy. In addition, the organization will need to consider other constraints or assumptions. Types of constraints and assumptions will be discussed later in this chapter.

Once a risk strategy is developed, a risk process can be defined and implemented that addresses risk assessment, risk response, and risk monitoring. The strategy describes the what. It describes what the organization is going to do regarding risk management, while the risk process describes how the organization will accomplish it. For example, a healthcare organization may decide that part of its risk strategy is a risk tolerance of zero breaches. If that is the case, then the organization will have to invest significantly in risk monitoring, data loss prevention, and information monitoring and ensure risk assessments are conducted on a more frequent basis.

Stakeholders within an organization decide what their risk tolerance is, but ultimately the head of the organization accepts the impact of the risk decisions. Risk stakeholders will be dependent on the size and structure of the organization. A smaller sized organization may designate the owner with his or her legal counsel as the risk strategy team, whereas a mid-size organization may elect all of its executive management, or a larger organization may elect a board of directors. In each case, the stakeholders will define the risk tolerance for the organization. Risk tolerance is the threshold for an acceptable level of risk for the organization. Different risk management frameworks may have different names for risk tolerance. For example, the Committee of Sponsoring Organizations (COSO) refers to it as "risk appetite" in its enterprise risk management framework.[7] It is still setting a threshold for the organization concerning risk.

Often risk tolerance is compliance based from a legal perspective for healthcare organizations. Compliance may be with HIPAA or the Data Protection Act and is dependent on the organizations and what regulatory environments impact them. Although the threshold may be defined in this manner, an organization may choose to raise or lower it depending on its organizational structure. For example, a smaller company may decide that one breach of information would incur a cost it could not recover from. The cost could be from a monetary or reputational perspective. On the other hand, a larger organization that has substantial funding and is well established may be able to accept a higher risk tolerance. In either situation, the risk tolerance will be defined and a risk strategy will be developed in conjunction with it.

6　http://csrc.nist.gov/publications/nistpubs/800-30-rev1/sp800_30_r1.pdf

7　http://www.coso.org/documents/ERM-Understanding%20%20Communicating%20Risk%20 Appetite-WEB_FINAL_r9.pdf

Organizations must decide how they will access, respond, and monitor risk even if that choice is to do nothing. For example, organizations may conclude they are not at risk and simply choose to not assess, respond, or monitor risk. Their process would be to do nothing, which is not the best risk management methodology. Even if an organization is not at risk at a given moment, changes within the organization or environment surrounding it may have introduced a new risk. In addition, the level for an already identified risk may have changed and will no longer be acceptable. Therefore, risk assessments should be performed continuously to ensure the organization is able to understand its risk and manage it.

Figure 4.1 illustrates the continuous nature of risk assessments and how it provides information to decision makers in the framing component and helps direct the response component when responding to information and privacy risks. This is why it is necessary for risk assessments to be well maintained and well communicated throughout the life cycle of the information.

Risk assessment (the term risk analysis is sometimes interchanged with risk assessment) is the process of identifying information risks, estimating the potential loss for each risk to the organization, and prioritizing the information risks. As an example, U.S. NIST SP 800-30 rev.1 provides a general overview of steps within a risk assessment process illustrated in *Figure 4.2*. The steps are:

- **Step 1** – Prepare for Assessment -An organization accomplishes this within the framing component of the risk management process.
- **Step 2** – Conduct Assessment - Factors to complete this step will be discussed in detail further in the chapter.
- **Step 3** – Communicate Results – Inform the stakeholders of the results of the risk assessment so they can make well-informed decisions.
- **Step 4** – Maintain Assessment - Ensure the documentation for risk assessment is kept up-to-date so that the information can be used in other assessments or to make risk based decisions. In addition, monitor the factors identified in the risk assessment for any significant changes.

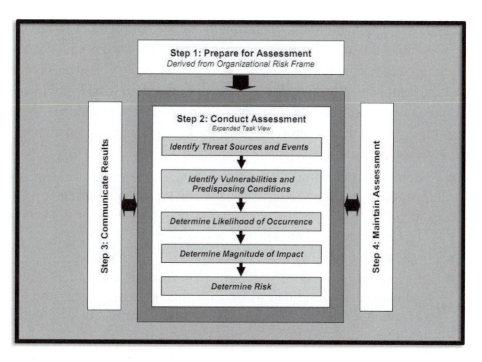

Figure 4.2 – **Risk Assessment Steps**

Approach

There are two approaches an organization can use to assess risk, qualitative and quantitative. Quantitative risk assessment is using something that is measurable. An example is calculating the Annual Loss Expectancy (ALE) of a medical billing system that was bought for $100,000, bills $120,000/year on average and can be exploited on a bi-monthly basis. This is a standard financial calculation where:

ALE = Annual Rate of Occurrence (ARO) x Single Loss Expectancy (SLE)

> **ARO** = *times it can be exploited/year = 6*
>
> **SLE** = *$100,000*
>
> **ALE** = *$600,000*

Therefore, the risk is measurable. Risk is generally not this simple to calculate. Often, the risk assessment an organization conducts is a mixture of both quantitative and qualitative.

Qualitative risk assessment is using something that is descriptive. A common approach is to describe risk in relative terms such as "high", "medium", and "low". It is important to note here that some organizations may state that their risk assessment is quantitative and based on scientific methods. Although scientific methods are generally quantitative, information security and privacy risk assessment

201

is generally performed using qualitative methods. For qualitative numbers or measures to be meaningful to the organization, a scale or criteria must be created. Giving something a rating of 9 on a scale of 1 to 10 is great but not on a scale of 1 to 100. Additionally, what is the difference between a risk of "9" and a risk of "8" in terms of the organization's mission? It is difficult to ascertain what is used when an organization creates its own scale. The criteria used to create the scale may be based on descriptions and is then interpretive and would not be considered quantitative. A qualitative risk assessment is typically conducted when:

- The risk assessors available for the organization have limited expertise in quantitative risk assessment; that is, assessors typically do not require as much experience in risk assessment when conducting a qualitative assessment.
- The timeframe to complete the risk assessment is short.
- Implementation is typically easier.
- The organization does not have a significant amount of data readily available that can assist with the risk assessment, and as a result, descriptions, estimates, and ordinal scales (such as high, medium, and low) must be used to express risk.
- The assessors and team available for the organization are long-term employees and have significant experience with the business and critical systems.

The assessment team requests documentation and sets up interviews with organizational members for the purposes of identifying vulnerabilities, threats, and countermeasures within the environment. All levels of staff should be represented, to include:

- Senior management
- Line management
- Business unit owners
- Temporary or casual staff (i.e., interns)
- Business partners, as appropriate
- Remote workers, as appropriate
- Any other staff deemed appropriate to task

It is important to note that staff across all business units within scope for the risk assessment should be interviewed. It is not necessary to interview every staff person within a unit; a representative sample is usually sufficient.

Once interviews are completed, the analysis of the data gathered can be completed. This can include matching the threat to a vulnerability, matching threats to assets, determining how likely the threat is to exploit the

4

vulnerability, and determining the impact to the organization in the event an exploit is successful. Analysis also includes a matching of current and planned countermeasures (i.e., protection) to the threat–vulnerability pair.

When the matching is completed, risk can be calculated. In a qualitative analysis, the product of likelihood and impact produces the level of risk. The higher the risk level, the more immediate is the need for the organization to address the issue and to protect the organization from harm. Once risk has been determined, additional countermeasures can be recommended to minimize, transfer, or avoid the risk. When this is completed, the risk that is left over—after countermeasures have been applied to protect against the risk—is also calculated. This is the residual risk, or risk left over after countermeasure application.

Information Asset Identification

Identifying information assets is essential in any risk assessment. All information has value and must be identified in order to assess risk appropriately. Without knowing what assets are critical and which would be most at risk within an organization, one would deem it not possible to protect those assets appropriately. For example, if an organization is bound by HIPAA regulations, but it does not know how electronic personally identifiable information may be at risk, the organization may make significant mistakes in securing that information, such as neglecting to protect against certain risks or applying too much protection against low-level risks.

Risk assessment also takes into account special circumstances under which assets may require additional protection, such as with regulatory compliance. Many times, these regulatory requirements are the means to completion of an appropriate risk assessment for the organization, as meeting compliance objectives requires the risk assessment to be done. It is important to note that enterprise tools exist to scan networks and can identify systems. Although some of those tools are able to identify certain types of information such as social security numbers, it is ultimately the organization's responsibility to understand the information it has and its value.

Asset Valuation

Organizational information will fall under a type of information asset valuation, tangible or non-tangible. Tangible assets are those that have a physical presence. For example, information may be stored on a computer and that computer has a value that is generally assessed by the original cost minus depreciation or market value. It is important to note that when determining the value of information systems, there are several components that must be accounted for. The physical cost of the equipment should be considered along with the configuration time spent, including controls implementation, documentation, risk assessments, etc. Non-tangible is far more difficult to assess.

How, then, is information value determined? Similarly to risk analysis, information valuation methods may be descriptive (subjective) or metric (objective). Subjective methods include the creation, dissemination, and collection of data from checklists or surveys. An organization's policies or the regulatory compliance requirements that it must follow may also determine information's worth. Metric, or statistical, measures may provide a more objective view of information valuation. Each of these methods has its uses within an organization.

Tangible Asset Valuation

Tangible assets are typically those that have a physical presence. These assets are typically valued based on the original cost of the assets minus depreciation. These assets are often depreciated to zero for account purposes. For a risk assessment purpose, the HCISPP needs to be aware of the original cost but more importantly the replacement cost. As suppliers and vendors come into the market and leave the market, the cost of replacing a specific appliance, server, or type of lock may change due to supply and demand. Additionally, assets originally depreciated may gain in value if the supply is less than the demand. Certain assets may also become outdated, and new assets may be required to replace the functionality or utility they provided. Ways to determine tangle asset value include:

- Original cost minus depreciation
- Actual market value through market research
  - Consider online auction sites that show what others are actually buying the asset for
  - Call vendors and get updated quotes for replacement cost comparison
- Cost of switching to a competing asset or capability

Intangible Asset Valuation

Intangible assets are assets that are not physical. Examples of intangible property include but are not limited to:

- Trademarks
- Patents
- Copyrights
- Business processes
- Brand recognition
- Intellectual property
- Protected Health Information

Intangible assets may also be further classified as definite or indefinite:

■ A definite intangible asset is an intangible asset with a definite expiration period. An example of a definite intangible asset is a patent. The patent has value only as long as it is enforceable. Once the patent expires, it no longer has value.

■ An indefinite intangible asset is an intangible asset with an indefinite expiration period. An example would be an organization's brand. The brand is expected to be maintained and preserved into the foreseeable future.

Intangible assets can be quite difficult to determine a value. What is the value of the "HCISSP^{SM}" service mark? It is valuable to the members who hold the credential, and it has a value to (ISC)^2, the organization that owns the trademark. But what is the total value of the service mark? To approximate the value of an intangible asset, the following methods are considered generally acceptable:

■ **Cost** – The cost to create the asset and the cost to replace the asset. This approach must be used cautiously because rarely does the value of intangible assets only equal the creation or acquisition cost.

■ **Capitalization of Historic Profits** – If getting a patent, creating a brand, or developing a new process directly led to increased profits or efficiencies, those profits or efficiencies can be considered part of the overall value of the asset.

■ **Cost Avoidance or Savings** – If acquiring the trademark of a product service allowed an organization to avoid paying royalties, those savings can be considered part of the asset's value.

The HCISPP should seek the aid of a financial expert when attempting to determine the intangible value of an asset. These are some of the most complex and valuable assets an organization has and require thorough valuation efforts.

Vulnerability

Part of a risk assessment is identifying vulnerabilities. The U.S. NIST SP 800-30 rev 1 states that "A vulnerability is a weakness in an information system, system security procedures, internal controls, or implementation that could be exploited by a threat source."[8] There are many software tools that can be used to scan and identify software vulnerabilities in an information system. It is important to highlight that vulnerabilities may exist in other areas other than the information system itself. A few examples of vulnerabilities are:

---

8   http://csrc.nist.gov/publications/nistpubs/800-30-rev1/sp800_30_r1.pdf page 9

- A secretary or guard who is absent from a security station that limits access to an information system.
- Neglecting to require users to sign an acknowledgement of their roles and responsibilities with regard to information security and privacy, as well as an acknowledgement that they have read, understand, and agree to abide by the organization's policies.
- Patching and configuration of an organization's information systems are done on an ad hoc basis and, therefore, are neither documented nor up to date.

Exposure

In the industry, there are some organizations that may use the term 'exposure'. For example, MITRE, a U.S. non-profit organization, maintains the Common Vulnerabilities and Exposures (CVE). It is a dictionary of names for common vulnerabilities and exposures that have been identified in the industry. MITRE defines an exposure as "a system configuration issue or a mistake in software that allows access to information or capabilities that can be used by a hacker as a stepping-stone into a system or network."[9] This is a subset of the definition for vulnerabilities discussed above. In addition to exposure is the term predisposing condition that is often used in the industry and is also a subset of vulnerabilities. U.S. NIST uses the term in *Figure 4.2* Risk Assessment Steps.

Threats

U.S. NIST SP 800-30 rev. 1 describes a threat as "any circumstance or event with the potential to adversely impact organizational operations and assets, individuals, other organizations, or the Nation through an information system via unauthorized access, destruction, disclosure, or modification of information, and/or denial of service." A threat may be a single circumstance or event or a set of related circumstances or events that can adversely have an impact. A threat event or circumstances are caused by threat sources. U.S. NIST also defines a threat source as "(i) the intent and method targeted at the exploitation of vulnerability; or (ii) a situation and method that may accidentally exploit a vulnerability."[10] Threat sources are described as not always malicious; they may also be accidental. Some common categories for threat sources are:

---

9   http://cve.mitre.org/about/terminology.html

10   http://csrc.nist.gov/publications/nistpubs/800-30-rev1/sp800_30_r1.pdf page 8

- **Human** – Malicious outsider or insider, human error
- **Natural** – Fire, flood, tornado, hurricane, snow storm, earthquake
- **Technical** – Hardware or software failure, malicious code, use of new technologies such as wireless
- **Environmental** – Hazardous waste, biological agent
- **Operational** – A process (manual or automated) that affects the confidentiality, integrity, or availability of the information

This list is not all-inclusive. Other categories and sources within each category exist along with other taxonomies that have been created in the industry. It is the HCISPP's responsibility to assist with identifying the threat sources during the risk assessment process that could leverage a vulnerability and impact the organization's information. It is important to note that different threat sources may have the same threat event as a result. For example, patient information on a server may not be available due to a snow storm that caused power failure for the server, or a denial of service attack may cause the server to be unavailable. Either way the threat event is the server and health information being unavailable. Both threat sources need to be considered in the process to ensure the organization can make well-informed decisions.

Likelihood

U.S. NIST 800-30 rev. 1 describes likelihood as "a weighted risk factor based on an analysis of the probability that a given threat is capable of exploiting a given vulnerability (or set of vulnerabilities)."[11] Likelihood is generally viewed as adversarial and non-adversarial. For the adversarial view, it is necessary to consider the adversary's capabilities, intent, and target. For the non-adversarial view, it is common to consider historical data. Initially, organizations that do not have trending analysis available to them may use an ordinal scale with labels such as low, medium, and high to score likelihood ratings. Other taxonomies exist in the industry such as the method presented in *Figure 4.3*.

---

11 http://csrc.nist.gov/publications/nistpubs/800-30-rev1/sp800_30_r1.pdf page 10

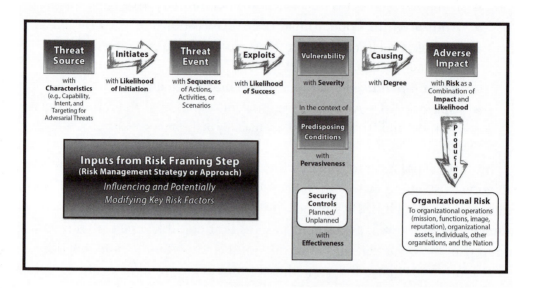

*Figure 4.3 –***Determining Likelihood of Organizational Risk**

Once a value has been determined for likelihood, it will be used in computing risk as discussed in the upcoming "Risk" section.

Impact

U.S. NIST SP 800-30 rev. 1 describes impact as "the magnitude of harm that can be expected to result from the consequences of unauthorized disclosure of information, unauthorized modification of information, unauthorized destruction of information, or loss of information or information system availability."[12] When a health organization considers impact, it needs to also consider other entities outside of itself. For example, a health organization may have PHI that belongs to a specific patient. Therefore, that patient needs to be considered along with any other organization or entity that may be impacted.

In addition, each organization needs to explicitly define definitions for impact, which may include anything such as loss of life, loss of money, or loss of reputation within their scale. Impact is considered in the same manner as likelihood and given a value that will be used in computing risk as discussed in the following section (on Risk). It is also important to note that within the industry, impact may be called consequence in some taxonomies.

---

12   http://csrc.nist.gov/publications/nistpubs/800-30-rev1/sp800_30_r1.pdf page 11

Risk

According to U.S. NIST SP 800-30, risk is defined as "a measure of the extent to which an entity is threatened by a potential circumstance or event, and is typically a function of: (i) the adverse impacts that would arise if the circumstance or event occurs; and (ii) the likelihood of occurrence."[13] If risk is a function of impact and likelihood and likelihood is a function of vulnerability and threat, then the factors that determine risk are impact, likelihood, vulnerability, and threats as illustrated in *Figure 4.4* Risk Factors.

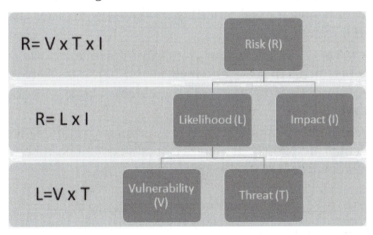

$R= V \times T \times I$ — Risk (R)

$R= L \times I$ — Likelihood (L), Impact (I)

$L=V \times T$ — Vulnerability (V), Threat (T)

Figure 4.4 – **Risk Factors**

Once all risks have been evaluated, they can then be prioritized because not all risks will receive the same amount of attention. Most organizations do not have unlimited amounts of resources to dedicate towards risks. Therefore, they need to be strategic when deciding how to respond to each risk by making use of the risk tolerance and risk strategy the organization has already defined.

Organizations may also decide to aggregate risk; this is when they roll up one or more lower prioritized risks into a higher prioritized risk. This may be done to better manage the scope or show the relationship between different risks such as a cause and effect.[14] When aggregating risk, an organization should not ignore the risk associated with those that are rolled up.

---

13   http://csrc.nist.gov/publications/nistpubs/800-30-rev1/sp800_30_r1.pdf page 12

14   http://csrc.nist.gov/publications/nistpubs/800-30-rev1/sp800_30_r1.pdf page 13

Controls

Controls regarding the security and privacy of healthcare information are safeguards and counter measures that are implemented to mitigate, lessen, or avoid a risk. Controls are generally grouped into different categories. U.S. NIST uses three classes in its descriptions of controls based on definitions from U.S. FIPS 200[15] that are based on a control's function:

- *Management* - Controls based on the management of risk and the management of information systems security. These are generally policies and procedures. These controls are also called "administrative controls."

- *Technical* - Controls that are primarily implemented and executed through mechanisms contained in the hardware, software, and firmware of the components of the system. These controls are also known as "logical controls."

- *Operational* - Controls that are primarily implemented and executed by people (as opposed to systems). These controls are also known as "physical controls."

In addition to these classes, U.S. NIST has defined 18 control families based on the minimum security requirements defined in U.S. FIPS 200. *Figure 4.5* illustrates their relationship to the classes.[16]

IDENTIFIER	FAMILY	CLASS
AC	Access Control	Technical
AT	Awareness and Training	Operational
AU	Audit and Accountability	Technical
CA	Security Assessment and Authorization	Management
CM	Configuration Management	Operational
CP	Contingency Planning	Operational
IA	Identification and Authentication	Technical
IR	Incident Response	Operational
MA	Maintenance	Operational
MP	Media Protection	Operational
PE	Physical and Environmental Protection	Operational
PL	Planning	Management
PS	Personnel Security	Operational
RA	Risk Assessment	Management
SA	System and Services Acquisition	Management
SC	System and Communications Protection	Technical
SI	System and Information Integrity	Operational
PM	Program Management	Management

Figure 4.5 – **Security Control Classes, Families, and Identifiers**

---

15   http://csrc.nist.gov/publications/fips/fips200/FIPS-200-final-march.pdf

16   http://csrc.nist.gov/publications/nistpubs/800-53-Rev3/sp800-53-rev3-final_updated-errata_05-01-2010.pdf page 6

The NIST framework is voluntary for healthcare organizations in the U.S. Other organizations within differing industries and economies may have different terms or a different number of categories depending on their definitions and how they choose to delineate their categories. For example, some relate control categories to the time line of a security incident as illustrated in *Figure 4.6*:

- **Directive** - Controls designed to specify acceptable rules of behavior within an organization.
- **Deterrent** - Controls designed to discourage people from violating security directives.
- **Preventive** - Controls implemented to prevent a security incident or information breach.
- **Compensating** - Controls implemented to substitute for the loss of primary controls and mitigate risk down to an acceptable level.
- **Detective** - Controls designed to signal a warning when a security control has been breached.
- **Corrective** - Controls implemented to remedy circumstance, mitigate damage, or restore controls.
- **Recovery** - Controls implemented to restore conditions to normal after a security incident.

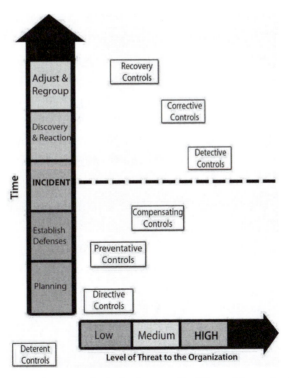

Figure 4.6 – **Continuum of Controls Relative to the Time Line of a Security Incident**

In either example, controls are still identified for the purpose of safeguards and countermeasures to address risk and different labels that can be used in conjunction with each other. An example is illustrated in *Figure 4.7* Control Example for Types and Categories.

	Directive	Deterrent	Preventative	Detective	Corrective	Recovery	Compensating
Administrative	Policy	Policy	User registration procedure	Review violation reports	Termination	DR Plan	Supervision
							Job rotation
							Logging
Technical	Config standards	Warning banner	Password based login	Logs	Unplug, isolate, & terminate connection	Backups	CCTV
			IPS	IDS			
							Keystroke monitoring
Physical	Authorized Personnel Only signs, traffic lights	Beware of Dog sign	Fence	Sentry	Fire extinguisher	Rebuild	Layered defense
				CCTV			

Figure 4.7 – **Control Example for Types and Categories**

Compensating controls are an important part of the risk management process. They are introduced when the existing capabilities of a system do not support the requirements of a policy. Compensating controls can be managerial, operational, or technical. Although an existing system may not support the required controls, there may exist other technology or processes that can supplement the existing environment, closing the gap in controls, meeting policy requirements, and reducing overall risk. For example, the access control policy may state that the authentication process must be encrypted when performed over the Internet. Adjusting an application to natively support encryption for authentication purposes may be too costly. Secure Socket Layer (SSL), an encryption protocol, can be employed and layered on top of the authentication process to support the policy statement. In addition, management processes, such as authorization, supervision, and administration, can be used to compensate for gaps in the control environment. The critical points to consider when addressing compensating controls are:

- Do not compromise stated policy requirements.
- Ensure that the compensating controls do not adversely affect risk or increase exposure to threats.
- Manage all compensating controls in accordance with established practices and policies.
- Compensating controls designated as temporary should be removed after they have served their purpose and another, more permanent control should be established.

Residual Risk

Keep in mind that it is typically not possible to completely eliminate the risk in a given area while still allowing functionality. The use of compensating controls allows an organization to reduce that risk down to a level that is acceptable or at least more manageable. This level of risk is called the residual risk. It is the risk leftover after a risk treatment option has been implemented. The section on *Risk Treatment* within this domain discusses risk treatment further and the options an organization has when addressing risk. The risk treatment term mitigating/remediating risk involves implementing compensating controls and can also be temporary solutions to accommodate a short-term change or support the evolution of a new application, business development, or major project. Implementing compensating controls is not the only choice an organization has to address risk. An important thing to note with residual risk is that allowing a system to continue to operate while implementing controls or not means that the residual risk is being accepted by default.

Risk Acceptance

Once the findings from the assessment have been consolidated and the calculations have been completed, it is time to present a finalized report to senior management. This can be done in a written report, by presentation or out brief, or by both means. Any written reports should include an acknowledgment to the participants, a summary of the approach taken, findings in detail (in either tabulated or graphical form), recommendations for remediation of the findings, and a summary. Organizations are encouraged to develop their own formats, to make the most of the activity and the information collected and analyzed. Once senior management has received the report, it is time for them in conjunction with any other stakeholders to select the risk treatment option for the risk(s) identified in the assessment. The section on "Risk Treatment" addresses options such as mitigation/remediation, transfer, avoidance, in addition to acceptance.

If the risk treatment option chosen is to accept risk, whether that be residual or all of the risk, the "Who is assigned and responsible for risk?" is a very serious question, with an intriguing answer: it depends. Ultimately, the organization (i.e., senior management or stakeholders) owns the risks that are present during operation of the company. Senior management, however, may rely on the business area or information owner/steward to assist in the identification of risks so that they can be mitigated, transferred, or avoided. The organization also likely expects that the owners/stewards will minimize or mitigate risk as they work, based upon policies, procedures, and regulations present in the environment. If expectations are not met, consequences such as disciplinary action, termination, or prosecution will usually result.

Here is an example: A claims processor is working with a medical healthcare claim submitted to his organization for completion. The claim contains electronic personally identifiable healthcare information for a person the claims processor knows. Although he has acknowledged his responsibilities for the protection of the data and the privacy of the patient, he calls his mother, who is a good friend of the individual who filed the claim. His mother in turn calls multiple people, who in turn contact the person who filed the claim. The claimant contacts an attorney citing a breach of privacy, and the employee and company are sued for the intentional breach of information. Several things are immediately apparent from this example. The employee is held immediately accountable for his action in intentionally exploiting a vulnerability (i.e., sensitive information was inappropriately released, according to United States federal law— HIPAA). While he was custodian of the data (and a co-owner of the risk), the court also determined that the company was co-owner of the risk and hence bore the responsibility for compensating the victim (in this example, the claimant). Organizations that choose not to manage risk will by default be placed in a position to accept it.

Understand Information Risk Management Lifecycles

A risk management lifecycle minimizes loss to information assets due to undesirable events through identification, measurement, and control. It encompasses the overall information security and privacy review, risk analysis, selection and evaluation of safeguards, cost–benefit analysis, management decision, and safeguard identification and implementation, along with ongoing effectiveness review. Risk management provides a mechanism to the organization to ensure that executive management knows current risks, and informed decisions can be made to use one of the risk management treatments: risk avoidance, risk transfer, risk mitigation, or risk acceptance.

Multiple frameworks and methodologies have been created to support security, auditing, and risk assessment including implemented security controls. These resources are valuable to assist in the design and testing of a risk management program. The following frameworks and methodologies have each gained a degree of acceptance within the auditing or information security and privacy community and assist with information security, privacy, and auditing. Although the origins of several of them were not specifically designed to support information security and privacy, many of the processes within these practices help professionals identify and implement controls in support of the confidentiality, integrity, and availability of their information.

In addition, some organizations have developed and implemented tools and frameworks to assist with the compliance of particular laws or regulations. An example is the U.S. Center for Medicaid Services (CMS) who created the Administrative Simplification Enforcement Tool (ASET),[17] which is a web-based application that enables the filing of HIPAA complaints by individuals or organizations against a healthcare provider, health plan, or clearinghouse. The complaint can be filed anonymously if selected but still provides demographic information and details for the alleged violation.

U.S. NIST SP 800–30, 800-37, 800-39 and 800–66

These methodologies are qualitative methods established for the use of the United States federal government and the global public, but they are particularly used in a voluntary fashion by regulated industries, such as healthcare. The 800–66 is written specifically with HIPAA clients in mind. While the 800-39 focuses on organizational risk management, 800-37 is the application of the risk management framework to information systems, and 800-30 focuses on risk assessments.

The 800-39 discusses the organizational tiers and how risk management is multi-tiered, as illustrated in *Figure* 4.8.[18] The document states that this is the best approach for implementing risk management into the organization so as to give a holistic view of risk through constant communication and still maintaining a shared interest in the business success of the organization.

STRATEGIC RISK

☑ Traceability and Transparency of Risk-Based Decisions

☑ Organization-Wide Risk Awareness

☑ Inter-Tier and Intra-Tier Communications

☑ Feedback Loop for Continuous Improvement

Tier 1
Organization

Tier 2
Mission/Business Processes

Tier 3
Information Systems

TACTICAL RISK

Figure 4.8 – **Multi-tiered organization-wide risk management**

---

17 https://htct.hhs.gov/aset/HIPAA%20Transactions%20and%20Code%20Sets.jsp?agree=yes

18 http://csrc.nist.gov/publications/nistpubs/800-39/SP800-39-final.pdf page 9

The 800-37 lists the steps for the Risk Management Framework (RMF) as illustrated in *Figure 4.9* and describes the tasks that are involved within each step. The RMF is designed to provide a structured process to implement information security and risk management activities into the system development life cycle.[19]

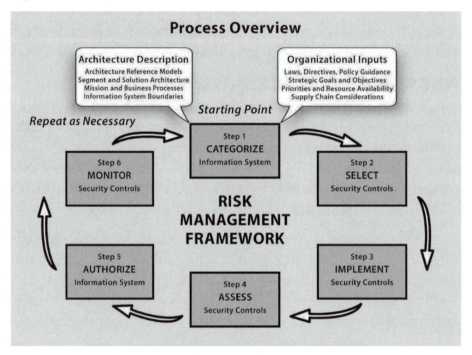

Figure 4.9 – **Risk Management Framework Steps**

ISO 27000 (Formally Known as ISO17799/BS7799)

The BS 7799/ISO 17799 standard can be used as a basis for developing security standards and security management practices. The U.K. Department of Trade and Industry (DTI) Code of Practice (CoP) for information security, which was developed with the support of the industry in 1993, became British Standard 7799 in 1995. BS 7799 was subsequently revised in 1999 to add certification and accreditation components, which became Part 2 of BS 7799. Part 1 of BS 7799 became ISO 17799 and was published as ISO 17799:2005, as the first international information security management standard by the International Organization for Standardization (ISO) and International Electrotechnical Commission (IEC). ISO 17799 was modified in June 2005 and renamed ISO/IEC 17799:2005. It contains 134 detailed information security controls based upon the following 11 areas:

---

19 http://csrc.nist.gov/publications/nistpubs/800-37-rev1/sp800-37-rev1-final.pdf page 8

1. Information security policy
2. Organizing information security
3. Asset management
4. Human resources security
5. Physical and environmental security
6. Communications and operations management
7. Access control
8. Information systems acquisition, development, and maintenance
9. Information security incident management
10. Business continuity management
11. Compliance

The ISO standards are grouped together by topic areas, and the ISO/IEC27000 series has been designated as the information security management series. For example, the 27002 Code of Practice has replaced ISO/IEC 17799:2005, "Information Technology—Security Techniques—Code of Practice for Information Security Management." This is consistent with how ISO has named other topic areas, such as the ISO 9000 series for quality management.

ISO/IEC 27002:2005 was released in October 2005 and specifies the requirements for establishing, implementing, operating, monitoring, reviewing, maintaining, and improving a documented information security management system, taking into consideration the company's business risks. This management standard was based on BS 7799, Part 2 and provides information on building information security management systems and guidelines for auditing the system.

COSO

The Committee of Sponsoring Organizations of the Treadway Commission (COSO) was formed in 1985 to sponsor the National Commission on Fraudulent Financial Reporting, which studied factors that lead to fraudulent financial reporting and produced recommendations for public companies, their auditors, the Securities Exchange Commission, and other regulators. COSO identifies five areas of internal control necessary to meet the financial reporting and disclosure objectives. These include:

1. Control Environment
2. Risk Assessment
3. Control Activities
4. Information and Communication
5. Monitoring

The COSO internal control model has been adopted as a framework by some organizations working toward Sarbanes–Oxley Section 404 compliance.

ITIL

The IT Infrastructure Library (ITIL) is a set of 34 books published by the British government's Stationary Office between 1989 and 1992 to improve IT service management. The framework contains a set of best practices for IT core operational processes such as change, release and configuration management, incident and problem management, capacity and availability management, and IT financial management. ITIL's primary contribution is showing how the controls can be implemented for the service management IT processes. These practices are useful as a starting point for tailoring to the specific needs of the organization, and the success of the practices depends upon the degree to which they are kept up to date and implemented on a daily basis. Achievement of these standards is an ongoing process, whereby the implementations need to be planned, supported by management, prioritized, and implemented in a phased approach.

COBIT

Control Objectives for Information and related Technology (COBIT) is published by the IT Governance Institute and integrates the following IT and risk frameworks:

- CobiT 5
- CobiT 4.1
- Val IT 2.0
- Risk IT
- IT Assurance Framework (ITAF)
- Business Model for Information Security (BMIS)

The COBIT framework examines the effectiveness, efficiency, confidentiality, integrity, availability, compliance, and reliability aspects of the high-level control objectives. The framework provides an overall structure for information technology control and includes control objectives that can be utilized to determine effective security control objectives that are driven from the business needs. The Information Systems Audit and Control Association (ISACA) dedicates numerous resources to the support and understanding of COBIT.

CRAMM

As described on the CRAMM (CCTA Risk Analysis and Management Method) website, residing on Siemens Insight Consulting's website: "CRAMM provides a staged and disciplined approach embracing both technical (e.g., IT hardware and software) and nontechnical (e.g., physical and human) aspects of security. To assess these components, CRAMM is divided into three stages: asset identification and valuation, threat and vulnerability assessment, and countermeasure selection and recommendation." The implementation of this methodology is much like the other methods listed in this chapter.

Failure Modes and Effect Analysis

Failure modes and effect analysis was born in hardware analysis but can be used for software and system analysis. It examines potential failures of each part or module and examines effects of failure at three levels:

1. Immediate level (part or module)
2. Intermediate level (process or package)
3. System-wide

The organization would then "collect total impact for failure of given modules to determine whether modules should be strengthened or further supported."

FRAP

The Facilitated Risk Analysis Process (FRAP) makes a base assumption that a narrow risk assessment is the most efficient way to determine risk in a system, business segment, application, or process. The process allows organizations to prescreen applications, systems, or other subjects to determine if a risk analysis is needed. By establishing a unique prescreening process, organizations will be able to concentrate on subjects that truly need a formal risk analysis. The process has little outlay of capital and can be conducted by anyone with good facilitation skills. FRAP is typically a good approach for small organizations or those with limited budgets.

OCTAVE

As defined by its creator, Carnegie Mellon University's Software Engineering Institute, OCTAVE "is a self-directed information security risk evaluation." OCTAVE is defined as a situation where people from an organization manage and direct an information security risk evaluation for their organization. The same people are responsible for making decisions about the organization's efforts to improve information security. In OCTAVE, an interdisciplinary team, called the analysis team, leads the evaluation.

Figure 4.10 illustrates that the OCTAVE approach is driven by operational risk and security practices. Technology is examined only in relation to security practices.

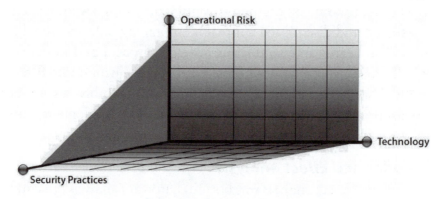

Figure 4.10 – **The OCTAVE approach is driven by operational risk and security practices**

The OCTAVE criteria are a set of principles, attributes, and outputs. Principles are the fundamental concepts driving the nature of the evaluation. They define the philosophy that shapes the evaluation process. For example, self-direction is one of the principles of OCTAVE. The concept of self-direction means that people inside the organization are in the best position to lead the evaluation and make decisions.

The requirements of the evaluation are embodied in the attributes and outputs. Attributes are the distinctive qualities, or characteristics, of the evaluation. They are the requirements that define the basic elements of the OCTAVE approach and what is necessary to make the evaluation a success from both the process and organizational perspectives. Attributes are derived from the OCTAVE principles. For example, one of the attributes of OCTAVE is that an interdisciplinary team (the analysis team) staffed by personnel from the organization leads the evaluation. The principle behind the creation of an analysis team is self-direction.

Finally, outputs are the required results of each phase of the evaluation. They define the outcomes that an analysis team must achieve during each phase. It is recognized that there is more than one set of activities that can produce the outputs of OCTAVE. It is for this reason that one does not specify one set of required activities.

Security Officers Management and Analysis Project (SOMAP)

The Security Officers Management and Analysis Project (SOMAP) is a Swiss nonprofit organization with a primary goal to run an open information security management project and maintain free and open tools and documentation under the GNU license. SOMAP has created a handbook, a guide, and a risk tool to help with understanding risk management. In the SOMAP risk assessment guide, the qualitative and quantitative methodologies are discussed. SOMAP identifies the importance of choosing the best methodology based on the goals of the organization. SOMAP illustrates risk assessment workflow as illustrated in *Figure 4.11*. More information, including the handbook, guide, and available tools can be obtained from www.somap.org.

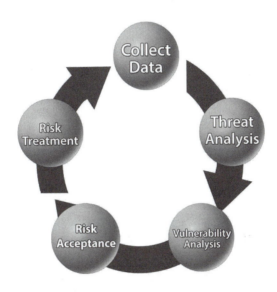

Figure 4.11 – **The SOMAP risk assessment workflow**

Spanning Tree Analysis

Spanning tree analysis "creates a 'tree' of all possible threats to or faults of the system. 'Branches' are general categories such as network threats, physical threats, component failures, etc." When conducting the risk assessment, organizations "prune 'branches' that do not apply."

VAR (Value at Risk)

In a paper presented by Jeevan Jaisingh and Jackie Rees of the Krannert Graduate School of Management at Purdue University, a new methodology for information security risk assessment titled value at risk (VAR) was introduced. The VAR methodology provides a summary of the worst loss due to a security breach over a target horizon. Many of the information security risk assessment tools are qualitative in nature and are not grounded in theory. VAR is identified as a theoretically based, quantitative measure of information security risk. It is believed that by using VAR the best possible balance between risk and cost of implementing security controls can be achieved. Many organizations identify an acceptable risk profile for their company. After determining the cost associated with this risk so that when the dollar value at risk for the organization exceeds that dollar amount, the organization can be alerted to the fact that an increased security investment is required. The VAR framework for information security risk assessment appears in *Figure 4.12*.

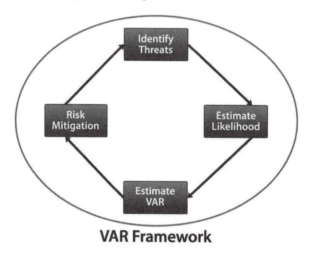

VAR Framework

Figure 4.12 – **The VAR framework for Information Security risk assessment**

Participate in Risk Management Activities

Because no organization has limitless dollars, resources, and time, it is sometimes difficult to persuade senior executives to undertake risk assessment, even in the face of regulatory requirements. How, then, might they be persuaded? One of the principle outcomes of risk assessment is the definition and identification of threats, vulnerabilities, and countermeasures present (or desired) within the organization. It would then be useful to "reuse" the data gathered during the risk assessment for other security initiatives, such as business continuity, security incident response, disaster recovery, and others. This reuse saves the organization dollars, time, and resources and can be demonstrated to senior management.

Depending on the healthcare professional's role within the organization, he or she may participate in the risk assessment itself, the risk-framing component prior to the assessment as discussed in the "Understanding Basic Risk Management Methodology" section, or the communication and documentation that occurs throughout the risk management lifecycle.

Participation may be required for the professional when an organization conducts a risk assessment with the evaluation of:

- Threats to its assets
- Vulnerabilities present in the environment
- The likelihood that a threat will "make good" by taking advantage of an exposure (or probability and frequency when dealing with quantitative assessment)
- The impact that the exposure being realized has on the organization
- Countermeasures available that can reduce the threat's ability to exploit the exposure or that can lessen the impact to the organization when a threat is able to exploit a vulnerability
- The residual risk (e.g., the amount of risk that is left over when appropriate controls are properly applied to lessen or remove the vulnerability)

If asked to participate with the selection of countermeasures to apply to risks in the environment, one should consider the many aspects of the countermeasure to ensure that he or she is a proper fit to the task. Considerations for countermeasures or controls include:

- Accountability (can be held responsible)
- Auditability (can it be tested?)
- Trusted source (source is known)
- Independence (self-determining)
- Consistently applied
- Cost-effective
- Reliable
- Independence from other countermeasures (no overlap)
- Ease of use
- Automation
- Sustainable
- Secure
- Protects confidentiality, integrity, and availability of assets
- Can be "backed out" in event of issue
- Creates no additional issues during operation
- Leaves no residual data from its function

Although this list appears rather lengthy, it is clear that countermeasures must be above reproach when in use for protection of an organization's assets.

The practitioner may be asked to assist with the documentation of evidence of the countermeasure in a deliverable called an exhibit or, in some frameworks, called "evidence." An exhibit can be used to provide an audit trail for the organization and, likewise, evidence for any internal or external auditors that may have questions about the organization's current state of risk.

In addition, it is crucial for an organization to ensure that appropriate policies, with detailed procedures and standards as appropriate that correspond to each policy item, be created, implemented, maintained, monitored, and enforced in the environment. It is highly recommended that the organization assigns resources that can be accountable to each task and tracks tasks over time, reporting progress to senior management and allowing time for appropriate approvals during this process. The practitioner may be asked to participate in any or all of the tasks that are related to the information he or she interacts with.

Remediation Action Plans

After the risk assessment is completed, a risk treatment(s) is chosen, and activities are identified, a plan is generally created that is called a corrective action plan, plans of action and milestones (POA&Ms), or fix it list. No matter the term, it should contain the list of activities, resources required, responsible person or people, and a date for completion. This should be well documented and reviewed continuously because it is a method for tracking progress. It is also evidence to provide for other assessments and audits and should be well maintained. Often, organizations will use spreadsheets or a project management application if there are many subtasks associated with the activities.

It is important to note that once risk assessment is completed and there is a list of remediation activities to be undertaken, an organization must ensure that it has personnel with appropriate capabilities to implement the remediation activities, as well as to maintain and support them. This may require the organization to provide additional training opportunities to personnel involved in the design, deployment, maintenance, and support of information security and privacy mechanisms within the environment.

Although strategic, tactical, and operational plans are interrelated, and each provides a different focus toward enhancing the information security and privacy of the organization, they may require different approaches such as timeframe for completion. The main focus of remediation plans is from an operational perspective, while a description of strategic and tactical is also given to ensure the practitioner has an understanding of what should be involved in each.

Strategic Planning

Strategic plans are aligned with the strategic business and information technology goals. These plans have a longer-term horizon (three to five years or more) to guide the long-term view of the security activities. The process of developing a strategic plan emphasizes thinking of the company environment and the technical environment a few years into the future. High-level goals are stated to provide the vision for projects to achieve the business objectives. These plans should be reviewed minimally on an annual basis or whenever major changes to the business occur, such as a merger, acquisition, establishment of outsourcing relationships, major changes in the business climate, introductions of new competitors, and so forth. Technological changes will be frequent during a five-year period, and so the plan should be adjusted. The high-level plan provides organizational guidance to ensure that lower-level decisions are consistent with executive management's intentions for the future of the company. For example, strategic goals may consist of:

- Establishing security policies and procedures
- Effectively deploying servers, workstations, and network devices to reduce downtime
- Ensuring that all users understand the security responsibilities and reward excellent performance
- Establishing a security organization to manage security enterprise-wide
- Ensuring effective risk management so that risks are effectively understood and controlled

Tactical Planning

Tactical plans provide the broad initiatives to support and achieve the goals specified in the strategic plan. These initiatives may include deployments such as establishing an electronic policy development and distribution process, implementing robust change control for the server environment, reducing vulnerabilities residing on the servers using vulnerability management, implementing a "hot site" disaster recovery program, or implementing an identity management solution. These plans are more specific and may consist of multiple projects to complete the effort. Tactical plans are shorter in length, such as 6–18 months, to achieve a specific security goal of the company.

Operational and Project Planning

Specific plans with milestones, dates, and accountabilities provide the communication and direction to ensure that the individual projects are completed. For example, establishing a policy development and communication process may involve multiple projects with many tasks:

1. Conduct security risk assessment

2. Develop security policies and approval processes

3. Develop technical infrastructure to deploy policies and track compliance

4. Train end users on policies

5. Monitor compliance

Depending upon the size and scope of the efforts, these initiatives may be steps of tasks as part of a single plan, or they may be multiple plans managed through several projects. The duration of these efforts is short term to provide discrete functionality at the completion of the effort. Traditional "waterfall" methods of implementing projects spend a large amount of time detailing the specific steps required to implement the complete project. Executives today are more focused on achieving some short-term, or at least interim, results to demonstrate the value of the investment along the way. Such demonstration of value maintains organizational interest and visibility to the effort, increasing the chances of sustaining longer-term funding. The executive management may grow impatient without realizing these early benefits.

Risk Treatment

Risk Mitigation/Remediation

Risk mitigation is the practice of eliminating or significantly decreasing the level of risk presented. Examples of risk mitigation can be seen in everyday life and are readily apparent in the information technology world.

For example, to lessen the risk of exposing personal and financial information that is highly sensitive and confidential, organizations put countermeasures in place, such as firewalls, intrusion detection/prevention systems, and other mechanisms, to deter malicious outsiders from accessing this highly sensitive information. In the underage driver example, risk mitigation could take the form of driver education for the youth or establishing policy not allowing the young driver to use a cell phone while driving or not letting youth before a certain age have more than one friend in the car at a time.

Risk Transfer

Risk transfer is the practice of passing on the risk in question to another entity, such as an insurance company. Let us look at one of the examples that were presented above in a different way. The family is evaluating whether to permit an underage driver to use the family car. The family decides that it is important for the youth to be mobile, so it transfers the financial risk of a youth being in an accident to the insurance company, which provides the family with auto insurance.

It is important to note that the transfer of risk may be accompanied by a cost. This is certainly true for the insurance example presented earlier and can be seen in other insurance instances, such as liability insurance for a vendor or the insurance taken out by companies to protect against hardware and software theft or destruction. This may also be true if an organization must purchase and implement security controls in order to make itself less desirable to attack than another.

It is important to remember not all risk can be transferred. While financial risk is simple to transfer through insurance, reputational risk may almost never be fully transferred. If a banking system is breached, there may be a cost in the money lost, but what about the reputation of the bank as a secure place to store assets? How about the stock price of the bank and the customers the bank may lose due to the breach?

Risk Acceptance

In some cases, it may be prudent for an organization to simply accept the risk that is presented in certain scenarios. Risk acceptance is the practice of accepting certain risk(s), typically based on a business decision that may also weigh the cost versus the benefit of dealing with the risk in another way.

For example, an executive may be confronted with risks identified during the course of a risk assessment for his or her organization. These risks have been prioritized by high, medium, and low impact to the organization. The executive notes that in order to mitigate or transfer the low-level risks, significant costs could be involved. Mitigation might involve the hiring of additional highly skilled personnel and the purchase of new hardware, software, and office equipment, while transference of the risk to an insurance company would require premium payments. The executive then further notes that minimal impact to the organization would occur if any of the reported low-level threats were realized. Therefore, he or she (rightly) concludes that it is wiser for the organization to forego the costs and accept the risk. In the young driver example, risk acceptance could be based on the observation that the youngster has demonstrated the responsibility and maturity to warrant the parent's trust in his or her judgment.

The decision to accept risk should not be taken lightly, or without appropriate information to justify the decision. The cost versus benefit, the organization's willingness to monitor the risk long term, and the impact it has on the outside world's view of the organization must all be taken into account when deciding to accept risk, even if accepting the risk and business decision to accept must be documented.

It is important to note that there are organizations that may also track containment of risk. Containment lessens the impact to an organization if or when an exposure is exploited through distribution of critical assets (i.e., people, processes, data, technologies, and facilities).

Risk Avoidance

Risk avoidance is the practice of coming up with alternatives so that the risk in question is not realized. For example, have you ever heard a friend or parents of a friend complain about the costs of insuring an underage driver? How about the risks that many of these children face as they become mobile? Some of these families will decide that the child in question will not be allowed to drive the family car, but they will rather wait until he or she is of legal age (i.e., 18 years of age) before committing to owning, insuring, and driving a motor vehicle.

In this case, the family has chosen to avoid the risks (and any associated benefits) associated with an underage driver, such as poor driving performance or the cost of insurance for the child. Although this choice may be available for some situations, it is not available for all. Imagine a global retailer who, knowing the risks associated with doing business on the Internet, decides to avoid the practice. This decision will likely cost the company a significant amount of its revenue (if, indeed, the company still has products or services that consumers wish to purchase). In addition, the decision may require the company to build or lease a site in each of the locations, globally, for which it wishes to continue business. This could have a catastrophic effect on the company's ability to continue business operations.

Another example can be described in the banking industry. A bank may wish to avoid Internet banking functions for its customers, but due to the competitive nature of the industry, the bank needs to make it available in order to avoid losing numerous customers to the competition.

4

Communications

The relationship between all the departments involved in information and privacy governance and executive management (including stakeholders) is a dotted-line relationship that may or may not be reflected on the organization chart. The information from the departments is providing the business direction and increasing the awareness of the information security and privacy activities that are impacting the organization on a continuous basis, which is extremely valuable. How frequently updates are given to senior management and stakeholders will depend upon the organizational culture (i.e., are monthly or quarterly oversight meetings held on other initiatives?), the number of security and privacy initiatives, and the urgency of decisions that need the input of the business units. Another form of communication in addition to update and feedback meetings is the reporting, and metrics will accompany those meetings and be produced on a predefined schedule to ensure the information is relevant and up-to-date.

Exception Handling

With any process there are always exceptions, including the risk management process. The most important thing to note with any exceptions is to be sure that they are well documented. Ensure the documentation describes the exception in detail, including the duration the exception will be allowed, the party requesting the exception, and most important all the risk the exception introduces. In addition, ensure that senior management and stakeholders are aware of the exception and that the appropriate parties have agreed to allow it. It is an acceptance of risk that needs to be documented just as any other risk decision is.

Reporting and Metrics

The information system security officer is responsible for understanding the business objectives of the organization, ensuring that a risk assessment is performed, taking into consideration the threats and vulnerabilities impacting the particular organization, and subsequently communicating the risks to executive management; if one is not assigned to the information system, this responsibility generally is the information owner/steward with the support of the system owner.

The makeup of the executive management team will vary based on the type of industry or government entity, but it typically includes individuals with C-level titles, such as the chief executive officer (CEO), chief operating officer (COO), chief financial officer (CFO), and chief information officer (CIO). The executive team also includes the first-level reporting to the CEO, such as the VP of sales and marketing, VP of administration, general counsel, and the VP of human resources.

The executive team is interested in maintaining the appropriate balance between acceptable risk and ensuring that business operations are meeting the mission of the organization. In this context, executive management is not concerned with the technical details of the implementations but rather with what is the cost/benefit of the solution and what residual risk will remain after the safeguards are implemented. For example, the configuration parameters of installing a particular vendor's router are not as important as the following:

- What is the real perceived threat (problem to be solved)?
- What is the risk (impact and probability) to business operations?
- What is the cost of the safeguard?
- What will be the residual risk (risk remaining after the safeguard is properly implemented and sustained)?
- How long will the project take?

Each of these must be evaluated along with the other items competing for resources (time, money, people, and systems).

The information system security officer or information owner/steward has a responsibility to ensure that the information presented to executive management is based upon a real business need, and the facts are represented clearly. Recommendations for specific controls should be risk based. Ultimately, it is the executive management of the organization that is responsible for information security (including privacy concerns). Presentations should be geared at a high level to convey the purpose of the technical safeguard and not be a rigorous detailed presentation of the underlying technology unless requested.

Measurements can be collected that provide information on long-term trends and illustrate the day-to-day workload. Measurement of processes provides the ability to improve the process. For example, measuring the number of help desk tickets for password resets can be translated into workload hours and may provide justification for the implementation of new technologies for the end user to self-administer the password reset process. Tracking how viruses spread or the frequency of reporting may indicate a need for further education or improvement of the antivirus management process. Many decisions need to be made when collecting metrics, such as who will collect the metrics, what statistics will be collected, when they will be collected, and what are the thresholds where variations are out of bounds and should be acted upon. An important first decision is to determine what metrics will be used to prove and whether the metric gathering effort will provide the necessary evidence or value desired.

KRIs

Key Risk Indicators (KRIs) are an early signal of emerging risks or increased risk exposure for the organization. Often, KRIs are mapped to a specific organizational objective. A good exercise that COSO describes to assist with the identification of a KRI is to take a risk event and work backwards.[20] This is because risk events are generally related to intermediate events that can be leading indicators and eventually a root cause. The closer the leading indicator is to the root cause, the more time is needed for management to react and implement mitigating controls. An example would be to consider a breach of healthcare personal information and to look at intermediate events such as the number of unencrypted laptops increasing. The root cause could be inappropriate asset inventory, increase in telework individuals, and lack of laptop encryption software. It would be appropriate to consider all 3 possibilities as root causes.

KPIs

Key Performance Indicators (KPIs) are metrics that allow for the identification of underperformance areas or others that will require more resources to meet demand. The example given above regarding the tracking of viruses is a KPI that illustrated a need for resources.

Establishing metrics is an important part of any program. It allows senior management and stakeholders to provide effective oversight. Metrics should be established to ensure that something is measureable. How can the organization determine if a program or project is successful or not without some form of metrics? The two well-known types of metrics in the industry, KPIs and KRIs, are very easily confused but are not interchangeable. Therefore understanding the difference is key for any practitioner. In addition, each organization should choose its own KRIs and KPIs that are appropriate for them. They are definitely not a one size fits all.

---

20 http://www.coso.org/documents/COSOKRIPaperFull-FINALforWebPostingDec110_000.pdf, page 9

More to Know

The following articles and documents contain more information about information and privacy security governance and risk management. They are freely available on the Internet.

» NIST Special Publication 800-39: Managing Information Security Risk: Organization, Mission, and Information System View (http://csrc.nist.gov/publications/nistpubs/800-39/SP800-39-final.pdf)

» Security Officers Management and Analysis Project (SOMAP.org)

» On-line Reference Database for NIST Special Publication 800-53 Security Controls (http://web.nvd.nist.gov/view/800-53/home)

» http://www.coso.org/documents/COSOKRIPaperFull-FINALforWebPostingDec110_000.pdf

Summary

Information security governance and risk management are core security activities that drive information security spending, policy, hiring, and ultimately impact. Organizations have survived or failed due to how they approach information security governance and risk management. Throughout this chapter the following concepts have been addressed:

■ The information governance concept including information about:
  ¤ Understanding security and privacy governance
  ¤ Governance structures
  ¤ Roles

- Understanding basic risk management methodology
  - Risk assessments and analysis methods including qualitative and quantitative risk assessments
  - Information asset identification
  - The value determination of tangible and intangible assets
  - Risk determination and its factors
- Identification of vulnerabilities and exposures
- Identification of threats
- Identification of impact
  - Risk and how controls (countermeasures and safeguards) can help mitigate vulnerabilities and risk including the different types of controls
  - Risk acceptance including residual risk and risk assignment to individuals and organizations
- Understanding information risk management lifecycles such as NIST, CMS, ISO, and other framework and methodologies
- Understanding of participation in risk management activities
  - Remediation plans
  - Risk treatment including mitigation/ remediation, transfer, acceptance, and avoidance
  - Communication to senior management and stakeholders
  - How exceptions to the risk management process are handled
  - Types of reporting metrics that can be used

Domain 4 – *Review Questions*

1. An organization maintains Protected Health Information in the cloud, on local systems in its offices, and on paper records. Which form of information has the greatest impact on the organization if it is breached?

   A. Paper based records

   B. Cloud based records

   C. Local system based records

   D. The impact is the same regardless of media

2. An oncology practice has outsourced its infrastructure to XYZ corporation. Due to no contract limitations, XYZ corporation has further sub-contracted the infrastructure work to another firm, ABC Group. The oncology practice's infrastructure is responsible for processing, storing, and transmitting the PHI of oncology patients. In this scenario, which organization is affiliated with the information owner/steward who would be held accountable in a breach?

   A. The oncology practice

   B. XYZ corporation

   C. ABC Group

   D. None as the contracting relationship has created a transference of risk.

3. The following represents four basic steps in managing risk. Place them in the correct sequential order:

   1. **Monitoring risk** – continuously monitor the risk environment

   2. **Assessing risk** – identify threats, vulnerabilities, impact, likelihood, and determine risk

   3. **Framing risk** – produce the risk strategy, identify risk tolerance, assumptions, and constraints

   4. **Responding to risk** – identify a consistent manner to respond to risk from an organization-wide perspective

   A. 1, 2, 3, 4

   B. 4, 3, 2, 1

   C. 3, 2, 4, 1

   D. 2, 1, 4, 3

4. Organizational risk tolerance is **BEST** established by _____

A. Senior leadership.

B. Information system owner.

C. Information system security officer.

D. Information owner.

5. An organization is reviewing its financial exposure should a breach occur. A senior penetration tester has determined in the past they have been breached two times a year, and each time it has cost the organization U.S. $100,000 to mitigate the breach and offer credit monitoring. What is the annual loss expectancy (ALE) for the organization?

A. U.S. $50,000

B. U.S. $25,000

C. U.S. $200,000

D. U.S. $250,000

6. Annual loss expectancy or ALE is a form of _____.

A. Qualitative risk assessment.

B. Quantitative risk assessment.

C. Qualitative and quantitative risk assessment.

D. Continuous monitoring.

7. Which of the following classes of controls are primarily implemented and executed through mechanisms contained in the hardware, software, and firmware of the components of the system?

A. Technical Controls

B. Managerial Controls

C. Operational Controls

D. Physical Controls

8. An organization has just completed a risk assessment. The assessment returned a single finding with a "low" risk to the organization. The cost to mitigate or transfer the risk would be U.S. $1.5 million dollars, and if the risk were exploited, no PHI or sensitive information would be lost, but the organization's public website would be down for 10 to 15 seconds no more than twice a year. The organization earns about U.S. $1 million dollars of revenue every year. What is the **BEST** risk treatment approach?

   A. Transfer risk

   B. Avoid risk

   C. Mitigate risk

   D. Accept risk

9. Consider the NIST risk management framework below: If an organization has adopted NIST as its risk management framework, which step is **MOST** important in ensuring proper risk management?

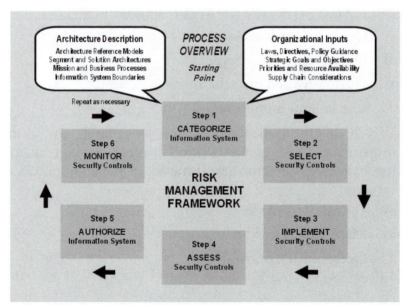

   A. Continuous monitoring

   B. Implement security controls

   C. Authorize information system

   D. Categorize information system

4

10. A remediation plan or plan of actions and milestones (POA&M) is **MOST** effective when it contains the following:

A. System downtime, resources required, responsible person, and a date for completion

B. List of activities, resources required, responsible person, and a date for completion

C. List of activities, system downtime, responsible person, and a date for completion

D. List of activities, resources required, responsible person, and system downtime

Domain 5

Information Risk Assessment

RISK IS DEFINED in the American Heritage Dictionary as "the possibility of suffering harm or loss."[1] Random House Dictionary defines risk management as "the technique or profession of assessing, minimizing, and preventing accidental loss to a business, as through the use of insurance, safety measures, etc."[2] (ISC)2 defines risk management as "a discipline for living with the possibility that future events may cause harm."[3] Further, (ISC)2 states that "risk management reduces risks by defining and controlling threats and vulnerabilities."

The National Institute of Standards and Technology defines risk in Special Publication 800-30 Rev. 1 as:

"the net mission impact considering (1) the probability that a particular [threat] will exercise (accidentally trigger or intentionally exploit) a particular [vulnerability] and (2) the resulting impact if this should occur . . . . [R]isks arise from legal liability or mission loss due to –

---

1   http://www.ahdictionary.com/word/search.html?q=Risk+&submit.x=12&submit.y=30

2   http://dictionary.reference.com/browse/risk+management

3   Official (ISC)2 Guide to the CISSP CBK

1. Unauthorized (malicious or accidental) disclosure, modification, or destruction of information

2. Unintentional errors and omissions

3. IT disruptions due to natural or man-made disasters

4. Failure to exercise due care and diligence in the implementation and operation of the IT system."[4]

In most organizations, there is often a balance between operational needs of the business and risk to the organization. In the healthcare field, this is compounded by the fact that the security and privacy risk decisions made by the organization may not only impact the bottom line of the business, but they could also impact the lives of those its mission is to heal and protect. When looking at information risk in healthcare, one will be guided in risk analysis activities by confidentiality, integrity, and availability. For instance, if the information in a system is breached, unintentionally disclosed, or becomes public, will that cause embarrassment or harm to patients? Alternatively, if an organization's database is corrupted and the information within can no longer be trusted, will those seeking help be given the right treatment? Additionally, if a system is taken offline due to an attack or utility outage, what impact will that have on providing health services? Ultimately, conducting a thorough information risk assessment will assist in "identifying, estimating, and prioritizing" privacy and security risks for both the organization and its patients.

---

4   http://csrc.nist.gov/publications/nistpubs/800-30-rev1/sp800_30_r1.pdf

TOPICS

- Understand Risk Assessment
  - Definition
  - Intent
  - Lifecycle/Continuous Monitoring
  - Tools, Resources, and Techniques
  - Desired Outcomes

- Identify Control Assessment Procedures from within Organizational Risk Frameworks

- Participate in Risk Assessment Consistent with Role in Organization
  - Information Gathering
  - Estimated Timeline
  - Gap Assessment
  - Corrective Action Plan
  - Mitigation Actions

- Participate in Efforts to Remediate Gaps
  - Types of Controls
    - Administrative
    - Operational/Physical
    - Technical
  - Controls Related to Time
    - Preventative
    - Detective
    - Responsive
    - Administrative

OBJECTIVES

According to the (ISC)[2] Candidate Information Bulletin (Exam Outline), a HCISPP candidate is expected to understand risk assessment concepts and demonstrate an ability to identify and participate in risk assessment practices. Additionally, HCISPP candidates should be able to:

- Identify control assessment procedures

- Participate in risk assessments consistent with their role in the organization

- Take action to remediate gaps.[5]

With this knowledge, practitioners can take an active role in the risk management process.

5   https://www.isc2.org/uploadedFiles/(ISC)2_Public_Content/Certification_Programs/
    HCISPP/HCISPP-brochure.pdf

5

Information Risk Assessment

Definitions

Vulnerability

The National Institute of Standards and Technology (NIST) Special Publication 800–30 Rev. 1, page 8, defines a vulnerability as "an inherent weakness in an information system, security procedures, internal controls, or implementation that could be exploited by a threat source."[6]

It is common to identify vulnerabilities as they are related to people, processes, data, technology, and facilities. Examples of vulnerabilities could include but are not limited to:

- Absence of a receptionist, guards, or other physical security mechanisms upon entrance to a facility
- Inadequate integrity checking in electronic health records
- Neglecting to require users to sign an acknowledgment of their responsibilities with regard to security and privacy, as well as an acknowledgment that they have read, understand, and agree to abide by the organization's security policies
- Patching and configuration of an organization's information systems are done on an ad hoc basis and, therefore, are neither documented nor up to date.

Threat

NIST Special Publication (SP) 800–30 Rev. 1, pages 7 – 8, defines threats as "any circumstance or event with the potential to adversely impact organizational operations and assets, individuals, other organizations, or the Nation through an information system via unauthorized access, destruction, disclosure, or modification of information, and/or denial of service."[7]

Generally there are three types of threat actors commonly cited when addressing information.

- Nation states
- Organized crime
- Hacktivists

---

6   http://csrc.nist.gov/publications/nistpubs/800-30-rev1/sp800_30_r1.pdf

7   http://csrc.nist.gov/publications/nistpubs/800-30-rev1/sp800_30_r1.pdf

However, given the nature of the healthcare industry and potential for fraud, waste, and abuse, the World Privacy Forum's 2006 Report on Medical Identity Theft discusses solo identity thieves, relatives of beneficiaries, and even malicious insiders of the healthcare field that can pose a threat to individual organizations or patient data.[8]

Impact

NIST Special Publication 800–30 Rev. 1 defines impact from a threat event as the magnitude of harm that can be expected to result from the consequences of unauthorized disclosure of information, unauthorized modification of information, unauthorized destruction of information, or loss of information or information system availability.

Harm can be experienced by a variety of organizational and non-organizational stakeholders, including the CEO, business owners, information owners, business process owners, information system owners, or public individuals relying on the organization. In short, anyone with a vested interest in the organization's operations, assets, or individuals could be impacted.

While there are many security and privacy risks to an organization, the impact of a breach could have a range of negative impacts to both the patient and the organization, including poor medical outcomes, financial loss to the organization or patient, loss of reputation, as well as legal or regulatory losses.

Adverse Medical Outcomes

In the case of a data breach, there are several ways that an individual can be impacted by poor or adverse medical outcomes. The most glaring example is that if the integrity of the data is compromised, then healthcare professionals may not have accurate data to provide a diagnosis. However, another way that individuals can receive incorrect treatment following a data breach is in the instance of medical identify theft.

According to the World Privacy Forum, "a stolen medical identity has a $50 street value… whereas a stolen social security number, on the other hand, only sells for $1."[9] The higher value represents the impact of two realities:

1. Medical identities can be used to fraudulently bill the government or insurance providers,[10] and

---

8   http://www.worldprivacyforum.org/wp-content/uploads/2007/11/wpf_medicalidtheft2006.pdf

9   http://www.govhealthit.com/news/glimpse-inside-234-billion-world-medical-id-theft

10 http://www.cms.gov/Medicare-Medicaid-Coordination/Fraud-Prevention/Medicaid-Integrity-Education/Provider-Education-Toolkits/Downloads/understand-prevent-provider-idtheft.pdf

> **2.** Unscrupulous individuals can use another person's medical identify to receive free medical treatment.[11]

In the latter instance, such use can litter an innocent person's medical history with false and otherwise incorrect information about medical conditions, procedures, and other diagnoses that can have significant impact on his or her health, reputation, and in some cases, credit.

For example, if a stolen medical identity is used to receive treatment for a chronic condition, information regarding that condition could show up on the original person's patient chart in an emergency room one day. In such a case, the patient may not be in a position to correct the healthcare provider regarding the alleged conditions and could therefore receive inappropriate or even harmful interventions, such as medicine to which he or she is allergic.

Financial Loss

To the healthcare industry, data breaches can have a significant impact on the bottom line of the business. According to the Ponemon Institute, "the average annual cost… could potentially be as high as almost \$7 billion."[12] In regards to medical identity theft, "1.42 million Americans were victims…in 2010," and it is estimated that "the annual economic impact of medical identity theft to be \$30.9 billion." In aggregate, these are not insignificant costs and negatively impact organizations and individuals alike.

When medical identities are stolen and used, there are still the normal co-pays and often portions of the bill not covered by the individual's insurance. In those instances, not knowing otherwise, the healthcare facility will bill the victim. Many times, the victim never receives a bill and is only notified when he or she is turned over to collections for services that were never received.

One example is of a woman who received "a bill from a local hospital for the amputation of her right foot." She made attempts to report this information as fraud but unfortunately made little progress, so she was forced to go into the hospital to prove that she still had both of her feet.[13] It is also just as likely that this fraud could have led to her insurance company denying her service for her own legitimate medical claims. This type of fraud can lead to out-of-pocket expenses and loss of credit rating.

Reputation Loss

Organizations around the world are subject to data breach notification laws. When a breach occurs in the U.S. for instance, there is a patchwork of state and

---

11 http://www.worldprivacyforum.org/wp-content/uploads/2007/11/wpf_medicalidtheft2006.pdf

12 Third Annual Benchmark Study on Patient Privacy & Data Security

13 http://www.businessweek.com/stories/2007-01-07/diagnosis-identity-theft

federal laws detailing the reporting requirements to affected individuals. When a breach becomes public, the reputation of the organization can be tarnished and can ultimately lead to a loss of business. Data breaches can have downstream effects due to medical identity theft that can cause reputation loss for individuals as well. For instance, one of the documented cases addresses when "a pregnant woman delivered a baby addicted to [cocaine] using another woman's social security number – and then abandoned the baby. Police arrested the victim and put her children into protective custody."[14] Such an instance would cause untold emotional and reputational harm to the woman and her family.

Legal/Regulatory Losses

Any time that a data breach occurs, the organization responsible for the breach is at risk of legal action for the methods in which it did, or did not, protect customer data, and healthcare is not immune to this liability. The Office of Civil Rights, the U.S. Department of Health and Human Services, a civil rights and health privacy rights law enforcement agency, "has the ability to levy fines and has entered into settlements for over one million dollars."[15] In most of these instances, OCR cites poorly implemented policies and procedures or failures to implement appropriate administrative and technical safeguards required under law to protect patient security and privacy. When these regulatory issues emerge, they often boil down to lack of due diligence, or due care, in that the organization did not make reasonable attempts to prevent harm or mitigate potential problems and vulnerabilities.

With the increased complexity of health IT and the current matrix of regulatory oversight, even more organizations are getting involved when a breach occurs. In the U.S. for example, the Federal Trade Commission determined that it can issue formal complaints and potential fines when it is deemed that a healthcare organization is accused of failing to "reasonably protect the security of consumers' personal data, including medical information."[16]

Risk Assessment

The National Institute of Standards and Technology (NIST), in Special Publication (SP) 800–30 Rev. 1, defines risk assessment as "the process of identifying, estimating, and prioritizing information security risks."[17]

---

14   http://www.govhealthit.com/news/glimpse-inside-234-billion-world-medical-id-theft

15   http://www.hhs.gov/ocr/privacy/hipaa/enforcement/examples/index.html

16   http://www.ftc.gov/news-events/press-releases/2013/08/ftc-files-complaint-against-labmd-failing-protect-consumers

17   http://csrc.nist.gov/publications/nistpubs/800-30-rev1/sp800_30_r1.pdf

When thinking of conducting a risk assessment and attempting to identify potential threats and vulnerabilities within an organization, one could learn from peer organizations in healthcare or industries that face similar threats. For instance, publicly available information on healthcare data breaches can shed light on common threats and vulnerabilities. In the United States, the Health Information Technology for Economic and Clinical Health (HITECH) Act requires reporting and publication of data breaches of protected or sensitive health information that impact more than 500 individuals. In the few years that the list has been published, it has accumulated over 700 discrete incidents. The incidents are grouped by the following categories: Hacking/IT Incident, Improper Disposal, Loss, Theft, Unauthorized Access/Disclosure, and Unknown/Other. The distribution of the 720 incidents is as follows:

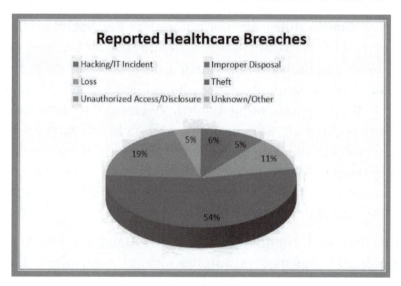

Figure 5.1 – **Chart Created From Data Provided by HHS HITECH ACT Breach Page**[18]

While the proportion of risk demonstrated by this list may not be directly applicable to any one organization, it may be possible to glean transferable insights for similarly situated organizations.

Intent

Risk assessment processes may vary between frameworks and industries, but at their core, the formulas remain largely the same. Risk is a function of threats, vulnerabilities, likelihood, and impact. Risk assessments may also be qualitative, quantitative, or a hybrid of the two. Qualitative risk assessments define risk in relative terms such as "high," "moderate," or "low". Quantitative

---

18   http://www.hhs.gov/ocr/privacy/hipaa/administrative/breachnotificationrule/breachtool.html

risk assessments attempt to provide specific measurements and impacts with dollar figures representing the expected loss. In many cases, these methods are combined for a hybrid approach to get the best of both worlds.

If a breach were to occur and sensitive health information were to be compromised, depending upon the scope of the breach, qualitatively there would be moderate to high reputational risk. However, the financial risk to the same breach could be quantified fairly using open source information. According to the Third Annual Benchmark Study on Patient Privacy & Data Security by the Ponemon Institute, healthcare had the highest "per capita data breach cost" at $233 per record, which is "substantially above the overall mean of $136."[19] Pharmaceuticals came in third at $207 per record. Per the same report, for most organizations, the number of breached records ranged from 2,300 to 99,000 records per incident. The average though was just over 23,000 per incident. The associated financial risk could be calculated as follows.

	Records	Cost Per	Total
Minimum	2,300	$233	$535,900
Average	23,000	$233	$5,359,000
High	99,000	$233	$23,067,000

Table 5.1 – **Financial Risk associated with a breach**

While these are the industry averages, there are many organizations that may have more than 100,000 records. For those, it is important to estimate cost of a breach on the high end of the financial risk spectrum given the total number of unique records maintained. It is also important to note that this does not capture the likely legal costs or regulatory fines.

As an organization becomes more sophisticated in its data collection and retention, and staff becomes more experienced in conducting risk assessments, an organization may find itself moving more toward quantitative risk assessment. The hallmark of a quantitative assessment is the numeric nature of the analysis. Frequency, probability, impact, countermeasure effectiveness, and other aspects of the risk assessment have a discrete mathematical value in a pure quantitative analysis. For example, when organizations initiate a risk assessment for the first time, their methods and processes may be nascent as there is a lack of historical data or, in some cases, a steady and mature operating environment. However, as the operating environment matures, it is possible to review system metrics and other data to generate a more informed view of the risk to the organization.

---

19 Third Annual Benchmark Study on Patient Privacy & Data Security, Ponemon Institute, December 2012

Information Lifecycle and Continuous Monitoring

Information Lifecycle

Information has a lifecycle that consists of creation, use, and finally destruction. Several important information security activities surround the lifecycle of information to protect it, ensure it is available to only those who require access to it, and finally to destroy it when it is no longer needed. Several concepts of information ownership need to be understood by the information security professionals as part of their duties.

When information is created, someone in the organization must be directly responsible for it. Often this is the individual or group that created, purchased, or acquired the information to support the mission of the organization. This individual or group is considered the "information owner." The information owner typically has the following responsibilities:

- Determine the impact the information has on the mission of the organization
- Understand the replacement cost of the information (if it can be replaced)
- Determine who in the organization or outside of it has a need for the information and under what circumstances the information should be released
- Know when the information is inaccurate or no longer needed and should be destroyed

Information owners must work with the information security program officer and other staff to ensure the protection, availability, and destruction requirements can be met. To standardize the types of information and protection requirements, many organizations use classification or categorization to sort and mark the information. Classification is concerned primarily with access, while categorization is primarily concerned with impact.

Classification is most often referred to when discussing military or government information. However, several organizations may use systems that are similar in function. The purpose of a classification system is to ensure information is marked in such a way that only those with an appropriate level of clearance can have access to the information. Many organizations will use the terms "confidential", "close hold", "restricted", "sensitive", or "Protected Health Information (PHI)" to mark information. These markings may limit access to specific members, such as board members, or possibly certain sections of an organization such as the Human Resources area.

Categorization is the process of determining the impact of the loss of confidentiality, integrity, or availability of the information to an organization. For example, public information on a webpage may be low impact to an organization as it requires only minimal uptime; it doesn't matter if the information is changed and it is globally viewable by the public. However, a healthcare organization will have significant amounts of patient data that if lost or altered may have an adverse impact on a patient's financial or physical health. This type of information would be categorized as "moderate" or, possibly, "high" impact. Several classification and categorization systems exist. Professionals who are responsible for protecting sensitive data should minimally be familiar with a few and understand which are common in the country and industry that they practice in.

An excellent example of categorization may be found in the United States' National Institute of Standards and Technology's (NIST) Federal Information processing standard 199 and NIST's special publication 800-60 "Guide for Mapping Types of Information and Information Systems to Security Categories." The United States federal civilian government is required to categorize information using these standards and guidelines. NIST SP 800-60 uses three levels of impact, such as low, moderate, and high, in addressing the key security goals of confidentiality, integrity, and availability. For example, a small physician's office will often have a need to protect different types of information. A sample categorization is as follows:

	Confidentiality	**Integrity**	**Availability**	**Categorization**
Patient Health Data	Moderate	Moderate	Low	Moderate

Table 5.2 – **A sample categorization of Patient Health Data**

In the case of patient health data, the categorization is predicated off of the highest marks in the categories. With moderate being the highest impact rating of the three security goals, that is the appropriate classification.

Classification and categorization is used to help standardize the defense baselines for information systems and the level of suitability and trust an employee may need to access information. By consolidating data of similar categorization and classification, organizations can realize economy of scale in implementing appropriate security controls. Security controls are then tailored for specific threats and vulnerabilities.

All information must eventually come to an end. Organizations often hoard old information, assuming it will be useful at some point when most information outlives its value and usefulness in a matter of years or even months.

Organizations should document retention schedules and requirements for information in their administrative policies. These schedules should mandate the destruction of information after a set date, period, or non-use trigger. The advantages of taking this approach are:

- Storage costs are reduced
- Only relevant information is kept and this can speed up searching and indexing
- Litigation holds and eDiscovery is less likely to encounter erroneous, pre-decisional, or deliberative information
- Compliance requirements are met

Continuous Monitoring

Risk analysis is often conducted as a point-in-time exercise and documented accordingly. However, the risk analysis process should be an ongoing activity. Healthcare organizations should conduct continuous risk analysis to identify when security measures need to be modified to keep up with operational realities. Additionally, any time that there is a significant update to policies, procedures, organization, or technologies, the security documentation should be updated to reflect the new or evolving risks. This will ultimately help reduce the effort required to remediate identified risks after the implementation of the change. It is also advantageous to set a regular review schedule (e.g., annually, bi-annually, or every 3 years) depending on needs of the organization.

From a technical perspective, there are numerous ways that risk assessment activities can be automated for IT support systems. Common activities at the host level include installing anti-virus software as well as Host-based Intrusion Detection (HIDS) suites. These tools will continually monitor risks associated with servers and user workstations. Network scanning tools should be deployed as well. Other tools including Network-based Intrusion Detection/Prevention, Network Access Control (NAC), and Data Loss Prevention (DLP) suites will respectively identify and attempt to block anomalous activity on the network.

The status of an organization's risk assessment will also change as new information becomes available. Vulnerability information for IT systems is released on a daily basis. As new vulnerabilities are discovered and released to the community, vendors work diligently to provide security patches for their products. It is up to individual organizations to gather this information and take the appropriate measures to patch the systems or identify other ways to mitigate the risk that a new vulnerability may pose. Importantly, although less frequently, new threat actors are identified. For instance, when a new, advanced fraud scheme is detected by law enforcement or an organized crime activity is increasing towards the healthcare industry or a peer organization, this information can directly feed into an update of an organizations risk assessment. Healthcare industry forums, annual security reports, open source intelligence, the National Health ISAC (NH-ISAC), and global Computer Security Incident Response Teams (CSIRT) are vital sources of information regarding emerging threats and vulnerabilities for healthcare organizations.

Given emerging trends in outsourcing, particularly in regards to cloud computing, continuous risk monitoring can culminate into a mix of technical, policy, and legal elements as well. While a private practice or public hospital may have technical systems on-site, these systems may effectively act as terminals that primarily interact with off-site servers and databases that manage electronic health records (EHR). In these instances, continuous monitoring activities are largely defined by internal policy controls around those that have access and the legal contracts that are in place with the various providers. While the individual healthcare organization customers manage access control (e.g., usernames, passwords, role-based privileges, etc.), the third-party service provider should be continuously monitoring for new threats and vulnerabilities and notifying its customers regarding changes and incidents. Specific terms will vary dramatically based upon the organization, regional laws, and contractual terms.

Tools, Resources, and Techniques

It is expected that an organization will make a selection of the risk assessment methodology, tools, and resources (including people) that best fit its culture, personnel capabilities, budget, and timeline. Many automated tools, including proprietary tools, exist in the field. Although automation can make the data analysis, dissemination, and storage of results easier, it is not a required part of risk assessment. If an organization is planning to purchase or build automated tools for this purpose, it is highly recommended that this decision be based on an appropriate timeline and resource skill sets for creation, implementation, maintenance, and monitoring of the tool(s) and data stored within for the long term.

NIST SP 800–30, 800-39 and 800–66

These methodologies are qualitative methods established for the use of the United States federal government and the global general public, but are particularly used by regulated industries, such as healthcare. 800-39 focuses on organizational risk management and 800-30 focuses on information system risk management.

The list of the NIST SP 800-30 Risk Assessment methodology process follows:

1. System characterization
2. Vulnerability identification
3. Threat identification
4. Countermeasure identification
5. Likelihood determination
6. Impact determination
7. Risk determination
8. Additional countermeasures recommendations
9. Document results

SP 800–66 is written specifically with Health Insurance Portability and Accountability Act (HIPAA) clients in mind (though it is possible to use this document for other regulated industries as well). HIPAA is a U.S. law that contains specific provisions for the security and privacy of health data. The Security Rule that was derived from this law requires healthcare organizations and business associates to "[c]onduct an accurate and thorough assessment of the potential risks and vulnerabilities to the confidentiality, integrity, and availability of electronic protected health information..."

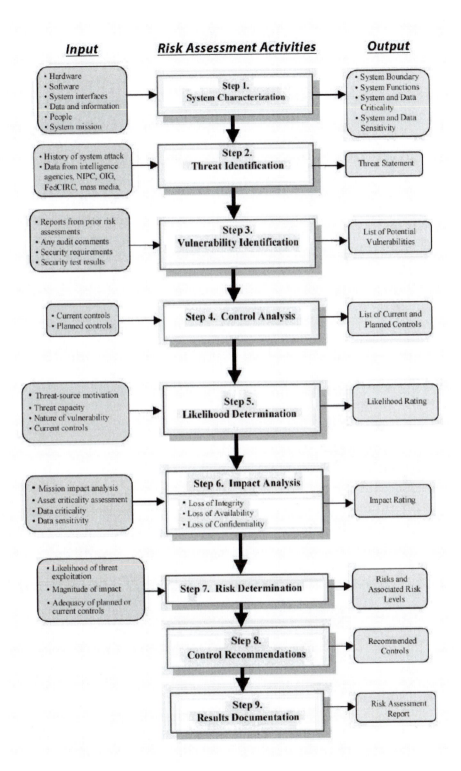

Figure 5.2 – **Risk Assessment Methodology Flowchart**
(By Gary Stoneburner [Public domain], via Wikimedia Commons)

HITRUST CSF

As described on the Health Information Trust Alliance (HITRUST), the Common Security Framework (CSF) Assurance Program "utilizes a common set of information security requirements with standardized assessment and reporting processes accepted and adopted by healthcare organizations." The goal is for "healthcare organizations and business associates to improve efficiencies and reduce the number and costs of security assessments." HITRUST partnered with the State of Texas to "create a formal Covered Entity Privacy and Security Certification Program to enable covered entities within the state to demonstrate their dedication to protecting patients' health information" and, in so doing, effectively created a safe harbor for participating organizations.[20]

HIMSS Risk Assessment Toolkit

The Healthcare Information and Management Systems Society (HIMSS) publishes a risk assessment and risk management toolkit that provides step-by-step instructions on conducting a thorough review of healthcare related threats and vulnerabilities. Additionally, there are numerous templates provided that target unique healthcare specific organizations (e.g., physician's office) and different information technology paradigms (e.g., cloud security).

Desired Outcomes

One of the principle outcomes of risk assessment is the definition and identification of threats, vulnerabilities, and countermeasures present (or desired) within the organization. It would then be useful to "reuse" the data gathered during the risk assessment for other security initiatives, such as business continuity, security incident response, disaster recovery, and others. The act of reusing data gathered during a risk assessment, when possible and appropriate, can save the organization dollars, time, and resources and can be demonstrated to senior management as a tangible value, or return on investment (ROI).

Role of Internal and External Audit/Assessment

Auditors provide an essential role for maintaining and improving information security. They provide an independent view of the design, effectiveness, and implementation of controls. The results of audits generate findings that require management response and corrective action plans to resolve the issue and mitigate the risk. Auditors often request information prior to the start of the audit to facilitate the review. Some audits are performed at a high level without substantive testing, while other audits will identify test samples to determine if a control is implemented and followed. The information security or assurance office, if available, cooperates with the internal and external auditors to ensure that the control environment is adequate and functional.

---

20 http://www.fierceemr.com/story/new-certification-program-provides-safe-harbor-privacy-security-compliance/2013-11-04

An internal audit department is responsible for evaluating the effectiveness and implementation of the organization's control structure, including the activities of the information security department. It would be difficult for the internal audit to provide an independent viewpoint. The internal audit department may have adversarial relationships with other portions of the company due to the nature of its role (to uncover deficiencies in departmental processes), and through association, the information security department or those responsible for information security and privacy may be perceived in a similar light. It is advisable that the security department establishes close working relationships with the internal audit department to facilitate the control environment. The internal audit manager most likely has a background in financial, operational, and general controls and may have difficulty relating to the technical activities of the information security department. On the positive side, both areas are focused on improving the controls of the organization. The internal audit department should have a preferable reporting relationship for audit issues through a dotted-line relationship with the company's audit committee on the board of directors. It is advisable for the information security function to have a similar path to report security issues to the board of directors as well, either in conjunction with the internal audit department or on its own. For smaller organizations and practitioner offices that do not have internal audit functions, periodic self-assessments would provide a similar benefit. However, it is important to ensure that there is separation of duties between the individual that implements the controls and the review staff.

External auditors provide an essential role for maintaining and improving information security. They provide an independent view of the design, effectiveness, and implementation of controls. The results of audits generate findings that require management response and corrective action plans to resolve the issue and mitigate the risk. Auditors often request information prior to the start of the audit to facilitate the review. Some audits are performed at a high level without substantive testing, while other audits will identify test samples to determine if a control is implemented and followed. The security department cooperates with the internal and external auditors to ensure that the control environment is adequate and functional.

In the United States, the U.S. Department of Health and Human Services, under HIPAA and the HITECH Act, has initiated an audit program for healthcare organizations and their business partners to ensure that appropriate privacy and security safeguards are in place to protect consumers. With this growing emphasis being placed on operational controls in the healthcare space, it is vital to have staff that is trained and experienced in providing safeguards for healthcare information.

Control Assessment Procedures from within Organizational Risk Frameworks

To aid in ensuring security and privacy requirements are met, many organizations adopt control frameworks to provide a governance program that is:

- **Consistent** – A governance program must be consistent in how information security and privacy is approached and applied. If two similar situations or requests result in different outcomes, stakeholders will lose faith in the integrity of the program and its usefulness.

- **Measurable** – The governance program must provide a way to determine progress and set goals. Organizations who implement frameworks that can be measured are more likely to improve their security posture over time. Most control frameworks contain an assessment standard or procedure to determine compliance and, in some cases, risk as well.

- **Standardized** – As with measurable above, a controls framework should rely on standardization so results from one organization or part of an organization can be compared in a meaningful way.

- **Comprehensive** – The selected framework should cover the minimum legal and regulatory requirements of an organization and be extensible to accommodate additional organization specific requirements.

- **Modular** – A modular framework is more likely to withstand the changes of an organization because only the controls or requirements needing modification are reviewed and updated.

An example of a control framework is the United States National Institute of Standards and Technology's Special Publication 800-53 Revision 4 (NIST SP 800-53). SP 800-53 is a control framework of over 300 controls in over 17 families and three classes. The framework includes the ability to scope and tailor controls to an organization's specific mission or requirements. NIST SP 800-53 is mandatory for United States federal agencies and their contractors. While frameworks such as these may seem daunting, they are designed to be applicable to almost every organization.

Another example is the International Standard Organization (ISO) 27001 Standard. Like NIST SP 800-53, ISO 27001 is designed to cover organizations of all sizes and types. The annex A of ISO 27001 contains the control framework with objectives and specifics about each control. ISO is a global framework adopted by numerous industries in most countries. Frameworks often map to each other as well. For example, NIST SP 800-53 has been mapped to the ISO 27001 standard. While there is considerable overlap, there are some areas that are not an exact fit. The following chart demonstrates a sample control framework comparison.

NIST SP 800-53 CONTROLS		ISO/IEC 27001 (Annex A) CONTROLS
AU-12	Audit Generation	A.10.10.1, A.10.10.4, A.10.10.5
AU-13	Monitoring for Information Disclosure	None
AU-14	Session Audit	None
CA-1	Security Assessment and Authorization Policies and Procedures	A.5.1.1, A.5.1.2, A.6.1.1, A.6.1.3 A.6.1.4, A.8.1.1, A.10.1.1, A.15.1.1, A.15.2.1
CA-2	Security Assessments	A.6.1.8, A.10.3.2, A.15.2.1, A.15.2.2
CA-3	Information System Connections	A.6.2.1, A.6.2.3, A.10.6.1, A.10.8.1, A.10.8.2, A.10.8.5, A.11.4.2
CA-4	**Withdrawn**	---
CA-5	Plan of Action and Milestones	None
CA-6	Security Authorization	A.6.1.4, A.10.3.2
CA-7	Continuous Monitoring	A.6.1.8, A.15.2.1, A.15.2.2
CM-1	Configuration Management Policy and Procedures	A.5.1.1, A.5.1.2, A.6.1.1, A.6.1.3, A.8.1.1, A.10.1.1, A.10.1.2, A.12.4.1, A.12.5.1, A.15.1.1, A.15.2.1
CM-2	Baseline Configuration	A.12.4.1, A.10.1.4
CM-3	Configuration Change Control	A.10.1.1, A.10.1.2, A.10.3.2, A.12.4.1, A.12.5.1, A.12.5.2, A.12.5.3
CM-4	Security Impact Analysis	A.10.1.2, A.10.3.2, A.12.4.1, A.12.5.2, A.12.5.3
CM-5	Access Restrictions for Change	A.10.1.2, A.11.1.1, A.11.6.1, A.12.4.1, A.12.4.3, A.12.5.3
CM-6	Configuration Settings	None
CM-7	Least Functionality	None
CM-8	Information System Component Inventory	A.7.1.1, A.7.1.2
CM-9	Configuration Management Plan	A.6.1.3. A.7.1.1, A.7.1.2, A.8.1.1, A.10.1.1, A.10.1.2, A.10.3.2, A.12.4.1, A.12.4.3, A.12.5.1, A.12.5.2, A.12.5.3
CP-1	Contingency Planning Policy and Procedures	A.5.1.1, A.5.1.2, A.6.1.1, A.6.1.3, A.8.1.1, A.9.1.4, A.10.1.1, A.10.1.2, A.14.1.1, A.14.1.3, A.15.1.1, A.15.2.1
CP-2	Contingency Plan	A.6.1.2, A.9.1.4, A.10.3.1, A.14.1.1, A.14.1.2, A.14.1.3, A.14.1.4, A.14.1.5
CP-3	Contingency Training	A.8.2.2, A.9.1.4, A.14.1.3
CP-4	Contingency Plan Testing and Exercises	A.6.1.2, A.9.1.4, A.14.1.1, A.14.1.3, A.14.1.4, A.14.1.5

Figure 5.3 – **NIST SP 800-53 and ISO 27001 sample control comparison**
(Joint Task Force Transformation Initiative Interagency Working Group 08, 01, 2009)

Risk Assessment Consistent with Roles within an Organization

Many different individuals within an organization contribute to successful information protection. As such, many will have a role to play in the risk assessment process. Security is the responsibility of everyone within the organization. Every end user is responsible for understanding the policies and procedures that are applicable to his or her particular job function and adhering to any and all security control expectations. Users must have knowledge of their responsibilities and be trained to a level that is adequate to reduce the risk of loss to an acceptable level. Although the exact titles and scope of responsibility of the individuals may vary from organization to organization, the following roles support the implementation of security controls. An individual may be assigned multiple roles for the organization. It is important to provide clear definition and communication of roles and responsibilities including accountability through the distribution of policies, job descriptions, training, and management direction, as well as providing the foundation for execution of security controls by the workforce.

5

Information Risk
Assessment

- **Executive Management** – Executive management maintains the overall responsibility for protection of the information assets. The business operations are dependent upon information being available, accurate, and protected from individuals without a need to know. Financial losses can occur if the confidentiality, integrity, or availability of the information is compromised. They must be aware of the risks that they are accepting for the organization. Risk must be identified through risk assessment so that management can make informed decisions. Furthermore, executive management is responsible for providing security leadership and governance for the organization.

- **Chief Information Officer** – The Chief Information Officer serves as the senior leader responsible for ensuring information technology and data processing initiatives align with the organization's mission or goals. This individual often reports to executive leadership, such as the CEO or COO, and manages technical operational risk for the organization including system authorization. As such, the CIO will review the residual risk for a new system or emerging risk for established systems and either establish plans to mitigate vulnerabilities or accept the associated risk.

- **Chief Information Security Officer** – The CISO directs, coordinates, plans, and organizes information security activities throughout the organization and works with many different individuals, such as executive management, management of the business units, technical staff, business partners, auditors, and third parties such as vendors. The CISO and his or her team are responsible for the design, implementation, management, and review of the organization's security policies, standards, procedures, baselines, and guidelines. In short, the CISO leads the information security office to manage information and information system security risks for the organization. This role is fundamental to the risk assessment process by leading security staff and communicating risk to the CIO.

- **Information System Security Officer** – Information System Security Officers maintain a subset of the responsibilities of the CISO. Specifically, the ISSO is responsible for the design, implementation, management, and review of the organization's security policies, standards, procedures, baselines, and guidelines. These responsibilities may be isolated to one system or a group of systems depending upon the structure of the organization. This individual is often uniquely situated within the organization to be able to highlight and identify security risks during the assessment process.

- **Privacy Officer –** The privacy officer will have knowledge of information systems, information security, privacy, and legal requirements and be able to identify and manage the associated risk and business impact to system changes, interconnections, and sharing practices. The privacy officer is responsible for reviewing organization practices and procedures to ensure the compliance with the relevant privacy laws and policies. Additionally, the privacy officer will be able to make risk management recommendations to prevent incidents of compromise and misuse of health or personal information.

- **Information Security Professional –** Drafting of security policies, standards and supporting guidelines, procedures, and baselines is coordinated through these individuals. Guidance is provided for technical security issues, and emerging threats are considered for the adoption of new policies. Activities such as interpretation of government regulations and industry trends and analysis of vendor solutions to include in the security architecture that advances the security of the organization are performed in this role. This individual possesses technical knowledge and is able to inform the risk assessment process for the organization.

- **Data/Information/Business Owners –** A business executive or manager is typically responsible for an information asset. These are the individuals that assign the appropriate classification to information assets. They ensure that the business information is protected with appropriate controls. Periodically, the information asset owners need to review the classification and access rights associated with information assets. The owners, or their delegates, may be required to approve access to the information. Owners also need to determine the criticality, sensitivity, retention, backups, and safeguards for the information. Owners or their delegates are responsible for understanding the risks that exist with regards to the information that they control. Given their role in the organization, they are usually the ones best situated to assess risk from a mission, goal, or business perspective and therefore must work closely with the technical security staff to ensure that organizational risk is adequately captured and mitigated.

- **Data/Information Custodian/Steward –** A data custodian is an individual or function that takes care of the information on behalf of the owner. These individuals ensure that the information is available to the end users and is backed up to enable recovery in the event of data loss or corruption. Information may be stored in files, databases, or systems whose technical infrastructure must be managed by systems administrators. This group administers access rights to the information assets. Individuals in this role

261

will have important business and operations knowledge to share to inform the risk assessment process and, like the data owners, must work closely with the technical security staff to ensure that organizational risk is adequately captured and mitigated.

■ **Information Systems Auditor/Assessor** – IT auditors determine whether users, owners, custodians, systems, and networks are in compliance with the security policies, procedures, standards, baselines, designs, architectures, management direction, and other requirements placed on systems. The auditors provide independent assurance to the management on the appropriateness of the security controls. The auditor examines the information systems and determines whether they are designed, configured, implemented, operated, and managed in a way ensuring that the organizational objectives are being achieved. The auditors provide top company management with an independent view of the controls and their effectiveness.

■ **Business Continuity Planner** – Business continuity planners develop contingency plans to prepare for any occurrence that could have the ability to impact the company's objectives negatively. Threats may include earthquakes, tornadoes, hurricanes, blackouts, changes in the economic/political climate, terrorist activities, fires, or other major actions potentially causing significant harm. The business continuity planner informs the risk assessment process and ensures that business processes can continue through the disaster and coordinates those activities with the business areas and information technology personnel responsible for disaster recovery.

■ **Information Systems/Information Technology Professionals** – These personnel are responsible for designing security controls into information systems, testing the controls, and implementing the systems in production environments through agreed upon operating policies and procedures. The information systems professionals work with the business owners and the security professionals to ensure that the designed solution provides security controls commensurate with the acceptable criticality, sensitivity, and availability requirements of the application. These professionals provide vital data around current systems vulnerabilities and controls that feed directly into the risk assessment process.

■ **Security Administrator** – A security administrator manages the user access request process and ensures that privileges are provided to those individuals who have been authorized for access by application/system/data owners. This individual has elevated privileges and creates and deletes accounts and access permissions. The security administrator also terminates access privileges when individuals leave their jobs or transfer between company divisions. The security administrator maintains records of access request approvals and produces reports of access rights for the auditor during testing in an access controls audit to demonstrate compliance with the policies. This professional will feed relevant system and security information into the risk assessment process.

- *Network/Systems Administrator* – A network or systems administrator (netadmin/ sysadmin) configures network and server hardware and the operating systems to ensure that the information can be available and accessible. The administrator maintains the computing infrastructure using tools and utilities such as patch management and software distribution mechanisms to install updates and test patches on organization computers. The administrator tests and implements system upgrades to ensure the continued reliability of the servers and network devices. He or she also provides vulnerability management through either commercial off the shelf (COTS) and/or non-COTS solutions to test the computing environment and mitigate vulnerabilities appropriately. This professional will feed relevant system and security information into the risk assessment process.

- *Physical Security* – The individuals assigned to the physical security role establish relationships with external law enforcement, such as the local police agencies, state police, or the Federal Bureau of Investigation (FBI) to assist in investigations. Physical security personnel manage the installation, maintenance, and ongoing operation of the closed circuit television (CCTV) surveillance systems, burglar alarm systems, and card reader access control systems. Guards are placed where necessary as a deterrent to unauthorized access and to provide safety for the company employees. Physical security personnel interface with systems security, human resources, facilities, and legal and business areas to ensure that the practices are integrated. This professional will feed relevant system and security information into the risk assessment process.

Information Gathering

A comprehensive risk assessment requires an accurate, thorough, and timely list of all potential risks and vulnerabilities to the confidentiality, availability, and integrity of health and personal information. Information relevant to the risk assessment will be gathered using a variety of methods. A foundational step will be to identify the lifecycle or flow of data through the organization. This includes where sensitive data, health information, or personal information are created, received, stored, maintained, processed, transmitted, shared, and, eventually, disposed. This step is vital to ensure that all vulnerabilities and threats are correctly identified. For example, if an organization uses tablet computers, it will need to get a sense of how the data on the device is stored, replicated, and backed up. While the organization's security controls may protect health information on the device, the information could be backed up to a cloud drive with varying levels of security.

At a base level, the first requirement is to create an inventory of all information and information systems that the organization owns, accesses, or otherwise utilizes under contract to store, process, or transmit data. This should include:

- Concentrations of files or databases that contain sensitive information
- Systems that contain or have access to sensitive data
- All IT systems and mobile devices that may access a specific network
- A list of interconnection with third parties including any security agreements or memorandums of understanding
- List of all software running on the devices on the network

Armed with this knowledge, the organization will be able to begin to address all risk to its information and information systems. It is incredibly important for the inventory to be thorough, accurate, and complete in order to allocate resources effectively and to mitigate risk down to an acceptable level.

Given the nature of health IT systems, electronic health records, and health exchanges, gathering information and maintaining an inventory of all third-party access and relationships will be one of the more complex relationships compared to other environments. These third parties could include the following:

- Cloud Service Providers (Infrastructure-as-a-Service, Platform-as-a-Service, or Software-as-a-Service)
- Other Healthcare Providers
- Insurers
- Law Firms
- Vendors/Maintenance
- Contractors

Depending upon the scope of access and information sharing with these organizations, the risks that they can pose can evolve over time. Maintaining an inventory of this information will help to identify changes as they occur and will help to highlight instances where changes with third parties could change the risk level to the organization.

Identify Vulnerabilities

Unlike a risk assessment, vulnerability assessments tend to focus on the technology aspects of an organization, such as the network or applications. Data gathering for vulnerability assessments typically includes the use of software tools, which provide volumes of raw data for the organization and the assessor. This raw data includes information on the type of vulnerability, its location, its severity (typically based on an ordinal scale of high, medium, and low), and sometimes a discussion of the findings.

Assessors who conduct vulnerability assessments must be expert in properly reading, understanding, digesting, and presenting the information obtained from a vulnerability assessment to a multidisciplinary, sometimes nontechnical audience. Why? Data that are obtained from the scanning may not truly be a vulnerability. False-positives are findings that are reported when no vulnerability truly exists in the organization (i.e., something that is occurring in the environment has been flagged as an exposure when it really is not); likewise, false-negatives are vulnerabilities that should have been reported and are not. This sometimes occurs when tools are inadequately "tuned" to the task, or the vulnerability in question exists outside the scope of the assessment.

Some findings are correct and appropriate, but they require significant interpretation for the organization to make sense of what has been discovered and how to proceed in remediation (i.e., fixing the problem). This task is typically suited for an experienced assessor or a team whose members have real-world experience with the tool in question.

There are also emerging, or at least evolving, technologies that will need to be reviewed, considered, and scoped into an organization's risk assessment where appropriate as they can introduce vulnerabilities to the organization. Some of these technologies include:

Electronic Health Records (EHR)

While there are countless benefits to EHR's, the digitization of health records can introduce security and privacy risks that may not have been previously considered. Sensitive files and patient records used to reside in the office filing cabinet and, in some cases, an off-site backup facility. However, when digitized, these files can be stored anywhere in the world, which opens them to common information security risks associated with the Internet.

Portable Devices

The consumerization of IT, or bring-your-own-device, trends have entered almost every aspect of business. Healthcare is obviously no different as the Ponemon Institute's Third Annual Benchmark Study on Patient Privacy & Data Security cites that "eighty-one percent of organizations permit employees and medical staff to use their own mobile devices such as smartphones or tablets to connect to their networks or enterprise systems such as email."[21] The expansion of these devices further erodes the concept of perimeter defenses as sensitive patient or organizational data can reside on any number of systems or devices that the organization does not control. If these devices are lost, stolen, or disposed of in a way that does not encrypt or securely delete the data they contain, these tools can act as means for a data breach.

Remote Access

As more of IT is outsourced to third parties, there is a greater chance that these vendors will want to remotely administer their systems and software. The credentials the vendors use to access these sites can be compromised and used to gain access to the organization's systems. If these connections are not regularly monitored to ensure that the administrators are not exceeding or abusing their access rights, risk can be introduced into the organization.

Cloud Computing

For cost or efficiency reasons, many systems and applications are purchased and run in the cloud. Per the Ponemon Institute, "sixty-two percent of organizations make moderate or heavy use of cloud services" and of those, "47 percent are not confident that information in the cloud is secure."[22] In these contracted relationships, patient and business data is still the organization's responsibility from a legal and regulatory perspective even if a breach occurs with the cloud service provider. As such, the organization will need to ensure that it fully understands any residual risk associated with the way these systems are managed. The best defense is to ensure that appropriate security, privacy, and regulatory controls are built into the contract before engaging with the cloud service provider.

---

21 Third Annual Benchmark Study on Patient Privacy & Data Security
22 Third Annual Benchmark Study on Patient Privacy & Data Security

Telehealth

As tools like video conferencing and wearable monitors proliferate, there are numerous privacy and security vulnerabilities that should be considered in the setup and operations of these tools. Additionally, it should be considered that "in telehealth models where one end of the communication is the patient, that endpoint falls outside the controlled and supervised environment of a HIPAA-regulated clinical care setting, magnifying existing privacy and security concerns."[23]

Embedded Medical Devices

The underlying technology chipsets and operations systems that support embedded medical devices are often the same that can be found and purchased in other consumer electronics. As such, there is the risk that vulnerabilities associated with this hardware and software transfer to the medical devices themselves, which makes them vulnerable to hacking. Furthermore, these devices are seldom updated or patched so they could be susceptible to older vulnerabilities for longer periods of time. Unfortunately, of the organizations that participated in the most recent Ponemon Patient Privacy and Data Security Study, "69 percent…do not secure medical devices."[24] The concern regarding the ongoing safety of these devices is such that, in the U.S., the Food and Drug Administration has issued a rule "mandating that device manufacturers and importers submit adverse event reports for medical devices electronically."[25]

Health Apps/Home Sensors

Health applications and in-home sensors that monitor the health of patients are ripe for security and privacy vulnerabilities. For instance, "home sensors intended to detect falls may also transmit information such as interactions with a spouse or religious activity, or indicate when no one is home."[26] Such breaches of privacy have already been introduced by home health sensors. For example, Fitbit, a daily health and activity tracker, "historically made users' profiles and activity public by default, to encourage social sharing and competitiveness. Some Fitbit users may not have realized this, given that the records of approximately 200 Fitbit users' [intimate activities] were showing up in Google search results."[27]

---

23 http://content.healthaffairs.org/content/33/2/216.
    full?ijkey=U93ciiUxE8bgc&keytype=ref&siteid=healthaff

24 Third Annual Benchmark Study on Patient Privacy & Data Security

25 FDA mandates electronic reporting for med device adverse events

26 http://content.healthaffairs.org/content/33/2/216.
    full?ijkey=U93ciiUxE8bgc&keytype=ref&siteid=healthaff

27 Fitbit Moves Quickly After Users' Sex Stats Exposed

Peer-to-Peer Software

Peer-to-Peer software can be useful for sharing or transmitting files within a closed network of peers. However, when the software is misconfigured or placed on systems that have access to sensitive healthcare information, there is a chance that these tools can introduce vulnerabilities that may not become known until after a data breach occurs. For example, in 2013, the U.S. Federal Trade Commission issued a complaint that alleged that a healthcare organization's "billing information for over 9,000 consumers was found on a peer-to-peer (P2P) file-sharing network and then...documents containing sensitive personal information of at least 500 consumers were found in the hands of identity thieves."[28]

Identify Threats

NIST, in Special Publication (SP) 800-30 Rev.1, defines a threat-source as "either (1) intent and method targeted at the intentional exploitation of a vulnerability or (2) a situation and method that may accidentally trigger a vulnerability."

Threat sources can be grouped into a few categories. Each category can be expanded with specific threats, as follows:

- ■ *Human* – Malicious outsider, malicious insider, (bio)terrorist, saboteur, spy or competitive operative, (medical) identity thief, loss of key personnel, errors made by human intervention, cultural issues
- ■ *Natural* – Fire, flood, tornado, hurricane, snow storm, earthquake
- ■ *Technical* – Hardware failure, software failure, malicious code, denial of service of medical devices, unauthorized use, use of emerging services such as wireless, new technologies
- ■ *Physical* – Closed-circuit TV failure due to faulty components, perimeter defense failure
- ■ *Environmental* – Hazardous waste, biological agent, utility failure
- ■ *Operational* – A process (manual or automated) that affects confidentiality, integrity, or availability

---

28 FTC Files Complaint Against LabMD for Failing to Protect Consumers' Privacy

Example:

	Intentional	Unintentional
Human	■ Data theft ■ Sabotage	■ Misconfigured server ■ Data entry error

Table 5.3 – **Sample definition of a threat source**

Many specific threats exist within each category; the organization will identify those sources as the assessment progresses, utilizing information available from groups such as (ISC)[2] and SANS and from government agencies such as the National Institute of Standards and Technology (NIST), the Department of Health and Human Services (HHS), and the National Health Service (NHS), among others.

Likelihood Determination

Likelihood is a component of a qualitative risk assessment. Likelihood, along with impact, determines risk. Likelihood can be measured by the capabilities of the threat and the presence or absence of countermeasures. Initially, organizations that do not have trending data available may use an ordinal scale, labeled high, medium, and low, to score likelihood rankings. Another method is presented in *Figure 5.4*:

Likelihood and Consequences Rating

Likelihood		Consequence	
Rare (Very Low)	E	**Insignificant** (Low - No Business Impact)	1
Unlikely (Low)	D	**Minor** (Low - Minor Business Impact, some loss of confidence)	2
Moderate (Medium)	C	**Moderate** (Medium - Business is Interrupted, loss of confidence)	3
Likely (High)	B	**Major** (High - Business is Disrupted, major loss of confidence)	4
Almost Certain (Very High)	A	**Catastrophic** (High - Business cannot continue)	5

Likelihood Qualification – How to Arrive at a Likelihood Rating

How to Qualify Likelihood	Rating
Skill (High Skill Level Required ⇨ Low or No Skill Required)	1=High Skill Required ⇨ 5=No Skill Required
Ease of Access (Very Difficult to Do ⇨ Very Simple to Do)	1=Very Difficult ⇨ 5=Simple
Incentive (High Incentive ⇨ Low Incentive)	1=Low or No Incentive ⇨ 5=High Incentive
Resource (Requires Expensive or Rare Equipment ⇨ No Resources Required)	1=Rare/Expensive ⇨ 5=No Resource Required
Total (Add Rating and Divide by 4)	1=E 2=D 3=C 4=B 5=A

Figure 5.4 – **Rating Likelihood and Consequences**

269

Once a value on the ordinal scale has been chosen, the selection can be mapped to a numeric value for computation of risk. For example, the selection of high can be mapped to the value of 1. Moderate can likewise be mapped to 0.5, and low can be mapped to 0.1. As the scale expands, the numeric assignments will become more targeted.

Determination of Impact

Impact can be ranked much the same way as likelihood. The main difference is that the impact scale is expanded and depends upon definition, rather than ordinal selections. Definitions of impact to an organization often include loss of life, loss of dollars, loss of prestige, loss of market share, and other facets. Organizations need to take sufficient time to define and assign impact definitions for high, medium, low, or any other scale terms that are chosen.

Once the terms are defined, impact can be calculated. If an exploit has the potential to result in the loss of life (such as a bombing or bioterrorist attack), then the ranking will always be high impact. In general, groups such as the government agencies view loss of life as the highest-priority risk in any organization. As such, it may be assigned the top value in the impact scale. An example: 51 to 100 = high; 11 to 50 = medium; 0 to 10 = low.

Determination of Risk

Risk is determined as the byproduct of likelihood and impact. For example, if an exploit has a likelihood of 1 (high) and an impact of 100 (high), the risk would be 100. As a result, 100 would be the highest exploit ranking available. These scenarios (high likelihood, high impact) should merit immediate attention from the organization.

As the risk calculations are completed, they can be prioritized for attention, as required. Not all risks will receive the same level of attention, based on the organization's risk tolerance and its strategy for mitigation, transfer, or avoidance of risk. *Figure 5.5* demonstrates a matrix view of risk.

Consequence

Likelihood	Insignificant 1	Minor 2	Moderate 3	Major 4	Catastrophic 5
A (almost certain)	H	H	E	E	E
B (likely)	M	H	H	E	E
C (possible)	L	M	H	E	E
D (unlikely)	L	L	M	H	E
E (rare)	L	L	M	H	H

E	*Extreme Risk:* Immediate action required to mitigate the risk or decide to not proceed
H	*High Risk:* Action should be taken to compensate for the risk
M	*Moderate Risk:* Action should be taken to monitor the risk
L	*Low Risk:* Routine acceptance of the risk

Figure 5.5 – **Rating Likelihood and Consequences**

Estimated Timeline

As noted in the risk matrix, each risk level should be labeled with a general action description to guide senior management decision making. The description identifies the general timeline (e.g., immediate action) and type of response needed (e.g., mitigate, monitor, accept) to reasonably and appropriately reduce the risk to acceptable levels. For example, a risk level of "Extreme Risk" could have an action description requiring immediate implementation of corrective measures to reduce the risk to a reasonable and appropriate level. Assigning action descriptions provides the covered entity additional information to prioritize risk management efforts.

Gap Assessment

A gap analysis is designed to recognize the current security posture of the organization and set realistic expectations of the targeted security posture. After assigning risk levels for all threat and vulnerability combinations identified during the risk assessment, one should document the gaps between identified risks and mitigating security controls.

Corrective Action Plan

A corrective action plan, similar to Plans of Actions and Milestones (POA&M), will take the output of the risk assessment and identify tasks needing to be accomplished to mitigate. The plans should enumerate all resources required to accomplish the elements of the plan (e.g., money, time, etc.), any milestones in meeting the tasks (e.g., phased completion), and scheduled completion dates for the milestones. Additionally, it is important to assign responsibility for each element and ensure that proper access and resources are allocated. For example, in the risk assessment process, it may be determined that there is a deficiency around Network Access Control (NAC). To mitigate this risk, the assessor will work with the system owner to identify possible mitigations for the deficiency and outline the resources required (e.g., hardware and personnel to implement). The mitigation options, resources, and projected timeline for milestones and completion dates will then be documented in a plan to be presented to senior management for approval.

Mitigation Actions

Risk mitigation is the practice of eliminating or significantly decreasing the level of risk presented. Examples of risk mitigation can be seen in everyday life and are readily apparent in the information technology world. For example, in order to lessen the risk of exposing sensitive personal and health information, organizations put countermeasures in place, such as firewalls, intrusion detection/prevention systems, and other mechanisms, to deter malicious outsiders from accessing this highly sensitive information.

The selection of countermeasures to apply to risks in the environment should be thoroughly evaluated, prioritized, and then implemented. Many aspects of the countermeasure must be considered to ensure that they are a proper fit to the task. Considerations for countermeasures or controls include:

- Accountability (can be held responsible)
- Auditability (can it be tested?)
- Trusted source (source is known)
- Independence (self-determining)
- Consistently applied
- Cost-effective
- Reliable
- Independence from other countermeasures (no overlap)

- Ease of use
- Automation
- Sustainable
- Secure
- Protects confidentiality, integrity, and availability of assets
- Can be "backed out" in event of issue
- Creates no additional issues during operation
- Leaves no residual data from its function

From this list, it is clear that countermeasures must be above reproach when deployed to protect an organization's assets.

It is important to note that once risk assessment is completed and there is a list of remediation activities documented in the corrective action plan to be undertaken, an organization must ensure that it has personnel with appropriate capabilities to implement the remediation activities, as well as to maintain and support them. This may require the organization to provide additional training opportunities to personnel involved in the design, deployment, maintenance, and support of security mechanisms within the environment.

In addition, it is crucial that appropriate policies with detailed procedures and standards that correspond to each policy item are created, implemented, maintained, monitored, and enforced throughout the environment. The organization should assign resources that can be accountable to each task and track tasks over time, reporting progress to senior management and allowing time for appropriate approvals during this process. All mitigation activities should have an identified scope, timeline, and budget.

Once the findings from the assessment have been consolidated and the calculations have been completed, it is time to present a finalized report to senior management. This can be done in a written report or by presentation. Any written reports should include an acknowledgment to the participants, a summary of the approach taken, findings in detail (in either tabulated or graphical form), recommendations for remediation of the findings, and a summary. Organizations are encouraged to develop their own formats and to make the most of the activity, as well as the information collected and analyzed.

5

Information Risk Assessment

Participate in Efforts to Remediate Gaps

Types of Controls

The following controls are broken out into three distinct categories:

1. Administrative
2. Operational/Physical
3. Technical

These controls are enumerated in NIST Special Publication 800-66 and specifically map to the requirements enumerated in the HIPAA Security Rule. However, they can also serve as recommended practices for healthcare organizations, entities, business associates, and organizations not covered by HIPAA or like laws.

Administrative

The National Institute of Standards and Technology (NIST) Special Publication 800–66 defines administrative controls as "actions and policies, and procedures to manage the selection, development, implementation, and maintenance of security measures to protect electronic protected health information and to manage the conduct of the covered entity's workforce in relation to the protection of that information."[29] Specific administrative control areas are as follows:

Security Management Process

The security management process encompasses all controls related to conducting a thorough risk assessment and implementing a risk management program. This includes developing and inventory, drafting policies and procedures, as well as establishing enforcement or sanction measurements for personnel that deviate from policy to risk practices.

Assigned Security Responsibility

"Who is assigned and responsible for risk?" is a very serious question, with an intriguing answer: it depends. Ultimately, the organization (i.e., senior management or stakeholders) owns the risks that are present during operation of the company. Senior management, however, may rely on business unit (or data) owners or custodians to assist in identification of risks so that they can be mitigated, transferred, or avoided. The organization also likely expects that the owners and custodians will minimize or mitigate risk as they work, based upon policies, procedures, and regulations present in the environment. In large healthcare organizations, there may be a single security officer assigned whereas in a smaller medical practice, the person with security responsibility may wear many hats. In either case, the assignment should be documented in policy.

---

29 NIST SP 800-66 Rev1: An Introductory Resource for Implementing the HIPAA Security Rule

Workforce Security

Individuals within an organization come to work every day to perform their jobs to the best of their ability. As such, these individuals have the appropriate intentions and seek out information on the best ways to perform their jobs, the training required, and what the expectations of their jobs are. Job controls, such as the segregation of duties, job description documentation, mandatory vacations, job and shift rotation, and need-to-know (least privilege) access, are implemented to minimize the risks to the data. Individuals must be qualified with the appropriate level of training, with the job roles and responsibilities clearly defined so that the interaction among departments can properly function.

Various activities should be performed prior to an individual starting in a position, such as developing job descriptions, contacting references, screening/investigating background, developing confidentiality agreements, and determining policies on vendor, contractor, consultant, and temporary staff access.

Personnel join and leave organizations every day. The reasons vary widely, due to retirement, reduction in force, layoffs, termination with or without cause, relocation to another city, career opportunities with other employers, or involuntary transfers. This extends to in-house staff and contractors. In both cases, clear termination procedures should be in place to ensure that their credentials and access to sensitive health data is removed upon their departure.

Information Access Management

Comprehensive access control policies and management ensure that personnel have access to only the sensitive health information that is needed to perform their job. There should be established procedures for authorizing and, if necessary, elevating access. Additionally, access rights should be reviewed on a regular basis to ensure that those with access still have a legitimate need to sensitive information.

Security Awareness and Training

Security awareness training is a method by which organizations can inform employees about their roles, and expectations surrounding their roles, in the observance of information security requirements. Additionally, training provides guidance surrounding the performance of particular security or risk management functions, as well as providing information surrounding the security and risk management functions in general. Finally, educated users aid the organization in the fulfillment of its security program objectives, which may also include audit objectives for organizations that are bound by regulatory compliance. It is important to note that ongoing security reminders and regular refresher training should be incorporated into a security awareness program.

Security Incident Procedures

Security incidents need to be investigated and followed up on promptly, as this is a key mechanism in minimizing losses from an incident and reducing the chance of a recurrence. Security officers are often responsible for implementing and operating incident response teams. These teams should be comprised of individuals with the necessary skills, including technical, management, and communications for evaluating the incident, evaluating the damage caused by an incident, and providing the correct response to repair the system and collect evidence for potential prosecution or sanctions.

Contingency Plan

A contingency plan is designed to prepare for any occurrence that could have the ability to impact the company's objectives negatively. The plan should document roles and responsibilities, preventative measures, and strategies to resume normal operations. The plan should be communicated and tested on a regular basis.

Third Party

Controls related to third parties are largely administrative as they are managed on a contractual rather than operational or technical basis. It is important to understand how all third parties share information and connect via IT systems. This information, along with your contractual security requirements and service level agreements, will allow you to manage the associated risk of these external relationships.

Operational/Physical

The National Institute of Standards and Technology (NIST) Special Publication 800–66 defines physical controls as "physical measures, policies, and procedures to protect a covered entity's electronic information systems and related buildings and equipment, from natural and environmental hazards, and unauthorized intrusion."[30] Specific operational/physical control areas are as follows:

Facility Access Controls

Facility access controls should manage the installation, maintenance, and ongoing operation of the closed circuit television (CCTV) surveillance systems, alarm systems, and card reader access control systems. Guards are placed where necessary as a deterrent to unauthorized access and to provide safety for the company employees. Physical security personnel interface with systems security, human resources, facilities, and legal and business areas to ensure that the practices are integrated. All security measures should be documented and incorporated into contingency planning activities as well.

---

30 NIST SP 800-66 Rev1: An Introductory Resource for Implementing the HIPAA Security Rule

Workstations

A workstation inventory should be well documented, including policies and procedures for effectively deploying servers, laptops, and network devices to reduce downtime.

Device and Media Controls

Device and media controls should be documented and enforced to include policies and procedures for adding to inventory and tracking throughout the lifecycle, including backup and, ultimately, disposal to ensure that sensitive health records are not lost or leaked.

In addition to digital information, such as electronic health records, physical records must also be securely managed to ensure the privacy and confidentiality for patients and organizations. Many offices collect information via printed forms or physicians' notes. Comprehensive protection of physical records includes creating policies around data collection, access control, copying, distribution, retention, and destruction.

Technical

The National Institute of Standards and Technology (NIST) Special Publication 800–66 defines technical controls as "the technology and the policy and procedures for its use that protect electronic protected health information and control access to it."[31] Specific technical control areas are as follows:

Access Control

Technical access control needs to be well managed to ensure that sensitive health information is only accessible to those that need it to perform their work. This includes the need to develop policies and procedures that allocate unique usernames to all staff, tracks and regularly reviews all access to sensitive data, and updates permissions accordingly.

Audit Controls

Information systems that contain sensitive health information should be monitored and audited on a regular basis. Depending upon the nature of a given system, there are system attributes and status information that are written into logs. These logs should be reviewed for anomalous activity, and procedure should dictate when certain activity should be reported for further investigation.

---

31 NIST SP 800-66 Rev1: An Introductory Resource for Implementing the HIPAA Security Rule

Integrity

Integrity is the principle that information should be protected from intentional, unauthorized, or accidental changes. Sensitive health information stored in files, databases, systems, and networks must be relied upon to make accurate diagnoses and recommendations. Controls are put in place to ensure that information is modified through accepted practices. Sample controls include error-correcting memory, magnetic disk storage, digital signatures, and check sum technology.[32]

Transmission Security

The core of transmission security is to establish policies and implement procedures for using encryption technology to ensure the confidentiality of sensitive health data while in transit. Healthcare organizations should review their networks as well as the interconnections with third parties to ensure that all egress points and weak spots in the network are covered by these procedures.

Controls Related to Time

Controls related to time allude to a subset of security controls that are of importance during various stages of an information system's lifecycle as it relates to an incident. Various security frameworks exist and each tend to use slightly different stages but, at a high level, tend to follow a similar pattern. For instance, in the U.S., NIST recently released a Framework for Improving Critical Infrastructure Cybersecurity. The stages addressed in this NIST Framework are as follows:

1. Identify
2. Protect
3. Detect
4. Respond
5. Recovery

Again, these categories are similar but slightly augmented for the purpose of critical infrastructure protection. An added use of this framework is that it provides an appendix with more specific security controls associated with each step and provides a reference mapping back to the international standards including Control Objectives for Information and Related Technology (COBIT), International Society of Automation (ISA), as well as the International Organization for Standardization (ISO) and the International Electrotechnical Commission (IEC).[33]

---

32 NIST SP 800-66 Rev1: An Introductory Resource for Implementing the HIPAA Security Rule

33 http://www.nist.gov/cyberframework/upload/cybersecurity-framework-021214.pdf

For the purposes of the HCISPP, this book uses the following control framework to identify controls related to time:

1. Preventative
2. Detective
3. Responsive
4. Recovery

Preventative

Preventative controls, as defined in NIST SP 800-66, are those "that deter, detect, and/or reduce impacts to the system." Preventative measures are preferable in that the cost is less than major recovery activities. For example, in the Software Development Life-Cycle, as in healthcare, prevention is better than cure. "Studies show that the relative cost of fixing defects in production is 30 to 100 times more expensive."[34] That is, the earlier in the development cycle that a defect, and possible future vulnerability, is identified, the less it costs to fix. Other examples of preventative controls include providing appropriate physical and logical access controls, managing remote access, providing security awareness training, ensuring that data is encrypted in transit and at rest, and having established change control procedures.

Detective

Detective controls reduce the risk of exposing sensitive personal and health information. Detective countermeasures include firewalls, intrusion detection/prevention systems, Data Loss Prevention, Network Access Control, and other mechanisms to deter malicious actors from accessing this highly sensitive information.

Even highly sophisticated technical organizations like the National Security Agency (NSA) are susceptible to data breaches. In fact, the NSA has publicly stated that it operates under the assumption that its networks have been compromised and that there are malicious actors on their network monitoring their activities.[35] The key is developing layered defenses and strong detective controls to identify when a breach has occurred and, to the extent possible, reduce the effectiveness of the breach.

---

34 http://www.isc2.org/uploadedFiles/(ISC)2_Public_Content/Certification_Programs/CSSLP/CSSLP_WhitePaper.pdf

35 http://www.reuters.com/article/2010/12/16/us-cyber-usa-nsa-idUSTRE6BF6BZ20101216

Responsive

Responsive controls relate to those activities required when addressing a security incident. Such controls include the activities of an incident response team to stop, limit, or reduce the impact of a security event. For example, if malware is discovered on a system, the incident response team may disconnect the machine from the network in order to ensure that it does not spread to other systems in the organization. Specific controls related to responsive activities include coordinating with stakeholders through the incident response plan, system compromise containment, and forensic analysis.

Recovery

Recovery controls relate to those activities that provide for the timely restoration of a system, service, or operation to a production state after a security incident. This is the time when recovery plans are executed, lessons learned are incorporated back into the recovery planning process, and the activities and outcomes are communicated with the relevant stakeholders. In the healthcare field, the recovery aspect may be of the utmost importance to the organization in order to be able to continue providing services. Additionally, if there was a data breach associated with the incident, this is where customer notification and other public relations activities would take place.

More to Know

The following resources provide additional information on Information Risk Assessment in the Healthcare Environment:
Official (ISC)² Guide to the CISSP CBK, Third Edition by Steven Hernandez

» *National Institute of Standards and Technology (NIST) Special Publication 800-30 Revision 1, Guide for Conducting Risk Assessments*

» *http://csrc.nist.gov/publications/nistpubs/800-30-rev1/sp800_30_r1.pdf*

» *National Institute of Standards and Technology (NIST) Special Publication 800-37 Revision 1, Guide for Applying the Risk Management Framework to Federal Information Systems*

» *http://csrc.nist.gov/publications/nistpubs/800-37-rev1/sp800-37-rev1-final.pdf*

» *National Institute of Standards and Technology (NIST) Special Publication 800-39, Managing Information Security Risk*

» *http://csrc.nist.gov/publications/nistpubs/800-39/SP800-39-final.pdf*

» *National Institute of Standards and Technology (NIST) Special Publication 800-66 Revision 1, An Introductory Resource Guide for Implementing the Health Insurance Portability and Accountability Act (HIPAA) Security Rule*

» *http://csrc.nist.gov/publications/nistpubs/800-66-Rev1/SP-800-66-Revision1.pdf*

» *National Institute of Standards and Technology (NIST) Special Publication 800-53, Revision 4, Security and Privacy Controls for Federal Information Systems and Organizations*

» *http://nvlpubs.nist.gov/nistpubs/SpecialPublications/NIST.SP.800-53r4.pdf*

» *National Institute of Standards and Technology (NIST) Special Publication 800-60 Guide for Mapping Types of Information and Information Systems to Security Categories*

» *http://csrc.nist.gov/publications/nistpubs/800-60-rev1/SP800-60_Vol1-Rev1.pdf*

» *U.S. Department of Health and Human Services Guidance on Risk Analysis Requirements under the HIPAA Security Rule*

» *http://www.hhs.gov/ocr/privacy/hipaa/administrative/securityrule/rafinalguidancepdf.pdf*

» *U.S. Department of Health and Human Services, HIPAA Security Series, Basics of Risk Analysis and Risk Management*

» *http://www.hhs.gov/ocr/privacy/hipaa/administrative/securityrule/riskassessment.pdf*

» *U.S. Department of Health and Human Services, HIPAA Breaches Affecting 500 or More Individuals*

» *http://www.hhs.gov/ocr/privacy/hipaa/administrative/breachnotificationrule/breachtool.html*

» *Federal Information Processing Standards Publication 199, Standards for Security Categorization of Federal Information and Information Systems*

» *http://csrc.nist.gov/publications/fips/fips199/FIPS-PUB-199-final.pdf*

» *HIMSS Healthcare Privacy & Security Risk Assessment Toolkit*

» *http://www.himss.org/library/healthcare-privacy-security/risk-assessment?&navItemNumber=21188*

» *A glimpse inside the $234 billion world of medical fraud*

» *http://www.govhealthit.com/news/glimpse-inside-234-billion-world-medical-id-theft*

» Fit*bit Moves Quickly After Users' Sex Stats Exposed*

» *http://www.forbes.com/sites/kashmirhill/2011/07/05/fitbit-moves-quickly-after-users-sex-stats-exposed/*

» 2013 Cost *of Data Breach Study: Global Analysis*

» *https://www4.symantec.com/mktginfo/whitepaper/053013_GL_NA_WP_Ponemon-2013-Cost-of-a-Data-Breach-Report_daiNA_cta72382.pdf*

» Th*ird Annual Benchmark Study on Patient Privacy & Data Security*

» *http://www2.idexpertscorp.com/assets/uploads/ponemon2012/Third_Annual_Study_on_Patient_Privacy_FINAL.pdf*

» NIST cybersecurity *framework: How it will impact healthcare*

» *http://www.fiercehealthit.com/story/how-nists-cybersecurity-framework-will-impact-healthcare/2014-02-13*

» Health *industry to test cybersecurity resilience*

» *http://www.fiercehealthit.com/story/health-industry-test-resilience-against-cyber-warfare/2014-01-13*

» FDA mandat*es electronic reporting for med device adverse events*

» *http://www.fiercehealthit.com/story/fda-mandates-electronic-reporting-med-device-adverse-events/2014-02-14*

» Diagnosis: Ident*ity Theft*

» *http://www.businessweek.com/stories/2007-01-07/diagnosis-identity-theft*

» HEALTHCARE INFORMATION SECURITY TODAY: 2013 Out*look: Survey Offers Update on Safeguarding Patient Information*

» *http://docs.ismgcorp.com/files/handbooks/HIS-Survey-2012/HIS_Survey_Report_2012.pdf*

» MEDICAL IDENTITY THEFT: The *Information Crime that Can Kill You*

» *http://www.worldprivacyforum.org/2006/05/report-medical-identity-theft-the-information-crime-that-can-kill-you/*

Case Examples and Resolution Agreements

» *http://www.hhs.gov/ocr/privacy/hipaa/enforcement/examples/index.html*

» *New certification program provides 'safe harbor' of privacy, security compliance*

» *http://www.fierceemr.com/story/new-certification-program-provides-safe-harbor-privacy-security-compliance/2013-11-04*

Domain 5 – *Review Questions*

1. How can a breach of protected health information (PHI) cause an adverse medical outcome due to integrity problems? Select the **BEST** response from the following:

   A. When data is breached, an attacker may attempt to use the victim's identity to obtain medical services. The victim's medical record then has erroneous information about the attacker that may cause adverse medical outcomes.

   B. When data is breached, a victim may attempt to use the attacker's identity to obtain medial services. The attacker's medical record then has erroneous information about the attacker that may cause adverse medical outcomes.

   C. A breach by definition affects the integrity of the data being breached and can therefore lead to adverse medical outcomes.

   D. Since PHI is considered low risk, there is no possibility of adverse medical outcomes due to breaches and resultant integrity problems.

2. An organization wishes to minimize risk throughout the organization after a risk assessment showed numerous high and moderate risks throughout the enterprise. Senior leadership wants to transfer as much risk as possible in the event of a breach. Which of the following **BEST** explains a risk transfer option?

   A. The organization may transfer all risk to another party. The party will be responsible and held accountable for all facets of risk and recovery should a breach occur. The organization will suffer no impact should a breach occur.

   B. The organization may not transfer any risk to another party. The organization is wholly responsible for all risk of information.

   C. The organization may transfer certain risk such as financial risk, but other risk such as reputation risk must be managed by the organization.

   D. The organization may transfer certain risk such as reputation risk, but financial risk must be managed by the organization.

3. The U.S. HITECH Act requires covered entities to report breaches of _____ people or more to the U.S. HHS Office of Civil Rights.

    A. 1

    B. 250

    C. 500

    D. 1000

4. Which of the following roles is **MOST** responsible for:

    -   Determining the impact the information has on the mission of the organization.
    -   Understanding the replacement cost of the information (if it can be replaced).
    -   Determining who in the organization or outside of it has a need for the information and under what circumstances the information should be released.
    -   Knowing when the information is inaccurate or no longer needed and should be destroyed.

    A. Senior leadership

    B. Information system security officer

    C. System owner

    D. Information owner/steward

5. Why should organizations use records retention schedules that mandate the destruction of information after a set date, period, or non-use trigger?

   A. Storage costs are reduced; only relevant information is kept, and this can speed up searching and indexing; litigation holds and eDiscovery are less likely to encounter erroneous, pre-decisional, or deliberative information; and to meet compliance requirements.

   B. Storage costs are increased; all information is kept, and this can speed up searching and indexing; litigation holds and eDiscovery is more likely to encounter erroneous, pre-decisional, or deliberative information; and minimize compliance requirements.

   C. Storage costs are reduced; litigation holds and eDiscovery is less likely to encounter erroneous, pre-decisional, or deliberative information; and to meet compliance requirements.

   D. Storage costs are reduced; only relevant information is kept, and this can speed up searching and indexing; and litigation holds and eDiscovery are less likely to encounter erroneous, pre-decisional, or deliberative information.

6. A small practice of thirty-five individuals wants to start performing continuous monitoring and assessment. Considerable debate has risen as to the best approach for performing the assessment. Which of the following approaches provides the **BEST** approach for a risk assessment?

   A. Have the organization's information system owner conduct the assessment as he or she already knows the most about the systems.

   B. Have an external or operationally separate entity perform the assessment so bias is minimized.

   C. Have the information system security officer conduct the assessment as he or she has the most knowledge of information security.

   D. Have the information owner/steward perform the assessment.

7. Information security and privacy is the responsibility of _____ in the organization. Please select the **BEST** answer from below:

   A. Everyone

   B. Senior leadership

   C. The information systems security officer

   D. The practice lead

8. Complete the following statement with the **BEST** response: Assessors who conduct vulnerability assessments must be experts in .

   A. Penetration testing, malware reverse engineering, and incident response.

   B. Properly reading, understanding, digesting, and presenting the information obtained from a vulnerability assessment and incident response.

   C. Properly reading, understanding, digesting, and presenting the information obtained from a vulnerability assessment to a multidisciplinary, sometimes nontechnical audience.

   D. Malware reverse engineering, incident response, and presenting the information obtained from a vulnerability assessment and incident response.

9. A rival healthcare provider has hired a hacker to illegally attempt to steal information from a healthcare organization. Which of the following **BEST** describes the hacker?

   A. Risk

   B. Likelihood

   C. Vulnerability

   D. Threat

10. A security management process is **BEST** described by which set of controls?

    A. Administrative/managerial

    B. Operational/physical

    C. Technical

    D. Detective

Domain 6

Third-Party Risk Management

THE HEALTHCARE ECOSYSTEM IS COMPLEX and multi-faceted, and it relies heavily on data and technology. Delivery of care may involve several entities to ensure that an individual's needs are met. It is a complex system when one considers the doctors, hospitals, pharmacies, insurance companies, government programs, counseling services, public health agencies, and so forth. When one adds third parties to the mix, the risk equation can grow exponentially. The challenge of the HCISPP with regard to third-party vendors is to help ensure that the confidentiality, integrity, and availability (CIA) of data is extended to outsourced service providers so that health care delivery is seamless and secure for the individual in need of its services.

TOPICS

- Understand the definition of third parties in healthcare context
- Maintain a list of third-party organizations
  - Health information use and processing storage and transmission
  - Third party role/relationship with the organization
- Standards and practices for engaging third parties
  - Relationship management
  - Compliance requirements
    - International variances
    - Implication of global trade restrictions
- Determine when third party assessment is required
  - Organizational requirements
  - Triggers of third-party assessments
- Third-party assessments and audits
  - Information asset protection controls
  - Compliance with information asset protection controls
  - Communication of findings
- Respond to notifications of security/privacy events
  - Internal processes for incident response
  - Relationship between organization and third-party incident report
  - Breach recognition, notification, and initial response
- Third-party connectivity
  - Trust models for third-party interconnections
  - Technical standards
  - Connection agreements
- Third-party program requirements (internal and external)
  - Information flow mapping and scope
  - Data sensitivity and classification
  - Privacy requirements
  - Security requirements
  - Risk associated with third parties
- Remediation efforts
  - Risk management activities
  - Risk treatment identification
  - Corrective action plans
  - Compliance activities documentation
- Third-party requests regarding privacy/security events
  - Organizational breach notification rules
  - Organizational information dissemination policies and standards
  - Risk assessment activities
  - Chain of custody principals

OBJECTIVES

IN THIS CHAPTER, the HCISPP candidate will explore the third-party vendor's role in the healthcare ecosystem and will develop an understanding of what it means to:

- Maintain a list of third-party organizations
- Determine when a third-party assessment is required
- Support third-party assessments and audits
- Respond to notifications of security/privacy events
- Support establishment of third-party connectivity
- Promote awareness of the third-party program requirements (internal and external)
- Participate in remediation efforts
- Respond to third-party requests regarding privacy/security events

6

Third-Party Risk Management

What is a Third Party in Healthcare?

Healthcare involves a variety of stakeholders—each of whom has a responsibility to safeguard the sensitive data with which it is entrusted. For purposes of the following discussion, the entity that has the direct relationship with the patient will be referred to as the primary entity. That could be a doctor, hospital, pharmacy, or health insurance company (also known as a payer). Any entity to which the primary entity sources a function or functions is considered a third-party vendor. In the United States, this relationship would be defined under the Health Insurance Portability and Accountability Act (HIPAA) as the covered entity (primary entity) and the business associate (third party) that will be using, storing, or transmitting Protected Health Information (PHI).

With the evolving nature of healthcare, it is common to see more and more services and functions sourced to third parties to reduce costs, introduce enhanced technology, supplement core services, and so forth. The expectation for third-party vendors who create, access, store, or process health information is that they must protect it at a level equal to or greater than the primary entity, though this does not absolve the primary entity of any responsibility for due diligence. Consider that, according to the Ponemon Institute's *2012 Study on Patient Privacy and Data Security*, healthcare entities reported that 42-percent of their breaches were caused by third parties.[1] The U.S. Department of Health and Human Services lists healthcare data breaches on its website if they impact more than 500 individuals.[2] The primary entity can suffer reputational damage as the result of an action by another party, as evidenced by the following case study from the United States involving the Los Angeles County Department of Health Services.

---

[1] Ponemon Institute released the Third Annual Benchmark Study on Patient Privacy and Data Security that is available for download with registration.

[2] http://www.hhs.gov/ocr/privacy/hipaa/administrative/breachnotificationrule/breachtool.html

CASE STUDY

Often the third-party vendor is not as well-known as the primary entity, so even though the vendor might be the cause of a breach, the primary entity suffers the "black eye". Consider an example involving the Los Angeles County Department of Health Services. The *Los Angeles Times* reported that the County had engaged Sutherland Healthcare Solutions, a billing and collections vendor as a third-party vendor (business associate under HIPAA). In February 2014, thieves stole computers from Sutherland's offices that contained Protected Health Information for more than 168,000 individuals.[3] Clearly, Los Angeles County is a well-known governmental body with much more name recognition than its vendor. As the well-known entity, the focus undoubtedly will be on Los Angeles County. Questions regarding the level of due diligence and due care in selection and operation of Sutherland will be the primary focus.

Vendors in the healthcare space can be as varied as a company that performs hardware destruction to one that handles medical claim processing, billing, or collections. Just as in other industries, vendor arrangements can vary, and each of them comes with a certain level of risk:

- Location
    - On-site at the primary entity's facility (e.g., nurses provided by a temporary agency)
    - Off-site at the third-party vendor's facility
    - Within the primary entity's country
    - Within a foreign country (often referred to as off-shore or near-shore)
- Service Offering
    - Business process outsourcing (e.g., medical transcription service)
    - Information technology outsourcing (e.g., system development / maintenance)
    - Cloud services (software-as-a-service, infrastructure-as-a-service, platform-as-a-service)

---

3   Sewell, Abby

Because sharing information is vital to ensuring that health care delivery provides for the needs of each individual, security and privacy of healthcare data poses some unique challenges. For example, the government or a health insurer (payer) requires information to be able to pay for the delivery of care. Providers (e.g., hospitals, doctors, pharmacies) must be capable of securely sharing patient information. Coordination among providers is required to give individuals an appropriate level of care. Although the data is sensitive and needs to be appropriately protected, care delivery depends on some level of openness to the data by authorized parties to be efficient and effective. At each step along the health care continuum, there are risks that must be anticipated and mitigated. When third parties are added to the mix, additional risk is introduced. It is precisely that risk which the HCISPP can help to identify, communicate, and manage.

The accountability for protection of health information ultimately lies with the primary entity; however, regulators are becoming more aware of the risks posed by downstream vendors. There are countless examples in the media of vendors who have caused data leakage or data breaches. It is important for a primary entity to ensure that its third-party vendors understand the laws and regulations to which the entity is held and to which compliance is expected of the vendor. Those regulations vary by country; often, additional laws exist within a country by state or province. Many regulations impose harsher penalties if there is negligence, so it is important to keep close watch over issues identified at a vendor to ensure they are corrected in an appropriate and timely manner. The organization that collected the PHI originally is responsible for the PHI even after it is passed on to a third party. The protection requirements for PHI follow the information onto whatever system or facility is processing, storing, transmitting, or disseminating the information.

In the United States, the primary regulation at the national level is the Health Insurance Portability and Accountability Act (HIPAA), more specifically the HIPAA Privacy and Security rules. Canada has the Personal Information Protection and Electronic Documents Act (PIPEDA) that addresses the security of sensitive information, including health information.[4] The European Union has the Directive on Data Privacy.[5] The EU directive, which guides the member countries in developing their specific laws, is often viewed as a strict standard that affords individuals greater control over the use of their data.[6] As the HCISPP candidate read in Chapter 1, the goal of these types of laws and regulations is to establish a framework that supports

---

4   http://www.priv.gc.ca/leg_c/leg_c_p_e.asp

5   http://ec.europa.eu/justice/data-protection/

6   Collmann, Jeff

the protection and confidentiality of patient information use and disclosure. Under the U.S. HIPAA law, the fines increase greatly if "willful neglect" is proven, meaning that the entity knew about an issue and failed to correct it. The maximum fine per violation is $1.5 million (U.S.).[7]

The U.S. Health Information Technology for Economic and Clinical Health (HITECH) Act of 2009 made business associates directly responsible for compliance with the HIPAA Security and Privacy Rules and provided the U.S. Department of Health and Human Services Office for Civil Rights (OCR) with enforcement powers over business associates. These actions place more accountability on business associates to understand and comply with the HIPAA rules. More recently, the HIPAA Omnibus Rule took effect. As of the September 2013 compliance date, business associates and their subcontractors, who create, receive, maintain, or transmit protected health information, are held to a more rigorous standard of security and privacy, putting them more on par with the covered entities. The rule also added some entity types to the definition of business associate, including data transmission service providers with routine access to protected health information, e-prescribing gateways, health information organizations, patient safety organizations, personal health record providers doing work on behalf of a covered entity, and subcontractors[8] (business associates must have appropriate agreements with subcontractors just as covered entities do with business associates).

Maintain a List of Third-Party Organizations

Health Information Use, Processing, Storage, and Transmission

A key responsibility of the primary entity is to know who its vendors are and what function or functions they perform on behalf of the organization. The information security professional should establish a collaborative and ongoing relationship with the areas of the organization responsible for procurement, contracting, and accounts payable. Those areas have a definite need for maintaining an inventory of vendors. Once there is an inventory, the HCISPP can begin to pair that with other information to create an overall picture of a vendor and identify specific types of risks that may be introduced. For example, the criticality of the vendor to health care delivery, the amount and type of data to which the vendor has access, the frequency with which data is shared with the vendor, and the way in which the vendor accesses sensitive data are all valuable inputs in determining a risk calculation.

6

Third-Party Risk Management

---

7   http://www.hhs.gov/news/press/2013pres/01/20130117b.html

8   http://www.gpo.gov/fdsys/pkg/FR-2013-01-25/pdf/2013-01073.pdf

Because healthcare data is so personal to an individual and highly regulated, it is imperative that the primary entity spell out for a third-party vendor the terms and conditions under which the data may be used, how it must be protected for transmission, and where and how it can be accessed and stored. For example, regulations may prohibit health information from being used to conduct certain types of marketing activities, or they may offer safe harbor if encryption is used in certain instances. This is where the intersection of security and privacy play out closely together. Privacy tells the HCISPP "what" needs to be protected so that security can determine "how" that protection should occur.

When it comes to transmission and storage, consideration must be made for not only the regulatory requirements but also the reputation of the primary entity and the harm to individuals if their health information is inappropriately obtained, released, or accessed. Encryption is generally accepted as the way to protect data in transmission, and it can be appropriate for data in storage as well. A layered security model is ideal, meaning that administrative, technical, and physical controls operate in concert to provide multi-faceted protection. A primary entity or a third-party vendor demonstrates due diligence when it can show that a variety of security controls exist and work together for overall data protection. Also, the better the understanding by the primary entity of how the data will flow from Point A to Point B and beyond is important. Once the data leaves the safety of the primary entity's environment, the primary entity needs assurance that it will be protected by the third party — where it will reside, how it will be stored, how it will be protected, etc.

Third Party Role/Relationship with the Organization

As shown in *Figure 6.1*, a key ally for the HCISPP is the primary entity business owner who maintains the day-to-day relationship with the vendor. This individual can become the eyes and ears in terms of changes at the vendor that could impact security controls, such as planned system changes or a physical location move. This does require investment on the part of the HCISPP to explain information security concepts and risks in non-technical language. The goal is to give the organization's leadership a foundational understanding of how a certain activity can affect information security controls. Also, the relationship that the primary entity has with the vendor is important to watch because it can help a HCISPP understand potential risks. For example:

- Is the business relationship established or not?
- Is the vendor performing a core service in parallel with the primary entity, or has the primary entity completely outsourced a core service?

- Is the vendor meeting the expectations of the business owner with regard to service-level agreements (SLAs)?
- Is the business owner pleased with the quality of service delivery?
- How long has the vendor been in business and performing these functions as a company?
- How financially sound is the vendor?
- What is the vendor's employee retention rate?
- What information security certifications or attestations, such as ISO or SSAE No. 16, does the vendor possess?

This demonstrates the need for the HCISPP to understand the business of healthcare and how security can help to minimize risks while allowing delivery of care to succeed. To individuals needing health care services, the security of their data should be the last thing with which they need to concern themselves. Security professionals who can make the connection between the business and technology and communicate well are in the best position to articulate risk.

Provides legal counsel regarding regulatory and contractual matters.

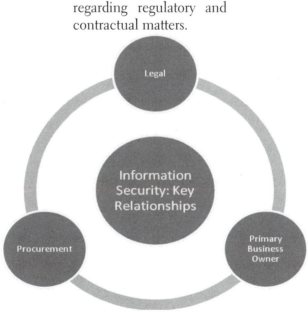

Negotiates with Third-Party vendors. Understand vendor landscape.

Maintains the operational relationship with the Third-Party vendor.

Figure 6.1 – **Key Relationships for Information Security**

In recent years, the healthcare industry, like many other industries, has begun to move toward cloud-based vendors. Cloud services offer economies of scale at a more reasonable cost than the primary healthcare entity can generally provide on its own. Although software-as-a-service (SaaS) vendors have provided solutions for a while, infrastructure-as-a-service and platform-as-a-service (development in the cloud) recently have become popular options. Like any other vendor, cloud providers introduce risks for a primary entity. *Table 6.1* offers some examples of information the primary entity should consider when working with a cloud service provider. Because of their operating model, cloud-based vendors are making investments in security, but they may not be as open to having a customer—the primary healthcare entity—conduct its own assessment or dictate as many of the contractual terms. Cloud vendors often do offer limited options for choice within their arrangements, as will be discussed under section 1.c: "Apply third-party management standards and practices for engaging third parties based on the relationship with the organization."

One item to note with cloud vendors, and another reason for information security to forge closer ties with the business, is that it is easier than ever for business owners to bypass internal controls for security and engage directly with a vendor. For example, consider the use of cloud-based document storage. A senior leader may believe that by signing up for a free account, he or she can conduct business and be more productive while at the same time keep costs low for the primary entity. However, there is no guarantee that the document storage vendor offers appropriate safeguards. So, as much as this chapter focuses on the ins and outs of formal third-party vendor relationships, the HCISPP must also consider ways in which policy, awareness, and technical controls need to evolve to keep up with changes in the ways individual employees can bring third parties into the mix.

Cloud Vendor Type	Definition & Some Considerations
Software-as-a-Service	Hosts software capability outside of primary entity's walls for primary entity to use. Some things for the primary entity to consider: ■ The physical location of the hosting, how the data processed in the application will be protected in transit and at rest. ■ How access to the software will be granted and terminated. The process for removing data from the cloud vendor's environment needs to be outlined if the relationship between primary entity and cloud vendor terminates. ■ Because this application supports the business, need to know how business continuity / disaster recovery is tested and handled. ■ How portable is the data if the primary organization decides it needs to move? What assurances of secure destruction of information are offered?
Infrastructure-as-a-Service	Hosts infrastructure capabilities, such as servers, outside of primary entity's walls. Primary entity may retain ability to manage and monitor hosted environment. Some things for the primary entity to consider: ■ The physical location of the hosting. ■ What level of rights the cloud vendor's team has to the environment. ■ If the cloud vendor provides technical support, how does cloud vendor ensure that its administrators do not abuse their rights? ■ How equipment destruction and disposal works. ■ Because the infrastructure supports business processes, need to know how business continuity / disaster recovery is tested and handled.
Platform-as-a-Service	Provides a hosted development environment for primary entity's developers to use. Some things for the primary entity to consider: ■ The location of the hosting. ■ If deemed necessary to use copies of production data for testing purposes, need to understand how the data will be protected in a test environment—for "real" data, controls should be equivalent to those used to protect production data. ■ May need to know how business continuity / disaster recovery is tested and handled if development is critical to the business and cannot be performed elsewhere.

Table 6.1 – **Cloud-Service Provider Considerations**

6

Third-Party Risk Management

Third-Party Management Standards and Practices

Although information security should participate across the vendor life cycle, as shown in *Figure 6.2*, the HCISPP needs to ensure that information security is embedded early in the vendor management life cycle. By building established relationships with the business operating divisions, the information security team can have a seat at the table when decisions are made on vendor selection. As an example, during the Request for Proposal (RFP) and vendor selection process, the HCISPP can evaluate the responses from potential third-party vendors with regard to information security controls. Even better, the HCISPP can provide security requirements during the development of the RFP to ensure appropriate assurances, attestations, security requirements, and service level agreements are included. An IS representative also can analyze previous audit/assessment reports provided by the third party, as well as determine if it has had past data breaches, how they were caused, and how they were handled. The IS representatives need an understanding from the third-party vendors of how they find and correct vulnerabilities. For example, does the third party engage an independent party to conduct network penetration testing on a regular basis?

Better yet, the HCISPP should try to participate when business leaders are deciding whether to outsource a particular function. If risk-based decisions can be made up-front in the life cycle, it greatly reduces potential issues down the road. In addition, it is important for the business to factor in the cost of compliance as a cost of outsourcing functions. Just as there are costs for doing business within an entity's four walls, there are costs to doing business externally, even when the goal is to save money. As an example, if the business believes that using a third-party vendor will save $2 million annually, but it will cost $25,000 to perform an annual audit, the savings are still significant. Factoring in the $25,000 annual cost still results in an overall savings, but it makes the case for information security compliance monitoring to be seen as a legitimate cost of doing business. When one considers that some healthcare data breaches have resulted in millions of dollars in fines and costs, all it would take is one major breach to wipe out the savings. The bottom line: up-front investment in information security controls and compliance monitoring is worth it.

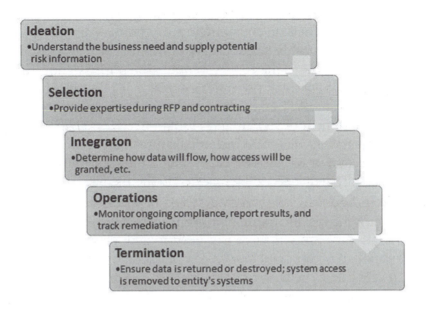

Figure 6.2 – **HCISPP Involvement in Third-Party Vendor Life Cycle**

Once the decision has been made to engage a third-party vendor, the contract becomes a key tool. Contracts with third parties are a critical component to the vendor management life cycle. Under the U.S. HIPAA rules, third-party vendors classified as business associates must execute a Business Associate Agreement that spells out privacy and security compliance expectations. On its website, the U.S. Department of Health and Human Services provides template language for the provisions that belong in a Business Associate Agreement.[9] In addition to the BA Agreement, many primary entities also elect to have additional contractual provisions to be more specific about security requirements, especially if the business associate is handling data over and above health information (e.g., confidential company information).

Not only must contracts include language required under specific laws and regulations to which the primary entity must adhere, but contracts should also articulate the terms that cover the primary entity's expectations regarding:

- ■ ***Compliance by the vendor*** with applicable information security and privacy laws and regulations.
- ■ ***Information security and privacy safeguards.*** Consider the administrative, physical, and technical controls required to adequately protect sensitive health information.
- ■ ***Right-to-audit.*** For example, how much notice does the primary entity have to give the vendor prior to conducting an audit?

---

9   http://www.hhs.gov/ocr/privacy/hipaa/understanding/coveredentities/contractprov.html

6

Third-Party Risk Management

- **Notification in the event of a data breach.** What timeframe must the vendor adhere to for notifying the primary entity? Will the primary entity notify its customers, or will that be a responsibility of the vendor? How is the vendor to notify the primary entity? This is especially important for business associates of U.S. primary/covered entities. The HITECH Act requires breaches to be reported to the Department of Health and Human Services (HHS). A breach involving more than 500 individuals must be posted to the HHS website, and in some cases, depending on the geographic area, the breach also may need to be reported to the media.

- **Where the data will be accessed, stored, or processed.** It is important to know the specific locations and ensure that the vendor will notify the primary entity if there is a need to add, change, or remove a location. It is important to set the expectation up front as to whether an activity can be performed in another country or not.

- **Data return or destruction when a contract terminates.** This includes how the data will be handled upon termination, as well as the expected timeframe for that action. It is important to also note that if data must be retained by a third party upon termination of a contract, it is expected that the third party will protect the data at the same level as under an in-force contract.

- **Employee background checks/employment verification.** The primary entity should know whether the vendor will be using its own employees, contracted labor, or a combination of both. What is included in the background check performed by the vendor (e.g., criminal history, credit history, educational verification, drug testing)?

- **Expectations for employee training.** How does the vendor provide specific training regarding the special considerations for handling of healthcare information? How often is refresher training mandated?

- **Ability of the vendor to subcontract work.** For example, the primary entity may require that it pre-approves any subcontractor that the vendor wishes to use to carry out the entity's work. If the primary entity is unaware of these relationships, it can introduce unnecessary risk. Consider *Figure 6.3* as an example of why this understanding is so important. The weakest link in the chain can reside far from the primary entity and thus be that much harder to locate if this information remains unknown. The HIPAA Omnibus Rule requires business associates to ensure that their subcontractors also abide by the privacy and security regulatory requirements.[10]

---

10 http://www.hhs.gov/news/press/2013pres/01/20130117b.html

■ ***Business continuity/disaster recovery plans.*** Within what timeframe must the vendor's function be recovered in the event of a disaster? How will the vendor notify the primary entity if a major outage or disaster occurs? Is the vendor prepared to move the work if its facility is unavailable (e.g., because of a fire or flood)?

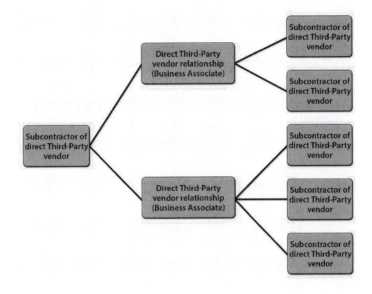

Figure 6.3 – **Subcontracting Chain Introduces Complexity & Risk**

It is important for the information security team to also build a strong relationship with the legal team. Conversations need to occur at the primary entity about which data protection points in vendor contracts are open for negotiation and which are mandated. Communication among the parties is a key to successfully ensuring that data is adequately protected. There should be no question at the third-party vendor of what the primary entity's expectations are. Having established and clear requirements also provides the primary entity with a way to measure compliance during subsequent audits or assessments.

As referenced above, cloud suppliers offer some unique challenges because by their nature, they need to operate within more defined parameters to be able to offer services at more competitive rates. Under cloud-services arrangements, the primary entity may not be able to customize an agreement to exact specifications, but many cloud providers—especially those wanting to conduct business within the healthcare industry—will offer some choice. The Cloud Security Alliance, which is a group of organizations who have banded together to promote best practices, issued a 2011 survey report in which 82-percent of cloud providers surveyed allow the customer some latitude in selecting where their data can be used or stored.[11]

11   Cloud Security Alliance

Third-Party Risk Management

6

Implication of Global Trade Restrictions

In the event that a vendor relationship crosses international boundaries, it is important to understand the laws under which both the primary entity and the vendor operate and how that affects the protection of health information. This has become especially relevant with the explosion of offshoring or near-shoring. It is important to understand the jurisdiction under which the third-party vendor resides with regard to laws and regulations. Some primary entities may want to make a decision to conduct business only with third parties whose ownership resides within the same country as their own, regardless of the location of services. That could allow the primary entity a better opportunity to pursue any legal action in its country's courts. Of course, as this is not a legal reference, individuals should consult with appropriate legal counsel when making decisions or recommendations on behalf of their companies.

Determine When Third-Party Assessment is Required

Organizational Requirements

A primary entity should include a formal audit or assessment in its contractual language with third parties. The contract should spell out:

- Who will perform the audit or assessment (e.g., primary entity or independent third party)
- How often it will be performed (e.g., annually)
- The timeframe for advance notice of the audit or assessment from the primary entity to the third party. In this instance, try to strike a balance between a fair timeframe for notice and the ability to adequately assess risk.
- Whether or not technical testing is a component (e.g., a penetration test of a third party would require some additional clarifications about scope and limitations)

According to a 2012 Ernst and Young survey report, 97-percent of organizations surveyed are driven by regulatory need to monitor their primary third-party vendors; 20-percent look at compliance activities of subcontractors (sometimes called fourth-party vendors).[12]

Many healthcare third-party vendors engage external auditing firms or certification bodies to provide clients with a certain level of comfort around their practices. For example, a third-party vendor may issue a Service Organization Controls (SOC) report to the primary entity to demonstrate the existence of effective controls. There are several flavors of SOC reports as outlined by information from the American

---

12 Ernst & Young

Institute of Certified Public Accountants (AICPA). The SOC1 report relays information on the controls that apply to processes influencing financial reporting, including some level of information security controls. The SOC2 can cover one or all of the following categories: security, privacy, availability, processing integrity, and confidentiality. Although some information security controls could be covered in a SOC1 report, a SOC2 report would take a broader and deeper look at security controls. There is also a SOC3, which is very similar to the SOC2, but it contains less detail and can be shared with a wider audience.[13]

Some third-party vendors elect to pursue a certification from an organization such as the International Standards Organization (ISO). A recent development for third-party vendors in the healthcare arena is the introduction of the Health Information Trust Alliance (HITRUST). This organization provides what is known as the Common Security Framework (CSF). The CSF brings together a series of information security controls from a variety of sources (HIPAA, International Standards Organization (ISO), National Institute of Standards and Technology (NIST), etc.) under one umbrella. Third-party vendors can use the CSF to conduct a self-assessment, but they can also elect to engage in a third-party assessment from an authorized entity. HITRUST aims to provide the healthcare industry with a common benchmark that covered entities can use to measure compliance at their business associates. The benefit to the vendors is that they would become HITRUST-certified, and they would not have to undergo as many client-specific assessments.[14] The goal for the primary entity is to receive information about the vendor that considers more of the unique healthcare security requirements.

With all of these options, many primary entities still feel the need to conduct their own assessments. Consider the compromise of using the audit reports available from the vendor as a way to determine what information the primary entity still needs to know or wishes to assess specific to its business relationship.

Triggers of Third-Party Assessments

The most likely trigger for a third-party assessment by the primary entity is as a result of a contractual requirement. The primary entity also may elect to put language in a contract allowing for a nonstandard assessment if the primary entity's data is breached as a result of an occurrence at the third party. In the instance of a breach, the primary entity should have contractual provisions that require the vendor to carry the cost of an assessment and associated remediation activities, including costs associated with notification and programs for impacted individuals (e.g., credit monitoring).

---

13   Bourke, James C.

14   http://www.hitrustalliance.net/about/

Under the HIPAA Omnibus Rule, the U.S. Department of Health and Human Services reserves the right to conduct its own audits of business associate practices. This is an activity that previously only applied to covered entities (primary entity).[15]

Third-Party Assessments and Audits

Information Asset Protection Controls

Although regulations generally provide guidance on the healthcare data elements that must be protected, healthcare is unique in that it brings together a host of personal information, including not only true healthcare elements (e.g., prescriptions, diagnosis) but also personal and financial (Social Security numbers, credit card payment information, bank account routing numbers). This creates a temptation for fraud. An article in *CIO* magazine estimates that the black market value of a health record is $50 (U.S.).[16] Also, the more information that the health record contains, the more ripe the record is to aid in a fraud scheme, such as allowing individuals to seek services and force payment using a legitimate patient's information. The U.S. Federal Bureau of Investigations (FBI) estimates that healthcare fraud costs about $80 billion (U.S.) annually.[17]

That said, some health information is obviously more valuable or sensitive than other types. For example, finding out that a person had an annual physical is not as sensitive as finding out that someone was enrolled in a substance abuse program or has schizophrenia. That does not mean that the information in the routine physical does not require protection, but it does mean that additional due care should be afforded to the substance abuse or mental health information.

Compliance with Information Asset Protection Controls

With third parties, it is important to spell out the controls that need to be applied to healthcare information. In those instances where healthcare is not the vendor's only line of business, this can be especially challenging. In the United States, the rules are tightening for business associates. The HITECH and HIPAA Omnibus Rules have made it clear that they are now held to the same HIPAA rules as the covered entities. Because compliance activities can introduce cost and overhead, some third-party vendors whose primary business is outside of the healthcare space are willing to perform services for healthcare entities as long as they do not have access to the data. In other words, some vendors are placing the onus

---

15   WEDI

16   CIO Magazine

17   http://www.fbi.gov/about-us/investigate/white_collar/health-care-fraud

back on the primary entity to ensure that the vendor can fulfill its responsibilities without accessing, using, or storing sensitive health data. In an article for the *Journal of the American Heath Information Management Association* (AHIMA), author Stephen Wu writes that "many of these vendors don't think of themselves as in the health field. Many are surprised to learn (usually from their health field customers) that they might be covered by the Omnibus Rule, and many vendors are pushing back to say they aren't business associates."[18] Compliance requirements can be seen as costly and onerous.

The primary entity must determine the level of assessment it will undertake for its third-party vendors. For example, will the primary entity rely on responses to a due diligence questionnaire, interview the representatives at the third party, and perform an on-site assessment? Will the assessment use inquiry and observation, testing or both? The primary entity may elect to change the method selected based on the perceived risk level of the third-party vendor. Although a facility walk-through may not always be feasible, it can be extremely enlightening for the primary vendor. If an HCISPP has the opportunity to visit a third party's facilities, activities such as how visitor check-in is handled, how a clean desk policy is practiced, and how sensitive printouts are disposed of can be monitored. Plus, the visit demonstrates to the vendor that the primary entity takes its due diligence responsibilities seriously. This also holds true for the internal business owner who maintains the relationship with the third-party vendor. When the business owner visits the vendor to assess operations, it also can have positive peripheral effects. When the vendor's employees understand their importance to the business operations of the primary entity, they are more likely to be engaged. Engaged employees look out for issues that could impact an organization. This author recalls an instance of visiting a third-party vendor and learning that the vendor's employees would welcome information, including security awareness materials that would provide information about the company for which the employees were performing functions. Developing a respectful business relationship with a third-party vendor gives the vendor added incentive to look out for the best interest of the primary entity.

Communication of Findings

When a primary entity or its designated assessor finds issues at a third party, those must be communicated to the third party's representatives. It is best to do this via a formal meeting where the third party can respond to the findings and agree upon corrective action and mitigation plans with the primary entity. The primary entity should have a mechanism to track the findings so that it

---

18   Journal of AHIMA

can follow up with the third party to confirm closure. According to a report issued by Ernst and Young, more than 60-percent of entities surveyed in 2012 indicated that after six months, well more than half of the issues identified with their third-party vendors remained open.[19] To conduct an assessment but not close the issues only gets the primary entity halfway, and one could argue that it puts the primary entity in a worse position because now there is a known issue that is not addressed. The primary entity can close this gap by ensuring remediation activities are documented and tracked to closure.

In those instances where a serious finding is found, the primary entity must consider whether or not it is prudent to continue business with the third party, such as in the case of grave contractual violations. It comes down to making a risk-based decision. This would be a serious situation most likely requiring a decision by business and IS senior management at the primary entity.

Notifications of Security/Privacy Events

Internal Processes for Incident Response

Incident reporting and response processes must be well defined for the primary entity and the third party, and it must be understood how those processes intersect when necessary. The primary entity needs to account for how its own incident response processes accommodate situations where a third party is the cause of a potential or actual breach. Roles and responsibilities need to be clearly defined to account for the flow of information internally at each organization, between organizations, and externally to individuals, regulatory bodies, and the media.

Relationship between Organization and Third-Party Incident Report

It is important for the primary entity to obtain a copy of an incident report from the third-party vendor. This helps to document the facts in an organized manner. The primary entity can use this as the baseline for coming back with questions or additional information requests. The primary entity needs to establish how often it will receive updates.

Breach Recognition, Notification, and Initial Response

In some cases, regulations require notification with specific timeframes to individuals whose information was breached. This is where a primary entity can lose valuable time if the third party does not immediately report a breach situation. For example, if a regulation like HITECH requires reporting to an individual within 60 days from the date that the breach was known to have

---

19 Ernst & Young

occurred, and the third party finds out about it on February 3 but doesn't report it to the primary entity until February 23, the covered entity has lost 20 days of valuable time to investigate, confirm facts, validate information for notification, and release the notification.

One other important consideration is who will release the notification. It should be spelled out in the contract if the primary entity wants to retain or delegate responsibility for individual notifications to a third party. The contract also should indicate who is responsible for costs associated with the investigation, remediation, notification, and customer care, such as offering credit monitoring for a time period. Bear in mind, some regulations may require reporting of the breach to a government agency and possibly the media.

Support Establishment of Third-Party Connectivity

Trust Models for Third-Party Interconnections

Data sharing between the primary entity and third parties must be done in accordance with applicable laws and regulations, as well as the terms of contracts/data sharing agreements. A key responsibility of the primary entity is to enforce minimum necessary/least privilege when determining the amount and type of data that needs to be used by the vendor to carry out its contractual responsibilities. For example, does the vendor need data that can be tied back to an individual, or would de-identified data be sufficient to fulfill its responsibilities? The primary entity must take care to limit the data elements that the third-party vendor can see. As an example, if the vendor does not need to see diagnosis information for individuals, the vendor should not have access to that information. Or, if the vendor only needs information on a subset of patients, it should not be granted access to the full population.

If the vendor's employees will be accessing the primary entity's systems, it will be important to ensure that the vendor is aware of the entity's policies and procedures. Processes will need to be in place to on-board and terminate vendor employee access to the primary entity's systems as vendor employees join, leave, or change responsibilities. These processes need to be clearly communicated to the primary entity's internal business owner and the third-party vendor.

When data must be transferred from one entity to another, it is important to consider the safeguards that need to be in place to ensure its protection. For example, encryption is a key consideration when data is sent over a public network or delivered via a storage device. Primary entities and third-party vendors must understand applicable regulations and what offers them safe harbor in the event of a security incident. The way a vendor will use and store information

6

Third-Party Risk Management

is critical to understanding the risk to the information. For example, will data be encrypted at rest? Are vendor employees allowed to use home PCs to access information? If so, how is the security handled for remote access (e.g., Virtual Private Network)?

A discussion around data sharing would not be complete without a mention of data destruction or return in the event that a relationship between a primary entity and a third-party vendor terminates. Not only should those terms be spelled out in contracts and agreements, but it is also incumbent upon the primary entity to ensure termination actions are carried out. Activities such as removing access to the data, appropriately destroying, disposing and/or returning the data, terminating network connections, and ensuring that files are no longer exchanged must all be taken into consideration.

CASE STUDY

Healthcare breaches are not confined to the United States. In one instance, unencrypted USB drives containing sensitive health data for millions of Canadians were shared by the government with researchers and third parties.[20] According to the Canadian Broadcasting Company (CBC), the government was unaware that several employees were copying data to the unencrypted devices and passing them off to the outside entities. The government was embarrassed because the data was released without authorization and was not appropriately protected. As a result of the incident, seven government employees lost their jobs.[21]

---

20   http://www.infosecurity-magazine.com/view/30247/bc-healthcare-breach-affects-5-million-canadians/

21   http://www.cbc.ca/news/canada/british-columbia/serious-deficencies-blamed-for-3-b-c-health-data-breaches-1.1354618

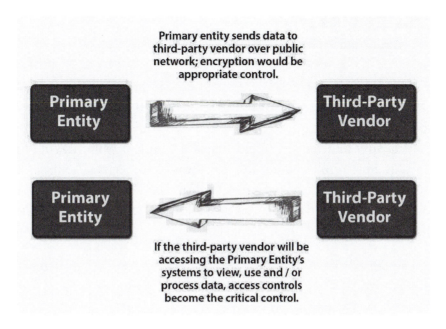

Figure 6.4 – **Data Exchange Considerations**

Technical Standards

Consider physical, logical, and network connectivity under technical standards. *Table* 6.2 provides a sampling of the technical standards that a primary entity should investigate with a third-party vendor. Specific regulations and standards (e.g., ISO 27001, HITRUST Common Security Framework) can help to drive out the specifics of a full listing for an organization.

Physical

This is an important area because it is one where weaker controls can easily be exploited without much sophistication. Poor physical security controls have been the cause of many breach situations reported by the media. Physical security controls help the primary entity have assurance that what happens outside the primary entity's four walls is in line with appropriate protections and safeguards. It is important to understand if any changes are planned in the vendor's locations where work is performed or data is stored on behalf of the primary entity. If a physical location move will take place, the primary entity needs to know how the third-party vendor will ensure that no sensitive data in paper or electronic form is inadvertently left behind.

6

Third-Party Risk Management

CASE STUDY

Blue Cross and Blue Shield of Tennessee learned a hard lesson about ensuring data is not left behind during a physical move. HHS fined the company $1.5 million (U.S.) after it was discovered that thieves entered a leased facility that was no longer used and stole 57 unencrypted hard drives that had remained at the location. The drives held sensitive health information for more than 1 million individuals.[22] The fine does not even account for the millions of dollars the company has spent on notification and remediation activities.

CASE STUDY

A quick scan of privacy websites shows many instances where unencrypted devices or media resulted in a breach situation. This is why it is crucial for the primary entity to understand the protections employed by the vendor.

As reported by Privacy Rights Clearinghouse, in 2013, Dynacare, a laboratory vendor for the city of Milwaukee, Wisconsin, USA, reported a breach to the city that resulted in the exposure of thousands of records containing information on city employees. The breach was caused when a laboratory employee's car was stolen. Inside the car was a USB drive that contained the records.[23] The HCISPP should be asking why a vendor employee would have the ability to save so much data to an unencrypted device and why the employee would be allowed to remove data from the facility.

---

22 http://www.hhs.gov/news/press/2012pres/03/20120313a.html

23 Privacy Rights Clearinghouse

CASE STUDY

Another example of poor physical security controls involves CVS Caremark, the retail pharmacy. Media reports showing that CVS disposed of Protected Health Information in unprotected Dumpsters caught the attention of both the Department of Health and Human Services Office for Civil Rights (HHS-OCR) and the Federal Trade Commission (FTC). Because CVS is a covered entity and a retail operation, HHS and the FTC both investigated and determined that CVS was disposing of such things as prescription drug bottle labels and medication instruction sheets into Dumpsters that anyone could access.

As a result of the government investigation, CVS was hit with a $2.25 million (U.S.) fine. The pharmacy chain also had to agree to implement information disposal policies and procedures, conduct enhanced training for its employees around appropriate disposal practices, and subject itself to both internal and external monitoring assessments.[24]

Logical

With regard to logical security, it is important to ensure that appropriate controls are in place to govern the access to the systems and data. This is most important when the third-party vendor will store data on its systems. However, it also plays out when the vendor will access the primary entity's systems. For example, there is responsibility on the third party to notify the primary entity if one of the vendor's employees has terminated employment so that the primary entity can remove the individual's system access. Also a consideration is how the third-party vendor governs and monitors the activities of system administrators and privileged users.

Network Connectivity

Network controls form the third leg of this technical standards triad. This is where the primary entity needs to gain an understanding of how the third party's network is set up, protected, and monitored. The primary entity needs assurance that the third party is doing everything in its power to prevent an unauthorized attack or intrusion. Also, with the proliferation of vendors offering web or mobile applications, the primary entity needs to understand how those will be protected. The "Connection Agreements" section in domain 5 provides information of how network agreements can help to define a great deal about network connectivity, controls, and use up front.

---

24 Federal Trade Commission

6

Third-Party Risk Management

CASE STUDY

There are countless examples inside and outside of healthcare regarding issues of compromised servers, exposing servers to the Internet that should not be, or exposing data on websites that is meant to be kept internal. Following are two examples from the HHS-OCR site where breaches of more than 500 individuals are listed.

The first one impacted the State of Delaware Health Plan, which was the covered entity. Its business associate, Aon Consulting, was supposed to release some non-sensitive information to the Internet but instead accidentally exposed health information for more than 22,000 individuals to a public website for five days.

The second involves Pinnacle Health Systems who contracted with a vendor called Gair Medical Transcription Services, Inc. Attackers were able to compromise a Gair server, resulting in an online health data exposure for more than 1,000 individuals. Pinnacle took this situation so seriously that it stopped doing business with Gair.[25]

Although these were two unique situations, they demonstrate the vulnerability of exposing sensitive data to the public via the Internet and emphasize the need for vigilance and monitoring.

---

25 http://www.hhs.gov/ocr/privacy/hipaa/administrative/breachnotificationrule/breachtool.html

Category	Considerations
Physical	■ Are visitors logged and escorted at the vendor's facilities? ■ Does the vendor's Data Center have strict physical access entry procedures? If the Data Center is managed by a hosting provider, is the hosting provider meeting or exceeding the requirements? ■ Are the facilities monitored (e.g., cameras, guards)? Is special care taken for sensitive areas of a facility (e.g., computer room of a Data Center)? ■ Does the vendor have procedures for identifying authorized personnel and allowing them access to the facility (e.g., badge readers, keypad entry)? ■ Is the Data Center equipped with appropriate environmental controls (e.g., fire protection, alternate power supplies)? ■ Do termination procedures exist for removing facility access in a timely manner if an individual's job changes or the individual no longer works for the vendor? ■ Are employees allowed to remove data in paper or electronic form (e.g., USB drive) from the vendor's facility? ■ Is printing of sensitive data allowed? ■ How does the vendor dispose of paper, media, or equipment containing sensitive information?
Logical	■ How does the vendor ensure that individuals receive only the access for which they are authorized and is required to perform their function? ■ Do the password standards meet or exceed those of the primary entity? If not, does the vendor have a way to comply? ■ Are laptops and other mobile devices adequately protected in the event they are lost or stolen (e.g., device encryption)? ■ Are termination procedures in place to remove system access timely if an individual's job changes or the individual no longer works for the vendor? ■ If the third-party vendor's employees will be accessing the primary entity's systems, in what timeframe and how will the third-party vendor notify the primary entity if an employee's access needs to be removed?
Network Connectivity	■ Does the vendor allow employees remote access to sensitive data (e.g., such as from an employee's home)? If so, how is authentication carried out (e.g., two-factor)? ■ Does the vendor have adequate network security to protect against external threats (e.g., firewalls with appropriate settings, network intrusion detection, antivirus solution)? ■ Does the vendor have standards and follow those standards for baseline configuration and patching? ■ Are the patching timeframes acceptable to address critical risks? ■ What level of network monitoring is in place to detect anomalies or suspicious events? ■ How will encryption of data in transit and at rest be handled? What encryption algorithms are used? U.S. covered entities will want to understand if those encryption standards comply with NIST.

Table 6.2 – **Physical, Logical, and Network Connectivity considerations**

6

Third-Party Risk Management

Connection Agreements

A third-party network connection agreement (also can be called a third-party network access agreement or an interconnection security agreement) dictates the terms under which the third party may access the primary entity's network. An example agreement published online by Health Service Executive of Ireland includes the following types of information:

- Third party will only use the primary entity's network for business purposes
- Only authorized employees of the third party are allowed to access the network
- Responsibility for network-related costs
- Confidentiality agreement language
- Explanation of privileges granted to the third party
- Statement that activity on the network will be monitored[26]

Third-Party Program Requirements (Internal and External)

Information Flow Mapping and Scope

A foundational piece to the third-party puzzle is understanding what data is going where and for what purpose. It helps the HCISPP to have knowledge of the business processes being supported and how the third-party vendor will gain access to the data needed to perform that function. Essentially, wherever and whenever information security can embed itself into discussions and decisions about the use of third-party vendors, it represents an opportunity to evangelize requirements that will help to minimize risk. The investment in education is worth the result. This also includes educating procurement and legal contacts as well.

Data Sensitivity and Classification

As with any industry, it is important that the primary healthcare entity understands the value of its data not only in context to regulatory requirements but also to its own business. Protected health information and related personally identifiable information are the obvious candidates in the context of this discussion, but the HCISPP cannot forget the business information that distinguishes the primary entity from its competitors. For example, strategic plans, new program offerings, pricing strategies and models, and proprietary system designs may not provoke notification if breached, but they certainly can have an impact on the

---

26 Health Service Executive

primary entity's business model and reputation. When the third-party vendor has its own data classification system, the primary entity needs the third party to demonstrate how its data fits into that classification to ensure that it is in line with the primary entity's expectations regarding data protection controls.

Privacy Requirements

This is an area where collaboration can occur if the primary entity has a privacy officer/department, as many large healthcare entities do. Information security and privacy representatives can collaborate to educate the internal business owner and third-party vendor. The focus is on what data needs to be used, in what manner, and for what purpose. It is important that they understand what to do if data is breached or even just improperly disclosed. For example, if a billing vendor accidentally sends a single bill for Patient A to Patient B, it does not rise to the level of a breach, but the disclosure should be tracked. That means the parties involved need to understand the instances that need to be reported, in what timeframes, and to whom they need to be reported.

Security Requirements

As stated earlier in the chapter, it is recommended that the HCISPP invest some time into helping the internal business owner, procurement, and legal understand security requirements at a high level. These individuals do not need to have a deep technical understanding of security but rather an overall awareness of what should be in place from an administrative, technical (logical and network), and physical standpoint. Again, the primary business owner is the individual who can be the eyes and ears day to day; it makes sense for the person to be equipped with some information security knowledge and awareness.

Security requirements can shift based on the arrangement in place with a third-party vendor. Most of this chapter is concerned with third-party vendors who perform work outside of the primary entity's walls; however, in healthcare, many situations occur where vendors may perform their functions at the primary entity's location, such as nurses contracted through a temporary agency. In those instances, it is important to ensure that the vendor's employees understand the security and privacy requirements under which the primary entity operates and how their activities need to conform. It benefits the primary entity to equip these on-site individuals with the same level of understanding regarding privacy and security controls that it gives to its employees.

Risk Associated with Third Parties

It is the primary entity's responsibility to perform due diligence to determine the level of risk introduced by a vendor. This activity should occur not only prior to engaging in a relationship with the vendor but also throughout the duration of a contract, especially because technology, business process, and regulations continue to evolve over time. The risk assessment should take into account the nature of the work performed by the vendor, the amount of sensitive data that will be handled, the frequency of the contact with the data, and the criticality of the vendor to the primary entity's business operations. Also, if the responsibilities of the vendor change or increase during the life cycle of the entity-vendor relationship, that can impact controls and how they are examined. This is why the partnership between the HCISPP and the internal business owner is so important. The business owner knows when operational changes will occur, and the HCISPP knows when those changes may modify the risk level.

Although "spend" would seem to be a likely candidate for risk analysis, in this case it is not always a valid measure of risk. An entity could spend $25,000 (U.S.) with a vendor or $200,000 (U.S.), but the risk posed by the smaller spend could conceivably be greater. For example, a smaller vendor may not be able to invest in best-in-class security controls because it is operating under tighter constraints. A smaller vendor may not have a dedicated information security team that can design and implement appropriate controls.

During the course of a vendor relationship, it is important for the primary entity to oversee and assess the controls that the vendor has implemented. A primary entity has to determine how much oversight is the appropriate amount. For example, if the vendor invests in audits (e.g., Service Organization Controls 1 or 2) and certifications (e.g., ISO) that appear to provide a high level of confidence in its control environment, the primary entity may be able to place more reliance on assessments performed by external entities. However, it is always good practice to ask questions specific to the business relationship and to inspect facilities where the work is being performed. This author recalls an anecdote shared by a colleague who related the experience of arriving at what he thought was the vendor's processing facility only to find out that the work was taking place several hours away at a facility of which he was unaware.

Remediation Efforts

Risk Management Activities

It is important for the primary entity to establish criteria on which to base risk. That holds true for the overall risk rating that determines the level of compliance monitoring to apply, as well as how identified issues will be assigned individual risk ratings. Both the primary entity and the third-party vendor need to be working from a common definition to avoid misunderstanding. It is important to communicate with the vendor what activities are associated with its risk level. For example, a primary entity may determine that all vendors who rank high in terms of criteria such as their criticality to the business, the amount and type of data they use, process or store and so forth, will be subject to an on-site assessment.

Risk Treatment Identification

Each finding during a third-party vendor assessment should be assigned a risk rating, such as critical, high, medium, or low. The primary entity needs to establish requirements at each of those levels. For example, it may be that a critical finding needs to be resolved in 14 days. The third-party vendor needs to understand the primary entity's stance on risk acceptance—perhaps only at a certain lower rating level. How will risk acceptance be agreed upon and documented? If the primary entity is not comfortable that a proposed remediation action will mitigate the identified risk and risk acceptance is not appropriate, the primary entity needs to have an escalation process in place to determine whether or not it makes sense to continue doing business with the third-party vendor. Follow-up timeframes could also vary by risk rating. The primary entity may want status weekly for critical risks but will only need to follow up quarterly on medium-risk findings.

Corrective Action Plans

When issues have been identified and assigned a risk level, it is important for an information security representative to meet with the internal business owner and the vendor's representative to discuss the issues and how the vendor plans to address them. The corrective action plan should indicate what the vendor plans to implement (e.g., new technology, enhanced policies and procedures, additional training) and the timeframe in which the activity will be carried out. In those instances where the vendor determines it cannot correct an issue, it will be the decision of the primary entity whether it can accept that risk or not. A decision will need to be made about the impact to the primary entity and if it makes sense to continue doing business with the known risk. Depending on the type of risk, this situation, which should be somewhat rare, will need to be escalated to senior management for a decision. That is where the HCISPP can provide valuable information about the risk and what it poses for the organization. This should be communicated in business language that can be understood by all parties involved in the decision-making process.

6

Third-Party Risk Management

319

Compliance Activities Documentation

As noted earlier, it is a responsibility of the primary entity to assess the risk associated with engaging in a relationship with a vendor. The role of the HCISPP is to serve as the Subject Matter Expert for assessing security risks, which in turn equips the business owner with information to make informed decisions. Risk levels need to be explained (e.g., critical, high, medium, and low) and defined for the business owners. Each associated level should be accompanied by an expected action timeline (e.g., critical risks must be remediated within 24 hours).

Again, if the security professional has invested in equipping the internal business owner with knowledge, tracking compliance activities can be incorporated into whatever process the business owner is using to track other metrics associated with the vendor (e.g., operational SLAs). For example, the internal business owner could periodically validate that the vendor has informed the primary entity of those individuals who have terminated employment with the vendor. It is a good practice for the internal business owner to embed ongoing compliance questions into the operational monitoring and reporting with primary entity senior management and the third-party vendor.

That is not to say that the information security department (if available) should not track the issues as well. On the contrary, IS should track all of the issues and stay in close contact with the internal business owners. The tracking not only shows progress on individual risks, but it also provides a repository of information that can be used to keep senior management informed and monitor trends. For example, over time, IS can show how a monitoring program is leading to overall reduced risk for the organization and help identify areas where standard contractual language could be enhanced moving forward.

Third Party Requests regarding Privacy/Security Events

Organizational Breach Notification Rules

In addition to any regulatory requirements regarding breach notification, it is imperative that the primary entity has policies and associated procedures to document its internal requirements and processes. Employees need to understand how and when to report a breach, and if employees are interacting with third-party vendors, they need to understand the requirements of the vendors as well. This takes an investment in awareness and training, which is where the HCISPP can provide a great deal of guidance. Because some regulations have specific timeframes for breach notification, it is worth the effort to train employees to avoid a situation that could lead to a regulatory violation for missed timeframes. Employees also need to understand what information to provide when reporting a potential or actual breach.

Although they may not have all of the information an investigator would like, the more information they can provide, the better. One recommendation is to provide more targeted training and awareness for employees who are the key contacts with the primary entity's third-party vendors. They should be familiar with the contractual obligations of the vendor for reporting a breach. They need to understand the responsibilities of their organization and the vendor's organization during a breach investigation and regarding notification to individuals. This is where incident reporting and response are of great help. When the primary entity is testing its incident response process, it would be beneficial to factor in scenarios where the third party identifies or causes an incident. Also, as part of due diligence, a primary entity needs to understand the incident response processes in place at its third parties.[27] The goal should be to foster as much consistency as possible regardless of the third party involved.

Organizational Information Dissemination Policies and Standards

The primary entity and the third-party vendor need established protocols for how information about a breach is communicated within their internal organizations, between their organizations, and externally. Facts about a breach should be communicated with non-essential parties on a need-to-know basis so that misinformation does not start to spread. It is important to have a method for identifying senior leadership and other corporate areas that should play their role (e.g., public relations for media inquiries). If all of these audiences and communication channels have been documented ahead of an actual incident, it takes the guesswork out when an issue occurs.

Risk Assessment Activities

When a security incident occurs, the purpose of the risk assessment is to determine the extent of the damage to the primary entity and, most importantly, to the individual whose data was exposed or compromised. The primary entity needs to factor in information such as:

- How many individuals are impacted
- The data elements involved (e.g., name, Social Security number, diagnosis, payment information)
- Whether the incident was caused by accidental or intentional action
- Whether or not the incident has been contained

---

27 http://www.govhealthit.com/news/4-steps-business-associates-comply-omnibus-hipaa

Under the U.S. HITECH breach notification rule, the covered entity or business associate needs to look at the facts to determine risk of financial, reputational, or other risk of harm to the individuals whose health information was exposed. According to guidance from the HHS Health Resources and Services Administration (HRSA), the following should be considered:

- Was identifiable protected health information impacted?
- If PHI was involved, was it appropriately secured or not (e.g., encrypted in transit)?
- Does the disclosure qualify for one of the exceptions, such as the disclosure "was made in good faith within the course or scope of employment or other professional relationship and does not result in further use or disclosure?"[28]
- What other factors were present that could cause harm to an individual (e.g., who used the compromised health information)?

When one is making a decision about whether or not breach notification is required, it is good practice to consult with legal counsel.

Chain of Custody

It is important to be prepared in case a breach happens at the third party. If everyone is aware of responsibilities ahead of time, it can prevent confusion and missteps when a breach occurs. The third party must be aware of who to contact at the primary entity (e.g., hotline, security office, help desk, business contact) and how to contact (e.g., phone, web form, email). The primary entity must ensure that its incident response procedures account for protocols that cover a breach reported by a third party. It is important that the primary entity understands if the breach has been or is in the process of being contained. In other words, is there still the possibility that additional data could be exposed? The primary entity needs to understand the volume and type of data that was breached. At the point a breach is reported, the third party may or may not know the exact individuals whose information is at risk. If they do not yet know that information, it is important for the primary entity and the third party to stay in regular contact so that data can be collected as quickly as possible.

As the investigation ensues, the primary entity needs to stay in close contact with the third party to understand the details and possibly even assist, especially if the primary entity has forensic security expertise. The principle of chain of custody is critical to ensure that the facts are in order and the evidence is appropriately collected, handled, logged, and maintained, especially if the situation requires involvement by law enforcement or potential legal action. The third party also must keep the primary entity aware of remediation activities designed to prevent future occurrences of the same type of breach.

---

28 http://www.hrsa.gov/healthit/toolbox/healthitadoptiontoolbox/privacyandsecurity/riskassessment.html

Summary

The HCISPP is an asset to a primary entity or third-party vendor that is trying to navigate the complex healthcare business and regulatory landscape. By working side-by-side with the business operating areas, the HCISPP can help to articulate and communicate risk so that sound decisions can be made. Regulatory requirements continue to mount and are definitely including the third-party vendor in the equation if the vendor creates, uses, transmits, or processes sensitive healthcare information. The primary entity has a vested interest from a legal, regulatory, and reputational aspect to remain involved and aware of the effectiveness of the controls in place at its third-party vendors.

Security compliance monitoring should be incorporated into the primary entity's program as a cost of outsourcing work to a third party. Up-front investment in understanding the landscape of third-party vendors used by the primary entity is important. The primary entity must know where sensitive health data is going, how it will be used, and how it will be protected. It is a responsibility of the primary entity to assess the vendor's continued compliance with information security regulatory and contractual requirements. Ongoing compliance monitoring, as well as issue identification, tracking, and closure, are essential to a sound third-party vendor management program.

The better the planning and preparation by a primary entity in conjunction with its third-party vendors, the more equipped each party will be if and when a security incident does occur. Well-defined roles and responsibilities, documented processes, and good communication are essential ingredients for success. Both the primary entity and the third-party vendor need to be aware of the regulatory requirements and documented processes associated with breach notification. Each party has clear stake in minimizing the damage. What should not be lost in all of this is that sensitive health data belongs to real people who may suffer embarrassment, financial loss, identity theft, and other ills should the information be breached or altered without authorization.

Managing information security risk associated with third-party vendors is a responsibility the HCISPP must take seriously because it provides assurance to all of those involved in healthcare, including the patient, that their sensitive data is safe and secure.

References

"About HITRUST." *HITRUST : About.* Accessed March 17, 2014, from http://www.hitrustalliance.net/about/.

"BC healthcare breach affects 5 million Canadians". *Infosecurity-Magazine.* January 16, 2013. Infosecurity-Magazine on the Web, accessed March 21, 2014.

Bourke, James C. "Explaining SOC: Easy as 1-2-3: What CPAs need to know about Service Organization Control reports." CPA2Biz, June 11, 2012, online, *CPA2Biz,* Available from AICPA, accessed March 17, 2014.

"Business Associate Contracts." *Business Associate Contracts.* U.S. Department of Health and Human Srvices, n.d. Web. March 17, 2014. http://www.hhs.gov/ocr/privacy/hipaa/understanding/coveredentities/contractprov.html.

Cloud Security Alliance, "Cloud Security Alliance Cloud Data Governance Cloud Consumer Advocacy Questionnaire and Information Survey (CCAQIS)", 2011. Available from Cloud Security Alliance, accessed March 15, 2014.

"Chronology of Data Breaches | Privacy Rights Clearinghouse." *Chronology of Data Breaches | Privacy Rights Clearinghouse.* Accessed December 1, 2013 from http://www.privacyrights.org/data-breach.

Collmann, Jeff, PhD, and Marcha, Margaret (ed.), Health Information and Management Systems Society, "Managing Information Privacy & Security in Healthcare European Union Privacy Directive Reconciling European and American Approaches to Privacy", February 2013. Available from Healthcare Information and Management Systems Society, accessed March 23, 2014.

Ernst & Young, "Lessons from Change: Key findings from Ernst and Young's 2012 financial service supplier risk management survey," 2013.

Federal Bureau of Investigations. "Rooting out healthcare fraud is central to the well-being of both our citizens and the overall economy". Available at http://www.fbi.gov/about-us/investigate/white_collar/health-care-fraud. Accessed March 22, 2014.

6

Third-Party Risk Management

Federal Trade Commission. "CVS Caremark Settles FTC Charges:Failed to Protect Medical and Financial Privacy of Customers and Employees;CVS Pharmacy Also Pays $2.25 Million to Settle Allegations of HIPAA Violations" Federal Trade Commission news release, February 18, 2009. Federal Trade Commission website. http://www.ftc.gov/news-events/press-releases/2009/02/cvs-caremark-settles-ftc-chargesfailed-protect-medical-financial, accessed on March 16, 2014.

"Guidance to Render Unsecured Protected Health Information Unusable, Unreadable, or Indecipherable to Unauthorized Individuals." *Guidance to Render Unsecured Protected Health Information Unusable, Unreadable, or Indecipherable to Unauthorized Individuals.* U.S. Department of Health and Human Services Office for Civil Rights, n.d. Web. 23 Mar. 2014. http://www.hhs.gov/ocr/privacy/hipaa/administrative/breachnotificationrule/brguidance.html.

Kam, Rick and Sher-Jan,Mahmood, "4 steps for business associates to comply with Omnibus HIPAA". *Government HealthIT.* September 20, 2013. Government HealthIT on the Web, accessed March 25, 2014.

"Modifications to the HIPAA Privacy, Security, Enforcement, and Breach Notification Rules Under the Health Information Technology for Economic and Clinical Health Act and the Genetic Information Nondiscrimination Act; Other Modifications to the HIPAA Rules; Final Rule," 78 Federal Register 17 (January 25, 2013), pp. 5566-5702.

Olavsrud, Thor, «Healthcare Industry CIOs, CSOs Must Improve Security.» *CIO.* March 6, 2012. CIO on the Web, accessed December 2, 2013.

Ponemon Institute, "Third Annual Benchmark Study on Patient Privacy and Data Security," December 2012.

Sewell, Abby. "Personal data on L.A. County medical patients stolen from contractor. " *Los Angeles Times.* March 6, 2014. Los Angeles Times on the Web, accessed March 15, 2014.

"'Serious deficiencies' blamed for 3 B.C. health data breaches: Personal health records of 4 million residents shared on unencrypted memory sticks". *CBC News.* June 26, 2013. CBC News on the Web, accessed March 21, 2014.

"Third Party Connection Agreement." *SANS Institute.* SANS Institute, Accessed March 26 2014 from. http://www.sans.org/security-resources/policies/Third_Party_Agreement.pdf.

U.S. Department of Health and Human Services. "HHS Settles HIPAA Case with BCBST for $1.5 Million" Health and Human Services news release, March 13, 2012. HHS website. http://www.hhs.gov/news/press/2012pres/03/20120313a.html, accessed on March 22, 2014.

U.S. Department of Health and Human Services Health Resources and Services Administration. "How does a covered entity or business associate perform a risk assessment to determine if a breach occurred?". Available at http://www.hrsa.gov/healthit/toolbox/healthitadoptiontoolbox/privacyandsecurity/riskassessment.html. Accessed on March 22, 2014.

WEDI, "Omnibus Final Rule – Modifications to the HIPAA Privacy, Security, Enforcement and Breach Notification Rules Under the HITECH Act and GINA Act; Other Modifications to the HIPAA Rules – Section by Section Comparative Summary", January 2013. Available from WEDI, accessed March 25, 2014.

6

Third-Party Risk Management

1. Third-parties can _____.
   A. Introduce additional risk to an organization if not properly assessed and monitored.
   B. Alleviate an organization of responsibility during a protected health information breach.
   C. Not outsource processing, storage, or transmission of sensitive PHI regardless of contract requirements.
   D. Only operate in countries where the original party resides.

2. What is the **BEST** reason a healthcare organization should create and maintain a list of third-party organizations it does business with?
   A. A list of vendors ensures the contracting office can quickly identify a list of potentially secure companies for new requirements.
   B. The listing can provide a means for the HCISPP to pair third-party provider information with the criticality of healthcare information frequency and sensitivity.
   C. The list can be used by the marketing firm to determine the best channels to market net electronic health record offerings.
   D. The third-party organization list is used by the HCISPP to determine the "How" of protection requirements.

3. Which of the following would **BEST** help a HCISPP determine if a third party has met an external attestation for information security or privacy?
   A. Financial soundness
   B. Length of time vendor has been in business
   C. ISO or SSAE No. 16 certifications
   D. Past performance reviews

4. Which of the following cloud service models requires the cloud provider to provide the majority of the security controls?
   A. Infrastructure as a service
   B. Software as a service
   C. Platform as a service
   D. Network as a service

5. What is the **BEST** way an HCISPP can ensure that information security and privacy is "built-in" to third-party cloud providers?

    A. Purchase whatever solution the majority of the market is consuming.

    B. Determine security and privacy requirements prior to researching cloud offerings and ensure any cloud providers can meet them.

    C. Purchase cloud services and then negotiate with the cloud provider to ensure the exact controls need are implemented

    D. Ensure the HCISPP is excluded from contract negotiations as security and privacy tend to increase price.

6. Which element of third-party management below has the **MOST** risk from data remnants?

    A. Integration

    B. Termination

    C. Operations

    D. Selection

7. When developing a contract with a third party to process, store, and transmit information, which of the following **BEST** protects the organization?

    A. Vendor compliance with laws and regulations, information security and privacy safeguards, right to audit clauses and full risk transfer to the vendor.

    B. Full risk transfer to the vendor, information security and privacy safeguards, right to audit clauses and data breach notification.

    C. Vendor compliance with laws and regulations, full risk transfer to the vendor, and right to audit clauses and data breach notification.

    D. Vendor compliance with laws and regulations, information security and privacy safeguards, right to audit clauses and data breach notification.

6

Third-Party Risk Management

8. Which of the following **BEST** explains when employee background investigations should be required of a third-party vendor?

    A. Only when working with a vendor outside of the organization's home country or jurisdiction.

    B. Only when working with a vendor inside of the organization's home country or jurisdiction.

    C. In any contract where the organization has a legal, regulatory, or risk management requirement to ensure information is protected against unauthorized disclosure.

    D. In any contract where the vendor will perform research using de-identified information from the organization.

9. An interconnection security agreement **BEST** serves to _____.

    A. Establish and memorialize security and privacy expectations for interconnecting parties.

    B. Establish fault after a breach and determine which party is most liable.

    C. Establish responsibility for network related costs.

    D. Memorialize employee access conditions for each party's data.

10. The _____ is **MOST** responsible to perform due diligence to determine the level of risk introduced by a vendor or third party.

    A. Sub-vendor

    B. Third-party assessor

    C. Business Associate

    D. Primary entity

Appendix A

Answers to Domain Review Questions

Domain 1 – **Healthcare Industry**

1. A Health Information Exchange (HIE) is an example of
   _____.

   A. Health Information Technology (HIT).
   B. Personal Health Record.
   C. An exclusion under HIPAA.
   D. An implantable medical device.

The correct option is **A**.

Health Information Technology consists of a wide variety of devices, networks, servers, platforms, and software that process, store, transmit, and disseminate health information. A personal health record is a patient centric and controlled record about a patient's health. HIPPA contains few exclusions, but a blanket exclusion for HIEs is not one of them. An HIE may relay information gathered and produced by an implantable medical device, but an implantable medical device is not an exchange.

2. Information security and privacy **MOST** benefit the healthcare industry by _____.

   A. Increasing organizational information technology costs.
   B. Allowing the organization to meet legal mandatory requirements.
   C. Ensuring risk is identified and managed in an appropriate and timely manner.
   D. Transferring risk from the organization to another party.

The correct option is **C**.

Information security and privacy ensure the organization is assessing risks to patient information and privacy on an ongoing basis. When risk is discovered, it must be managed. Organizations have options as to how they manage risk, but they can never fully transfer all risk. Meeting mandatory requirements is a necessary first step, but organizations must understand they are responsible for going beyond the minimum and ensuring their risk management approach is appropriate for their enterprise.

3. Two of the MOST important features of a Health Information Exchange are _____.

    A. Scalability and patient "ease of use".

    B. Scalability and security.

    C. Interoperability and security.

    D. Interoperability and patient "ease of use".

The correct option is **C.**

> Interoperability ensures information from various systems and manufacturers can be ingested and imported into other systems. Security is also very important as patient information must be protected in transit. Scalability and ease of use are also important. However, security and interoperability must be in place, or every time the exchange is scaled the risk is also scaled with it. Ease of use is also an important function; however rarely does an HIE have a patient interface. Instead, the HIE is focused on business to business or practitioner to practitioner data transfer.

4. Which of the following **BEST** describes the general benefits of a Health Information Exchange?

    A. Providing a vehicle for improving quality and safety of patient care, providing a basic level of interoperability among electronic health records (EHRs) maintained by individual physicians and organizations, and reducing healthcare fraud and abuse.

    B. Providing a vehicle for improving quality and safety of patient care, reducing healthcare fraud and abuse, and providing the backbone of technical infrastructure for leveraging by national and state-level initiatives.

    C. Reducing healthcare fraud and abuse, providing a basic level of interoperability among electronic health records (EHRs) maintained by individual physicians and organizations, and providing the backbone of technical infrastructure for leveraging by national and state-level initiatives.

    D. Reducing healthcare fraud and abuse, providing a basic level of interoperability among electronic health records (EHRs) maintained by individual physicians and organizations, and providing the backbone of technical infrastructure for leveraging by national and state-level initiatives.

The correct option is **A.**

The primary generic features of an HIE are:

1. Providing a vehicle for improving quality and safety of patient care;
2. Providing a basic level of interoperability among electronic health records (EHRs) maintained by individual physicians and organizations;
3. Stimulating consumer education and patients' involvement in their own healthcare;
4. Helping public health officials meet their commitment to the community;
5. Creating a potential loop for feedback between health-related research and actual practice;
6. Facilitating efficient deployment of emerging technology and healthcare services; and
7. Providing the backbone of technical infrastructure for leveraging by national and state-level initiatives.

5. Select the **BEST** response from the following to complete the phrase: Medical coding _____
   A. Is used as part of an organization's information security and privacy risk management process.
   B. Has unified the practice of healthcare internationally and established a standard for billing and payment from private and government programs.
   C. Provides an effective way to determine data classification.
   D. Provides a standard to determine an information's confidentiality, integrity, and availability impact.

The correct option is **B**.

6. When designing a workflow for sensitive patient information, which of the following is **MOST** important in terms of privacy?
   A. Data integrity checks and audit logs.
   B. "Minimum necessary use" and data integrity checks.
   C. Audit logs and availability tests.
   D. "Minimum necessary use" and audit logs.

The correct option is **D**.

Minimum necessary use ensures only those who must have access to the information to do their job can have access. Audit logs ensure if access is not appropriate, the offender can be located and disciplined as needed. These are the most important aspects of ensuring privacy in a workflow. Data integrity checks are important for patient safety and organizational efficiency, but they do not offer privacy protection. Availability tests are also important for patient safety, but they do not offer privacy protections.

7. In the United States under HIPAA, doctors, clinics, pharmacies, and psychologists are **BEST** defined as _____.
   A. Health information clearing houses.
   B. Providers of services.
   C. Healthcare Plans.
   D. Business Associates.

The correct option is **B**.

HIPAA clearly identifies the following:

Direct Covered Entities		
1. Health Plans	2. Providers of Services	3. Health Information Clearinghouses
Includes an individual or group plan who provides and pays for health care (Medicare and the components of government agencies)	Radiologists, Physicians, Laboratories, etc.	Organizations that can be used to translate either to or from the standard format
Business Associates		
Companies that work on behalf of or subcontract with a covered entity		

8. How does the U.S. HIPAA privacy and U.S. HIPAA security rule differ?
   A. No difference exists; they mandate the same requirements.
   B. The privacy rule applies to electronic transmissions while the security rule applies to physical and verbal matters.
   C. The security rule applies to electronic transmissions while the privacy rule applies to physical and verbal matters.
   D. The privacy rule contradicts the security rule regarding electronic health records.

The correct option is **C**.

The security rule applies to electronic transmissions while the privacy rule applies to physical and verbal matters." They are separate and distinct requirements that do not conflict with each other.

9. The U.S. HIPAA Privacy Rule de-identification requirement _____.

   A. Allows patient data to be used for research without consent if the data is from less than eighteen people.

   B. Allows patient data to be used for research without consent if an expert determines the data has been de-identified or if eighteen specific identifiers are removed.

   C. Allows research on data of individuals over the age of eighteen without their consent.

   D. Allows the selling of fully identifiable patient data to non-covered entities.

The correct option is **B**.

There is no volume or group size specified as part of the requirement and no age determination either for inclusion of protection.

10. Which of the following **BEST** explains the relationship between the U.S. HIPAA and U.S. HITECH laws?

    A. HIPAA enhances HITECH by specifying that the U.S. Food and Drug Administration must administer a PHI breach notification and enforcement program.

    B. HITECH nullifies HIPAA and acts as a holistic replacement designed with electronic health records in mind.

    C. HITECH enhances HIPAA by specifying the U.S. HHS Office of Civil Rights as the enforcer of HIPAA privacy and security rules.

    D. HIPAA nullifies HITECH and acts as a holistic replacement designed with electronic health records in mind.

The correct option is **C**.

Chronologically, HITECH came after HIPAA and was largely an enhancement in addition to providing more specificity about the adoption of electronic health records in the U.S. While the U.S. Food and Drug Administration has wide enforcement authority over several aspects of the U.S. healthcare system, the U.S. HHS Office of Civil rights is empowered by law through HITECH to enforce the HIPAA security and privacy rule.

Domain 2 – **Regulatory Environment**

1. An organization needs to use data flow modeling to develop a system that will boot securely, perform routine checks to ensure the system is still secure, and perform security checks based on certain activities. Which data flow model **BEST** describes this approach?

    A. State Machine Model

    B. Multilevel Lattice Model

    C. Noninterference Model

    D. Information flow Model

The correct option is **A.**

State Machine Model is concerned with the "state" of the system at a given point in time and therefore follows a process of checking the machine state based on events or triggers such as time or actions to determine how safe the machine is. Multilevel security models describe strict layers of subjects and objects and define clear rules that allow or disallow interactions between them based on the layers they are in. These are often described using lattices, or discrete layers with minimal or no interfaces between them. Most lattice models define a hierarchical lattice with layers of lesser or greater privilege. The goal of a noninterference model is to help ensure that high-level actions (inputs) do not determine what low-level users can see (outputs). Most of the security models presented are secured by permitting restricted flows between high- and low-level users. A noninterference model maintains activities at different security levels to separate these levels from each other. Information flow models focus on how information is allowed or not allowed between individual objects. Information flow models are used to determine if information is being properly protected throughout a given process.

2. The Bell-LaPadula security model allows _____.
   A. Objects to read information from subjects at a similar classification level or at lower levels, but they are barred from reading any information from objects classified at a higher level of confidentiality.
   B. Subjects to read information from objects at a higher classification level or at lower levels, but they are barred from reading any information from objects classified at a lower level of confidentiality.
   C. Subjects to read information from objects at a similar classification level or at lower levels, but they are barred from reading any information from objects classified at a higher level of confidentiality.
   D. Subjects to read information from objects at a similar classification level or at higher levels, but they are barred from reading any information from objects classified at a lower level of confidentiality

The correct option is **C**.

3. To avoid disclosure according to the "* property", _____.
   A. The subject would be able to write information to objects at a similar classification level or lower levels but would be barred from writing any information to objects classified at a higher level of confidentiality.
   B. The object would be able to write information to subjects at a similar classification level or higher levels but would be barred from writing any information to subjects classified at a lower level of confidentiality.
   C. The object would be able to write information to subjects at a similar classification level or lower levels but would be barred from writing any information to objects classified at a higher level of confidentiality.
   D. The subject would be able to write information to objects at a similar classification level or higher levels but would be barred from writing any information to objects classified at a lower level of confidentiality.

The correct option is **D**.

This can seem very odd at first glance, but remember that the goal is to prevent disclosure. Writing something at a higher level will not result in disclosure, even if it makes it impossible for the original subject to read it! It also has some practical value in some cases. For example, an organization's president may wish a set of subordinate officers to make reports to their superiors in such a way that they cannot read each other's reports while still allowing their superiors to read and collate information across reports from their subordinates.

4. The biba simple integrity model ensures _____.
    A. The subject is prevented from reading from more accurate objects but can read from objects that are less accurate than the subject needs.
    B. The object is prevented from reading from less accurate subjects but can read from subjects that are more accurate than the object needs.
    C. The object is prevented from reading from more accurate subjects but can read from subjects that are less accurate than the object needs.
    D. The subject is prevented from reading from less accurate objects but can read from objects that are more accurate than the subject needs.

The correct option is **D**.

In the simple integrity property, a given subject has the ability to read information from different types of objects with differing levels of integrity or accuracy. In this case, less accurate information than what the subject would expect could result in corruption, so the subject must be prevented from reading from less accurate objects but can read from objects that are more accurate than the subject needs.

5. Which of the following models focuses on preventing conflict of interest when a given subject has access to objects with sensitive information associated with two competing parties?
    A. Clark-Wilson
    B. Brewer-Nash
    C. Biba
    D. Bell-LaPadula

The correct option is **B**.

The principle is that users should not access the confidential information of both a client organization and one or more of its competitors. At the beginning, subjects may access either set of objects. Once, however, a subject accesses an object associated with one competitor, they are instantly prevented from accessing any objects on the opposite side.

This is intended to prevent the subject from sharing information inappropriately between the two competitors, even unintentionally. It is called the Chinese Wall Model because, like the Great Wall of China, once on one side of the wall, a person cannot get to the other side. It is an unusual model in comparison with many of the others because the access control rules change based on subject behavior.

6. Which of the following is designed to protect the goodwill a merchant or vendor invests in its products by creating exclusive rights to the owner of markings that the public uses to identify various vendor or merchant products or goods?

    A. Copyright

    B. Criminal Law

    C. Due Diligence

    D. Trademark

The correct option is **D**.

A trademark is designed to protect the goodwill of an owner based on unique markings.

7. An organization wishes to use 1,500 patient health records for research. The organization operates in the United States and is subject to HIPAA. The organization has decided to remove eighteen personal identifiers from each record to de-identity the information in accordance with HIPAA. The act of removing the information in accordance with the law is **BEST** described as _____.

    A. Safe Harbor

    B. Expert Determination

    C. Risk Transference

    D. Risk Avoidance

The correct option is **A**.

A safe harbor is typically a set of "good faith" conditions, which if met, may temporarily or indefinitely protect an organization from the penalties of a law or regulation. Expert determination is another way of using patient information according to HIPAA but is not the same as simply removing all eighteen personal identifiers. Risk has not been transferred in this situation as there is not a recipient. Risk also has not been avoided as the organization has decided to perform the research. Risk may be mitigated by using a safe harbor approach; however risk reduction was not provided as a possible response for this question.

8. A nurse working the floor is approached by an individual claiming to be a psychotherapy patient's mother. The person requests access to the patient's psychotherapy notes. According to HIPAA, which of the following responses **BEST** describes what the nurse can disclose?

    A. Once the individual is verified as the patient's mother, the nurse may disclose critical psychotherapy information pertinent to the care of the patient.

    B. Nothing. The nurse may not disclose any information related to the psychotherapy information to anyone except the patient or the creator of the notes.

    C. Once the individual is verified as the patient's mother, the nurse must ask the mother to complete a non-disclosure agreement. After the agreement is completed, the nurse may provide the information.

    D. Nothing. The nurse may not disclose any information related to the psychotherapy to anyone including the patient or the creator of the notes.

The correct option is **B**.

HIPAA specifically addresses psychotherapy notes in its regulations. As stated on the Health and Human Services website, psychotherapy notes are not only the personal information of a patient but the notes of a professional therapist. "Therefore, with few exceptions, the Privacy Rule requires a covered entity to obtain a patient's authorization prior to a disclosure of psychotherapy notes for any reason, including a disclosure for treatment purposes to a health care provider other than the originator of the notes."

9. The U.S. Affordable Care Act requires _____.

    A. Operating rules for each of the HIPAA covered transactions; a unique, standard Health Plan Identifier (HPID); and a standard and operating rules for Electronic Funds Transfer (EFT) and Electronic Remittance Advice (ERA) and PHI processing when performed within the law and scope of "public interest."

    B. Operating rules for each of the HIPAA covered transactions; a unique, standard Health Plan Identifier (HPID); and a standard and operating rules for Electronic Funds Transfer (EFT) and Electronic Remittance Advice (ERA) and claims attachments.

    C. PHI processing when performed within the law and scope of "public interest" and a standard and operating rules for Electronic Funds Transfer (EFT) and Electronic Remittance Advice (ERA).

D. Operating rules for each of the HIPAA covered transactions; PHI processing when performed within the law and scope of "public interest"; and a standard and operating rules for Electronic Funds Transfer (EFT) and Electronic Remittance Advice (ERA) and claims attachments.

The correct option is **B**.

"PHI processing when performed within the law and scope of 'public interest'" is part of the EU Data Privacy Directive.

10. An information security assessment has determined numerous controls are not in place to help protect an organization's information system. The organization's leader states they will differ acceptance of any risk but refuses to shut down or limit the operation of the affected systems. Can the leader do this?

A. Yes because she is the leader of the organization, and it is her decision to make.

B. Yes, major risk management frameworks such as ISO and NIST support not accepting risk while allowing system operation.

C. No, the organizational leader is not the ultimate authority for risk acceptance decisions.

D. No, it is not possible to be aware of risks due to system operation and not accept them by default if a system is running.

The correct option is **D**.

While the leader of an organization is the ultimate risk acceptance official, he or she must still abide by the reality of due care and due diligence. Knowing about risk and refusing to act on it is by default accepting the risk. Major risk management frameworks such as NIST and ISO do not allow a leader to know about risk without accepting it as long as the system is operational. If the system is shutdown, risk is avoided, but service is disrupted. Many organizational leaders have information security professionals advise them regarding information security risk matters and may also include counsel.

Domain 3 – **Privacy and Security in Healthcare**

1. The pillars of information security consist of _____.
   A. Confidentiality, Integrity, and Availability.
   B. Privacy, Integrity, and Availability.
   C. Confidentiality, Privacy, and Availability.
   D. Confidentiality, Integrity, and Privacy.

The correct option is **A**.

Privacy is a specialized form of the application of confidentiality and the rights of individuals.

2. A patient wants to ensure the email they received from their primary care specialist is actually from the person they expect and not an impostor. Which concept will **BEST** ensure the sender of the email is actually the primary care specialist?
   A. Availability
   B. Confidentiality
   C. Digital Signatures
   D. Hashing

The correct option is **C**.

Digital signatures are a special application of integrity and hashing with public key infrastructure. When properly implemented, digital signatures provide an extremely high level of confidence in the sender's identity.

3. During _____ the subject's purported identity is validated by one or more credentials from the three main categories of factors: something the subject knows (password or passphrase), something the subject has (smartcard, token, or certificate), or something the subject is (a biometric such as a fingerprint or retina scan).
   A. Identification
   B. Accountability
   C. Access Control
   D. Authentication

The correct option is **D**.

4. HIPAA provides safe harbor against a breach if _____.
   A. The data was collected more than five years ago.
   B. The data was breached by a third party doing work on behalf of the original provider.
   C. The organization didn't understand information security and privacy.
   D. The information was properly encrypted.

The correct option is **D**.

Organizations under HIPAA are responsible for not only their own use of information but also the use of data by their business associates. Furthermore, fines by the HHS OCR have shown ignorance is not a defense when a breach occurs. HIPAA has no safe harbors related to time.

5. Public Key Infrastructure or PKI is a form of _____.
   A. Asymmetric encryption.
   B. Symmetric encryption.
   C. Hashing functions.
   D. Digital signatures.

The correct option is **A**.

Symmetric encryption requires all parties to have the same private key. Hashing functions are one way functions used for integrity. Digital signatures use PKI, but PKI is not only used for digital signatures. Asymmetric encryption describes a system where each party has two keys, a public key any party may have and a private key known only to the possessing party.

6. Complete the following with the **BEST** answer: Sharing of login credentials _____.
   A. Should be encouraged because it greatly reduced administrative burdens.
   B. Should be used only for workstations where the users know and trust each other very well.
   C. Should be discouraged but tolerated as employee moral must be preserved.
   D. Should be discouraged because non-repudiation will be violated.

The correct option is **D**.

The concept of non-repudiation ensures an individual cannot deny he or she performed an action. Having numerous people use the same username and password (credentials) provides an opportunity to blame another for a crime or administrative violation.

7. _____ are the points at which assets are susceptible to an exploit or attack and are often attributed to unintended design flaws in the implementation of a hardware device, software application, or a system.
   A. Threats
   B. Vulnerabilities
   C. Likelihoods
   D. Risks

The correct option is **B**.

Threats exploit vulnerabilities with a certain likelihood that results in risk.

8. Separation of duties is **BEST** used in situations where _____

   A. There must be a high level of certainty about who performed an action.
   B. Systems must be available for several days no matter the circumstances.
   C. An individual must not have access to modify a record without permission.
   D. A process requires checks and balances that force collusion.

The correct option is **D**.

Separation of duties ensures at least two people must conspire together to commit a crime or fraud. This requirement not only lowers the opportunity for crime, fraud, or undesirable acts, but it also aids in the investigation because incongruent statements can quickly turn one party on another.

9. An organization works mostly with older patients and wants to perform research on their patient population. The organization is subject to HIPAA, and an HCISPP has informed them they will need to remove all date information for patients older than 89 years of age. What is the **BEST** reason the organization must do this?

    A. HIPAA provided an arbitrary age to limit the population of studies.

    B. After the age of 89, there are considerably fewer people alive to match information to, and therefore an attacker can easily guess the individual.

    C. The organization believes the HCISPP is an "expert" and therefore is relying on them for an expert determination.

    D. Research on patients over 89 years of age is covered by legislation other than HIPAA.

The correct option is **B**.

Some may wonder why birth year has to be removed for individuals over age 89. Consider that one of the oldest living individuals in the United States is 114. For de-identification to work, organizations cannot tie the data back to an individual. If just birth year is listed and not birthdate, an attacker could still easily find out that there are only one or two people of that age. It would be relatively easy to figure out who they were, even if the attacker did not have much other information. To prevent the possibility of identification, one should remember that the specific birth year cannot be included for individuals over age 89.

10. Least privilege is a form of _____.

    A. Minimum necessary.

    B. Non-repudiation.

    C. Rotation of duties.

    D. Mandatory vacations.

The correct option is **A**.

Both least privilege and minimum necessary describe ensuring an individual has access to the only information that is necessary to perform his or her job. Non-repudiation is important in ensuring minimum necessary access. Rotation of duties is used to detect fraud or problems as is mandatory vacations.

Domain 4 – **Information Governance and Risk Management**

1. An organization maintains Protected Health Information in the cloud, on local systems in its offices, and on paper records. Which form of information has the greatest impact on the organization if it is breached?
   A. Paper based records
   B. Cloud based records
   C. Local system based records
   D. The impact is the same regardless of media

The correct option is **D**.

Remember information has the same impact to the organization during a breach regardless of form. Therefore a database on a server, a database in the cloud, and a file cabinet full of paper all have the same impact if the information is breached. The HCISPP must remember to keep a vigilant eye over all information regardless of its form.

2. An oncology practice has outsourced its infrastructure to XYZ corporation. Due to no contract limitations, XYZ corporation has further sub-contracted the infrastructure work to another firm, ABC Group. The oncology practice's infrastructure is responsible for processing, storing, and transmitting the PHI of oncology patients. In this scenario, which organization is affiliated with the information owner/steward who would be held accountable in a breach?
   A. The oncology practice
   B. XYZ corporation
   C. ABC Group
   D. None as the contracting relationship has created a transference of risk.

The correct option is **A**.

While XYZ and ABC have access to the information and maintains the infrastructure, they did not collect the information from patients. The oncology practice collected the information for their work, and therefore they are responsible for protecting it even if they trust other providers to maintain their infrastructure. Even if the oncology practice included punitive financial damages in the contract in the event of a breach, patients and the public would still look at the provider as the responsible party because the provider chose the contractor.

3. The following represents four basic steps in managing risk. Place them in the correct sequential order:

   1. Monitoring risk - continuously monitor the risk environment
   2. Assessing risk – identify threats, vulnerabilities, impact, likelihood, and determine risk
   3. Framing risk - produce the risk strategy, identify risk tolerance, assumptions, and constraints
   4. Responding to risk – identify a consistent manner to respond to risk from an organization-wide perspective

   A. 1, 2, 3, 4
   B. 4, 3, 2, 1
   C. 3, 2, 4, 1
   D. 2, 1, 4, 3

The correct option is **C**.

The correct approach for managing risk is

   1. *Framing risk* – Produce the risk strategy, identify risk tolerance, assumptions, and constraints
   2. *Assessing risk* – Identify threats, vulnerabilities, impact, likelihood, and determine risk
   3. *Responding to risk* – Identify a consistent manner to respond to risk from an organization-wide perspective
   4. *Monitoring risk* – Continuously monitor the risk environment

4. Organizational risk tolerance is **BEST** established by _____
   A. Senior leadership.
   B. Information system owner.
   C. Information system security officer.
   D. Information owner.

The correct option is **A**.

Information system owners may not know the full impact of the information to the organization's mission. Information owners may be knowledgeable about their information but may not have a holistic view of the organization; information system security officers have a deep understanding of the information security aspects of a system but may not be in tune with the strategy and tactics of senior leadership.

5. An organization is reviewing their financial exposure should a breach occur. A senior penetration tester has determined in the past they have been breached two times a year, and each time it has cost the organization U.S. $100,000 to mitigate the breach and offer credit monitoring. What is the annual loss expectancy (ALE) for the organization?
   A. U.S. $50,000
   B. U.S. $25,000
   C. U.S. $200,000
   D. U.S. $250,000

The correct option is **C**.

ALE is expressed as:

ALE = Annual Rate of Occurrence (ARO) x Single Loss Expectancy (SLE)

6. Annual loss expectancy or ALE is a form of _____.
   A. Qualitative risk assessment.
   B. Quantitative risk assessment.
   C. Qualitative and quantitative risk assessment.
   D. Continuous monitoring.

The correct option is **B**.

There are two approaches an organization can use to assess risk, qualitative and quantitative. Quantitative risk assessment is using something that is measurable. In this example, the ALE is measurable in dollars and times an event has occurred. Therefore, the risk is measurable. Risk is generally not this simple to calculate. Often the risk assessment an organization conducts is a mixture of both quantitative and qualitative. Qualitative risk assessment is using something that is descriptive. A common approach is to describe risk in relative terms such as "high", "medium", and "low". It is important to note that some organizations may state their risk assessment is quantitative and based on scientific methods. Although scientific methods are generally quantitative, information security and privacy risk assessment is generally performed using qualitative methods. This is because a scale or criteria must be created to understand the meaning of any measurement or number.

7. Which of the following classes of controls are primarily implemented and executed through mechanisms contained in the hardware, software, and firmware of the components of the system?

    A. Technical Controls

    B. Managerial Controls

    C. Operational Controls

    D. Physical Controls

The correct option is **A**.

Managerial controls are implemented through policies, procedures, standards, and guidance. Operational controls are implemented through people and processes that incorporate people, such as ensuring new hires have a background investigation. Physical controls are also commonly called operational controls as physical controls are most often used to protect assets from people or control the physical security of personnel.

8. An organization has just completed a risk assessment. The assessment returned a single finding with a "low" risk to the organization. The cost to mitigate or transfer the risk would be U.S. $1.5 million dollars, and if the risk were exploited, no PHI or sensitive information would be lost, but the organization's public website would be down for 10 to 15 seconds no more than twice a year. The organization earns about U.S. $1 million dollars of revenue every year. What is the **BEST** risk treatment approach?

    A. Transfer risk

    B. Avoid risk

    C. Mitigate risk

    D. Accept risk

The correct option is **D**.

Given the information provided above, the best approach would be to accept the risk. As the maximum down time would amount to less than 30 seconds a year and the cost to mitigate is 150% of the organization's revenue, the best decision would be to accept risk. The only time this may change is if a regulatory requirement demanded the risk be completely eliminated. If that is present (which for this question it was not), the organization must mitigate, transfer, or avoid the risk.

9. Consider the NIST risk management framework below: If an organization has adopted NIST as its risk management framework, which step is **MOST** important in ensuring proper risk management?

    A. Continuous monitoring

    B. Implement security controls

    C. Authorize information system

    D. Categorize information system

The correct option is **D**.

While all steps are important in the risk management framework, the first step of categorization will determine control baseline selection, assessment methodology and rigor, and the impact of the system to the organization. Misunderstanding or improperly scoping the categorization of a system will result in a cascading error and lead to an inaccurate picture of risk.

10. A remediation plan or plan of actions and milestones (POA&M) is **MOST** effective when it contains the following:

    A. system downtime, resources required, responsible person, and a date for completion

    B. list of activities, resources required, responsible person, and a date for completion

    C. list of activities, system downtime, responsible person, and a date for completion

    D. list of activities, resources required, responsible person, and system downtime

The correct option is **B**.

System downtime is important for many organizations; however, not all corrective actions will require downtime, and it is less significant than the other elements provided in remediation.

Domain 5 – **Information Risk Assessment**

1. How can a breach of protected health information (PHI) cause an adverse medical outcome due to integrity problems? Select the **BEST** response from the following:
   A. When data is breached, an attacker may attempt to use the victim's identity to obtain medical services. The victim's medical record then has erroneous information about the attacker that may cause adverse medical outcomes.
   B. When data is breached, a victim may attempt to use the attacker's identity to obtain medial services. The attacker's medical record then has erroneous information about the attacker that may cause adverse medical outcomes.
   C. A breach by definition affects the integrity of the data being breached and can therefore lead to adverse medical outcomes.
   D. Since PHI is considered low risk, there is no possibility of adverse medical outcomes due to breaches and resultant integrity problems.

The correct option is **A**.

PHI should always be considered sensitive, and the definition of a breach involves the failure of confidentiality and privacy of PHI.

2. An organization wishes to minimize risk throughout the organization after a risk assessment showed numerous high and moderate risks throughout the enterprise. Senior leadership wants to transfer as much risk as possible in the event of a breach. Which of the following **BEST** explains a risk transfer option?
   A. The organization may transfer all risk to another party. The party will be responsible and held accountable for all facets of risk and recovery should a breach occur. The organization will suffer no impact should a breach occur.
   B. The organization may not transfer any risk to another party. The organization is wholly responsible for all risk of information.
   C. The organization may transfer certain risk such as financial risk, but other risk such as reputation risk must be managed by the organization.
   D. The organization may transfer certain risk such as reputation risk, but financial risk must be managed by the organization.

The correct option is **C**.

Financial risk is often transferred through an insurance policy or similar. In the event of a breach, the insurance pays to provide credit monitoring and help the company repair its systems from the breach. However, the insurance will do nothing for the reputation of the organization. The organization will continue to be held accountable for its own reputation and goodwill among its peers, partners, and customers.

3. The U.S. HITECH Act requires covered entities to report breaches of _____ people or more to the U.S. HHS Office of Civil Rights.
   A. 1
   B. 250
   C. 500
   D. 1000

The correct option is **C**.

In the United States, the Health Information Technology for Economic and Clinical Health (HITECH) Act requires reporting and publication of data breaches of protected or sensitive health information that impact more than 500 individuals.

4. Which of the following roles is **MOST** responsible for:
   - Determining the impact the information has on the mission of the organization.
   - Understanding the replacement cost of the information (if it can be replaced).
   - Determining who in the organization or outside of it has a need for the information and under what circumstances the information should be released.
   - Knowing when the information is inaccurate or no longer needed and should be destroyed.
   A. Senior leadership
   B. Information system security officer
   C. System owner
   D. Information owner/steward

The correct option is **D**.

Information owners must work with the information security program officer and other staff to ensure the protection, availability, and destruction requirements can be met. To standardize the types of information and protection requirements, many organizations use classification or categorization to sort and mark the information. Classification is concerned primarily with access, while categorization is primarily concerned with impact.

5. Why should organizations use records retention schedules that mandate the destruction of information after a set date, period, or non-use trigger?

   A. Storage costs are reduced; only relevant information is kept, and this can speed up searching and indexing; litigation holds and eDiscovery are less likely to encounter erroneous, pre-decisional, or deliberative information; and to meet compliance requirements.

   B. Storage costs are increased; all information is kept, and this can speed up searching and indexing; litigation holds and eDiscovery is more likely to encounter erroneous, pre-decisional, or deliberative information; and minimize compliance requirements.

   C. Storage costs are reduced; litigation holds and eDiscovery are less likely to encounter erroneous, pre-decisional, or deliberative information; and to meet compliance requirements.

   D. Storage costs are reduced; only relevant information is kept, and this can speed up searching and indexing; and litigation holds and eDiscovery are less likely to encounter erroneous, pre-decisional, or deliberative information.

The correct option is **A**.

A properly implemented records retention schedule provides all these benefits.

6. A small practice of thirty-five individuals wants to start performing continuous monitoring and assessment. Considerable debate has risen as to the best approach for performing the assessment. Which of the following approaches provides the **BEST** approach for a risk assessment?

   A. Have the organization's information system owner conduct the assessment as they already know the most about the systems.

   B. Have an external or operationally separate entity perform the assessment so bias is minimized.

   C. Have the information system security officer conduct the assessment as they have the most knowledge of information security.

   D. Have the information owner/steward perform the assessment.

The correct option is **B**.

> While an external party may not know everything about the system or organization, they only have one objective - an impartial assessment. The system owner may be worried about protecting his system and may minimize or hide findings. The information owner/ steward may care deeply about their information but may lack the technical expertise to perform and assessment and may end up in a confrontational relationship with the system owner. The information system security officer is also responsible for day to day operational security and therefore would be assessing part of her own work, which could minimally lead to the appearance of bias.

7. Information security and privacy is the responsibility of _____ in the organization. Please select the **BEST** answer from below:
    A. Everyone
    B. Senior leadership
    C. The information systems security officer
    D. The practice lead

The correct option is **A**.

> Security is the responsibility of everyone within the organization. While day to day security and risk management functions fall on specific roles such as the information systems security officer and senior leadership, all members of the organization have a responsibility to protect sensitive information. Every end user is responsible for understanding the policies and procedures that are applicable to their particular job function and adhering to any and all security control expectations. Users must have knowledge of their responsibilities and be trained to a level that is adequate to reduce the risk of loss to an acceptable level. An individual may be assigned multiple roles for the organization. It is important to provide clear definition and communication of roles and responsibilities including accountability through the distribution of policies, job descriptions, training, and management direction, as well as providing the foundation for execution of security controls by the workforce.

8. Complete the following statement with the **BEST** response: Assessors who conduct vulnerability assessments must be experts in _____.
   A. Penetration testing, malware reverse engineering, and incident response.
   B. Properly reading, understanding, digesting, and presenting the information obtained from a vulnerability assessment and incident response.
   C. Properly reading, understanding, digesting, and presenting the information obtained from a vulnerability assessment to a multidisciplinary, sometimes nontechnical audience.
   D. Malware reverse engineering, incident response, and presenting the information obtained from a vulnerability assessment and incident response.

The correct option is **C**.

While incident response, reverse malware engineering, and penetration testing can all aid the assessor in a vulnerability assessment, these skills are worthless if the assessor cannot convey the vulnerability information to management and other non-technical audiences.

9. A rival healthcare provider has hired a hacker to illegally attempt to steal information from a healthcare organization. Which of the following **BEST** describes the hacker?
   A. Risk
   B. Likelihood
   C. Vulnerability
   D. Threat

The correct option is **D**.

A threat-source is "either (1) intent and method targeted at the intentional exploitation of a vulnerability or (2) a situation and method that may accidentally trigger a vulnerability."

10. A security management process is **BEST** described by which set of controls?
    A. Administrative/managerial
    B. Operational/physical
    C. Technical
    D. Detective

The correct option is **A**.

A security management process is part of an overarching security program that is driven by management buy-in and enforced through policies, procedures, standards, and guidelines.

Domain 6 – **Third-Party Risk Management**

1. Third parties can _____.
   A. Introduce additional risk to an organization if not properly assessed and monitored.
   B. Alleviate an organization of responsibility during a protected health information breach.
   C. Not outsource processing, storage, or transmission of sensitive PHI regardless of contract requirements.
   D. Only operate in countries where the original party resides.

The correct option is **A**.

A third party can never alleviate the responsibility of the primary party during a breach; however they may choose to share the blame. Unless contractually specified, third parties may outsource further to other parties without informing the primary organization of the decision and any risk implications. Third parties may also operate in their country of choice if not explicitly specified as part of a contractual agreement.

2. What is the **BEST** reason a healthcare organization should create and maintain a list of third-party organizations it does business with?
   A. A list of vendors ensures the contracting office can quickly identify a list of potentially secure companies for new requirements.
   B. The listing can provide a means for the HCISPP to pair third-party provider information with the criticality of healthcare information frequency and sensitivity.
   C. The list can be used by the marketing firm to determine the best channels to market net electronic health record offerings.
   D. The third-party organization list is used by the HCISPP to determine the "How" of protection requirements.

The correct option is **B**.

Contracting and marketing are important functions, but for the HCISPP, protection of healthcare information is the first priority. The third-party list provides the "Who" of protection. Further analysis of interconnections and business agreements results in the appropriate "How."

3. Which of the following would **BEST** help a HCISPP determine if a third party has met an external attestation for information security or privacy?

   A. Financial soundness

   B. Length of time vendor has been in business

   C. ISO or SSAE No. 16 certifications

   D. Past performance reviews

The correct option is **C**.

The HCISPP is responsible for determining the best approach to risk when dealing with third parties. While financial performance, length of time in business, and past performance reviews all help paint a picture of business health, only ISO or SSAE No. 16 reviews require an external review of information technology practices.

4. Which of the following cloud service models requires the cloud provider to provide the majority of the security controls?

   A. Infrastructure as a service

   B. Software as a service

   C. Platform as a service

   D. Network as a service

The correct option is **B**.

Software as a service providers must not only provide security controls for the software they develop, but also the underlying platforms and infrastructures they rely on for service.

5. What is the **BEST** way an HCISPP can ensure that information security and privacy is "built-in" to third-party cloud providers?

   A. Purchase whatever solution the majority of the market is consuming.

   B. Determine security and privacy requirements prior to researching cloud offerings and ensure any cloud providers can meet them.

   C. Purchase cloud services and then negotiate with the cloud provider to ensure the exact controls needed are implemented.

   D. Ensure the HCISPP is excluded from contract negotiations because security and privacy tend to increase price.

The correct option is **B**.

The HCISPP should be involved in any contract negotiations, as he or she should determine if there is a security or privacy implication as part of any concession or demand. The HCISPP should also avoid getting into a situation where he or she will need to negotiate after the fact for more security and privacy. This is often very expensive and may not be implemented quickly enough for adequate risk management. HCISPPs should be aware of what the market as a whole is consuming, but they should also understand their own organization's requirements and regulations. They should then determine what is right for their organization regardless of the market.

6. Which element of third-party management below has the **MOST** risk from data remnants?
   A. Integration
   B. Termination
   C. Operations
   D. Selection

The correct option is **B**.

Termination is when the third party is expected to annihilate and destroy any records trusted to them. If they do not, the resultant information is often called a data remnant. These remnants are dangerous because the organization is still responsible for the data even though they have severed their relationship with the third party.

7. When developing a contract with a third party to process, store, and transmit information, which of the following **BEST** protects the organization?
   A. Vendor compliance with laws and regulations, information security and privacy safeguards, right to audit clauses and full risk transfer to the vendor.
   B. Full risk transfer to the vendor, information security and privacy safeguards, right to audit clauses and data breach notification.
   C. Vendor compliance with laws and regulations, full risk transfer to the vendor, and right to audit clauses and data breach notification.
   D. Vendor compliance with laws and regulations, information security and privacy safeguards, right to audit clauses and data breach notification.

The correct option is **D**.

No organization can transfer all risk to the other organization because the primary organization is still responsible for protecting the information they collected. Even if an organization has a financial agreement to cover costs, they will still need to accept the risks of public perception and market loss should a breach occur.

8. Which of the following **BEST** explains when employee background investigations should be required of a third-party vendor?

    A. Only when working with a vendor outside of the organization's home country or jurisdiction.

    B. Only when working with a vendor inside of the organization's home country or jurisdiction.

    C. In any contract where the organization has a legal, regulatory, or risk management requirement to ensure information is protected against unauthorized disclosure.

    D. In any contract where the vendor will perform research using de-identified information from the organization.

The correct option is **C**.

Background investigations ensure the people trusted with protected health information have been screened to avoid potential theft or conflicts of interest. While jurisdiction may matter in successful background investigation authority, it should not determine whether one is needed or not. If research is using de-identified information, a background investigation will most likely not be necessary.

9. An interconnection security agreement **BEST** serves to _____.

    A. Establish and memorialize security and privacy expectations for interconnecting parties.

    B. Establish fault after a breach and determine which party is most liable.

    C. Establish responsibility for network related costs.

    D. Memorialize employee access conditions for each party's data.

The correct option is **A**.

Interconnection security agreements often contain information related to: security and privacy controls, network use expectations, employee access limitations, network or security related cost sharing, confidentiality requirements, privileges granted, and possibly network monitoring information. The most important aspect of the information security agreement is the consensus of security and privacy expectations. This agreement drives all other areas mentioned.

> **10.** The _____ is **MOST** responsible to perform due diligence to determine the level of risk introduced by a vendor or third party.
>
> A. Sub-vendor
>
> B. Third-party assessor
>
> C. Business Associate
>
> D. Primary entity

The correct option is **D**.

The primary entity is ultimately responsible for ensuring a vendor or third party does not introduce risk. While a sub-vendor and a business associated may take part in sharing the risk, the primary entity is still most responsible. The third-party assessor may be employed by the primary entity to assess risk, but the assessment is used by the primary entity as part of their due diligence of risk.

Index

A

Access Limitation, 140, 167

Accountability, 43, 69, 106, 149, 168, 259, 294, 295

Accuracy/Completeness/Quality, 168

Activation and Notification, 160

Administrative Law, 86

Affordable Health Care for America Act, 14

AHIMA. *See* Journal of the American Heath Information Management Association (AHIMA)

AICPA. *See* American Institute of Certified Public Accountants (AICPA)

ALE. *See* Annual Loss Expectancy (ALE)

American Institute of Certified Public Accountants (AICPA), 165, 304, 305, 325

Anatomical Therapeutic Chemical Classification System (AT, or ATC/DDD), 20

Annual Loss Expectancy (ALE), 201, 235

Annual Rate of Occurrence (ARO), 201

Appendices, 160

ARO. *See* Annual Rate of Occurrence (ARO)

Assessing Risk, 198

Assessment. *See* Audit

Asset Valuation, 192, 203, 204

Audit, 35, 36, 41, 44, 57, 92, 96, 114, 196, 224, 256, 257, 263, 275, 300, 301, 304, 305, 329

Authentication, 146, 184

Availability, 140, 142, 145, 167, 184, 251

B

BA Agreement, 166, 301

Bell-LaPadula Confidentiality Model, 73

Biba Integrity Model, 76

Breach Notification, 28, 31, 34, 35, 39, 140, 170, 180, 320, 326, 327

Breach Recognition, 308

Brewer-Nash (Chinese Wall) Model, 81

Business
Continuity, 217, 262, 303
Relationship, 43, 296, 305, 307, 318

Business Associate Agreement, 177, 301

Business Continuity, 114, 140, 145, 158, 262

Business Continuity Planner, 262

C

Capitalization of Historic Profits, 205

CCTA Risk Analysis and Management Method (CRAMM), 219

CDC. *See* Center for Disease Control (CDC)

CDT. *See* Current Dental Terminology (CDT)

Center for Disease Control (CDC), 45

Center for Medicare & Medicaid Services (CMS), 18, 19, 32, 49, 50, 192, 215, 233

Chain of Custody, 322

I

Index

I

Index

369

I

Index